SPEAKING *for* MYSELF

Politics and Other Pursuits

Duff Roblin

GREAT PLAINS
PUBLICATIONS

Great Plains Publications
3—161 Stafford Street
Winnipeg, Manitoba R3M 2X9

The publisher acknowledges the financial assistance of The Canada Council and
the Manitoba Arts Council in the production of this book.

The author would like to thank the *Winnipeg Free Press* for its
kind permission to use some of the images featured in this book.

Cover photo by Gerry Kopelow
Design & Typography by Taylor George Design
Printed in Canada by Friesens

CANADIAN CATALOGUING IN PUBLICATION DATA

Roblin, Duff 1917 -

    Speaking for myself: politics and other pursuits

    ISBN 1-894283-09-0

1 Roblin, Duff, 1917 —   2. Prime ministers —
Manitoba – Biography.   I. Title

FC3376.1.R62 A3 1999   971.27'03'092   C99-920153-0
F1063.R623 1999

Dedicated to the friends of a life time
be they known or unknown.

TABLE *of* CONTENTS

ABOVE: Premier Duff Roblin prepares to celebrate the Centennial, August 1967

PREFACE

———◆———

LET THE READER BE AWARE THAT WHAT I RECORD IN THIS VOLUME IS A personal memoir of events in my life in politics and in the world as I perceive them. It is something more than a stream of consciousness or recollections summoned up from the past, and something less than an impartial and considered historical account. It is not a history. It is a personal testimony flavoured by opinion, and if there is a bias, it is in favour of the author. Thus, a memoir tells something about what I did, when I did it, and why I did it.

For some time, I had toyed with the notion of setting down reminiscences of my times, but I allowed procrastination to rule the day. Then James Carr presented himself as a catalyst. He was pressing and persuasive; and without his saying so, I felt "time's wingéd chariot hurrying near" and, moreover, he offered to help. As a journalist, academic, and politician, being formerly the Deputy Leader of the Liberal Party in Manitoba, he seemed to me to be an ideal collaborator and so it turned out.

The preparation of this work was straightforward. The archives were not extensively consulted, but two sets of press clippings were. The first set was kept by my mother up to 1958. She only clipped the favourable notices. After 1958, when I married Mary MacKay, she clipped everything—good and bad. These reminders of the day-by-day public record gave me the best database I could wish, and for me, were well worth the many labours they entailed. My debt to my two compilers is deep. Thus refreshed, I consulted with old friends like Sterling Lyon, the only survivor with me of my first cabinet, Arthur Mauro, Ralph Hedlin, Clay Gilson, James Burns and my 1967 federal leadership team and others.

That done, I made notes to guide my remarks and, sitting down across the table from James Carr, I recited my story into the tape recording machine... Jimmy monitored, stimulated, and focused. When these tapes were transcribed, the editorial team took over. Besides Jimmy's journalistic and academic skills, John Dafoe—one-time editorial page editor of the *Winnipeg Free Press*—who happily as a young journalist had been a witness to many of the events I describe—was called in to lend his impressive experience. Statements of fact were examined by Lewis Stubbs for accuracy. The text was read by Margo Goodhand for literacy and grammatical consistency, while Miriam Fenster transcribed with intelligent perception. I thank them all.

To those who are mentioned by name, and to those who are not, particularly those interested in politics who made my cause their own, I express my deepest thanks for the invaluable part they played in this record.

I hope my son, Andrew, and my daughter, Jennifer, will take pleasure in this account of my doings. My deepest gratitude and love I offer to my wife, Mary, whose selfless, unconditional, and loving support for 40 years is my strength, my comfort, and my stay.

one

FAMILY MATTERS

MY EARLIEST CLAIM TO A NORTH AMERICAN PROGENITOR IS A CERTAIN Pietro Cesere Alberti. He was a native of Venice who, around 1640, for reasons which are obscure, found himself a crewman on a privateer called the *Konnick David*, which I take is Dutch for King David. It was a vessel that carried 14 guns and 25 men, and was bound for New Amsterdam, which in those days was a Dutch colony. It later became New York. Pietro had a difference of opinion with the captain, so when the ship reached Manhattan, he jumped off and landed in North America. Shortly after that, he married into the Dutch community and, in the course of time, the name Alberti was Dutchified to Albertus and then to Bertus. He took up farming in what is now called Brooklyn. I'm the 11th in descent from Pietro, and his strain came into the Roblin family through my great-grandmother, Deborah Kotchapaw.

The Roblin family is thus of American origin. The 11 Roblin generations took us through a line of Dutch, English, and Huguenot origins, and when my mother's family came along, Scottish and Alsatian, so I'm a genuine North-American mixture. Our family's religion varied from Dutch Reformed to Quaker to Methodist. The name Roblin is thought to be English, though perhaps Huguenot. The French Church of Threadneedle Street, London, records Roblins from the last year of the reign of Queen Elizabeth I. I must also report there are Roblins aplenty in France. In fact, there's a Hôtel Roblin in Paris, though I've never stayed.

The Roblins were farmers. At the time of the American War of Independence in 1776, they found themselves at Smith's Clove, Orange County, New York State. Some of the Roblins were Loyalists and served in the King's army. Some of them just tried to keep out of trouble. In the course of the revolution, my forebears' farmstead was raided. When the wife of the family, Elizabeth Miller Roblin, was dared to swear allegiance to King George III, she replied, "My king yesterday. Why not my king today?" Fortunately, she suffered no harm, but her husband, Philip, was badly wounded in this fracas. The Roblins considered these goings-on to be rather unfriendly, so they joined history's long list of displaced persons and, with the full approval of their revolutionary neighbours, came to Canada in 1783. Elizabeth, before she left, allegedly complained to General George Washington, who promised a redress, which she never got.

The Roblin family tree, from the arrival of the United Empire Loyalists in 1783 and onwards, is minutely detailed. There were usually about 10 children in every generation. Consequently, half of the people in eastern Ontario are potentially related to me. When I grew up in Winnipeg, I thought my family was the only Roblins in existence. What a mistake! They're all over the place. The Roblins settled in the Bay of Quinte district in eastern Ontario, then a complete wilderness, first landing at a place which is now called Adolphustown. At that site, the tombstones of several of the early Roblins and others have been set into a United Empire Loyalist pioneers memorial wall. Not all the Roblins left New York. In fact, the Canadian Roblins and the American Roblins used to correspond, up until the time of the American Civil War. At that time, the American Roblins decided that the Canadian Roblins were beyond the pale because they were thought to favour the South, so the connection was broken.

In the late 1700s, life in the Bay of Quinte was primitive indeed. Everything that the family required, it provided for itself, except perhaps iron for ploughshares, and salt and tea. But clothing, food, fuel and shelter were things that it found for itself. The family matriarch of the day was the same Elizabeth Miller, the wife of Philip Roblin Sr., previously mentioned. She was an Iron Lady. When her husband died as a result of his wounds in the

American scuffle, she took over as head of the family. She helped organize a Methodist Church in the area, and was the driving force behind what became Roblin's Mill, where grain was ground into flour. Incidentally, Roblin's Mill was later removed to Toronto to be reincarnated as the Black Creek Pioneer mill.

As the family made its way in this pioneer situation, some members became interested in politics. In fact, in the early 1800s, John Roblin, Philip's son, ran for the legislature of what was then Upper Canada as a Reformer, not once but three times. He was successful on all three occasions but never took his seat in the legislature. He was a lay preacher, a Methodist circuit rider to be precise, at a time when the clergy were barred from sitting in the legislature. The Family Compact, to which he was firmly opposed, cleverly, if dubiously, invoked the clergyman rule (three times) to keep him out of his seat. The second member of the family, of the next generation—also called John—was a Clear Grit member of Parliament of Upper Canada. For 16 years he was a strong supporter of William Lyon Mackenzie and the radical tradition in eastern Ontario. It is alleged that Sir John A. Macdonald found his contribution to the legislative discussions highly irritating. He was also an agent for the Bank of Montreal. A portrait of John P. Roblin hung in the Bank of Montreal's head office. Fred McNeil, when he was president of the bank, gave me a photocopy. Later on, in 1854-61, in the Parliament of the united Canadas, David Roblin was a two-term member of that legislature. Add my grandfather and me to the list, and you get five politicians and, as you might say, a family tradition.

My mother's family had a quite different story. Her father—my grand-father—Andrew Murdoch, was born at Ballater, Scotland, near Balmoral Castle. He came with his parents to Canada in the 1850s at the age of three months, when it took a month to cross the ocean by sailing ship. His father was an employee, probably a gardener, on the royal estate of Balmoral. When he left to emigrate, he received a letter from the queen's secretariat, wishing Mr. Murdoch every good fortune in his adventures in the colonies. It didn't say which colony, which was rather a good thing, because there were two Murdoch cousins, one going to Australia and one going to Canada. My ancestor was headed for Australia, but the birth of his son interfered with the travel plans so he switched with his cousin and he came to Canada instead.

His son, my grandfather, Andrew Murdoch, was a life-long Ontario Scottish Grit, of which there are no grittier. He once shook hands with Sir Wilfrid Laurier on a railroad platform in the course of an election campaign and that sealed the bargain and fixed his politics. His wife came from an Alsace-Lorraine family who had settled in Montreal, so I put them down as half French and half German. Andrew Murdoch and Ella May Eckhardt were the grandparents on my mother's side, and so complete the family tree.

Family background may, in adult life, be of some personal interest, yet among children it can usually be regarded as a subliminal influence at best. In my case, however, my grandfather, Rodmond Palen Roblin, was too large a figure in my childhood recollections to be overlooked. I recall grandfather R.P., as everyone called him, in his late sixties and long retired from public life, as the family patriarch, the revered and dominant personality in the family circle.

R.P. was one of those Roblins from the Bay of Quinte in Ontario. As a young man, he married Adelaide de Mille. They were travelling with their first-born by sleigh someplace in eastern Ontario when the horse bolted, startled by a railway engine. R.P. was thrown out with his wife and child, and he broke his leg. (The name of the child was Wilfrid Laurier Roblin, which shows what his politics were in those days.) While he was convalescing from this accident, he read a piece of literature about the great golden West, and decided he had to take a look at it. His trade as a cheese maker had declined after the United States abrogated its reciprocity treaty with Canada, so he was ready to move. From Georgian Bay he sailed to Duluth, and from Duluth reached Warren's Landing, Minnesota, and then travelled by boat—six days down the Red River—landing in Winnipeg on May 31, 1877, with nothing but what he could carry. He went to work as a labourer, turning the printing press at the local newspaper, but not for long. He decided that Winnipeg—population 2,722—didn't look very promising, so he and a friend decided to move on to Edmonton with the ox-carts. They started out on foot from Winnipeg and got as far as Headingley. The muddy going was so heavy that R.P. gave up on Edmonton; gave his partner a revolver, which he was carrying, and decided to look for some place closer at hand.

The place he found was Carman, 40 miles southwest of Winnipeg, but accessible only on horseback or on foot. It was then called Boyne Crossing after the river that runs through it. There was not much there, but he opened a store, a trading post, to trade with the Indians and the growing population of new settlers. The main product the Indians had to offer was seneca root—there might have been the odd buffalo hide—but mostly seneca root, good for pharmaceuticals. One day he traded off the top hat, and the morning coat he was married in, to an Indian chief for a large supply of seneca root. R.P.'s description of the Indian chief trying to tell him in sign language that he wanted to buy a laxative is best left to the imagination. He decided to call this place Carman after one of his former teachers at Albert College in Belleville. He kept store there for a while, took up a homestead, and then became a pioneer in the new grain export business in Manitoba. He next gravitated into politics.

R.P. was first elected as a Liberal in 1888. He broke with the Greenway government on its railway policy, and later was the only Protestant member to oppose its bill to change the constitutional school rights of franco-Manitobans. The terms of the original Manitoba Act of 1870, respecting language and education rights, were not lightly to be abrogated. But they were under threat, and this concerned him. He crossed the floor first as an Independent, then in 1896 was elected leader of the Conservative party, in opposition to the Greenway government.

The election of 1899 was then drawing near, and my grandfather knew his position on the Manitoba school question had made him no friends in the powerful Orange Order. He thought the party required a leader with an estab-lished Conservative pedigree so he retired to make way for Hugh John Macdonald (the son of Sir John A.) who had sat in the federal Parliament. Hugh John was not eager, but Sir Charles Tupper, federal party leader, and other heavyweights from eastern Canada persuaded him to take the job. He won the election and became premier. My grandfather was in the legislature but not in the cabinet. However, in 1900, Hugh John decided to return to federal politics, and my grandfather then succeeded him as premier in October 1900. Hugh John later became a Chief Magistrate in Winnipeg and was a highly revered figure in the pioneer community.

R.P.'s life in politics was over before I was born, and the record of his 15 years as premier is no part of my memoirs. Nevertheless, as I grew up, the echoes of those events reverberated around me and in my consciousness and should not go unremarked. I could list his policies on railway building, the agricultural college, normal school, workmen's compensation, public utilities, the Manitoba Telephone System, hospital institutions, good roads, the extension of the provincial boundaries north to the 60th parallel, his fight for farmers against the Grain Exchange, public finances including a direct corporation tax initiative and other policies of an active administration. But it is the events of his last year in 1914 that linger in the public memory. Nellie McClung, a brilliant advocate, interested in sterilization, prohibition and especially votes for women, raised a major challenge. R.P., grounded in the pioneer tradition of his early days and, let it be said, in his Victorian ethos, refused female suffrage. He was decidedly on the wrong side of the issue, as my mother reported, both for herself and her mother-in-law. Mrs. McClung won the public debate hands down. Even though up until then, R.P. had represented majority opinion in the province, it soon turned with a vengeance in favour of women's rights.

The final blow, however, was the charge of corruption in the construction of the new legislative building. Malfeasance was exposed. The government was blamed, and R.P. accepted his responsibilities and resigned. Ministers were purported to be parties in a fraudulent transaction. A long and dreary trial in the courts ensued. Meanwhile, in other proceedings, the provincial architect was implicated and the building contractor was sent to gaol. R.P.'s trial ended in the jury's disagreement, and in the outcome the courts discharged him.

Duff Roblin

ABOVE: MATERNAL GRANDFATHER MURDOCH   ABOVE: PATERNAL GRANDFATHER ROBLIN

I make no comment on R.P. in politics, lest an undue filial piety be thought to unbalance the account. But I do refer to the analysis of W.L. Morton. Morton was the son of a cabinet colleague of Premier D.L. Campbell, and one of Manitoba's pre-eminent historians. His book, *A History of Manitoba*, came out in 1955. In a review of the political scene in 1913, Morton describes a society moving from an agricultural base to an industrial one as a challenge to political parties and "an especial challenge to the Conservative Party which was completing its fourth term of highly successful administration. That party had governed the province well; it had moved with the times. It could point to a long record of concrete achievement. It had, in fact, been progressive in its practical measures and while it had been conservative in that it stood by what was established as in the school question and demanded that the need of reform be thoroughly proved before adoption ..."

Morton goes on to reprobate the extreme partisanship of Manitoba politics at that time and to wonder about the ability of the government to respond fully to a new spirit of the time. Morton also offered a character sketch of R.P. as "a man of great energy, simplicity and directness of mind and possessed of a trenchant grasp of principles ... These qualities were modified by a broad tolerance of different views, a vigilant realism in reading public opinion and a keen sense of human foibles and weaknesses." Morton continues: "A certain pomposity of speech and manner, a self confidence, that verged on arrogance, a personal loyalty which approached a blind trust in colleagues were to mar the strong characteristics of Roblin as they hardened into fixed habit."

So far, so good. Now Morton speaks of the effects of the legislative building scandal. He condemned a political machine captured by blind partisan politics. He identifies the responsibility of party leaders and concludes "the old kind of politics would no longer do and had to go. The pity of it is that men of marked ability and fine achievements had to be swept away with it. Sir Rodmond Roblin deserved a better fate and the historic party he had led with such distinction a more loyal and honest service from its agents."

As for R.P.'s final discharge by the courts, Morton observes "no further public service, it was clear was to be rendered by pressing charges against a man known to be personally honourable but who had been engulfed by the under-world of politics everyone hoped was now destroyed." As for me, from the long perspective of my many years, I have reflected on the human condition and observed the struggles of men with time, circumstances and themselves to shape their own ends. R.P. was the outstanding Manitoba personality of his times and a strong leader among men. I am not willing that the good should be interred with his bones. I will take him, and I will take him warts and all.

In those days without movies, radio, or television, politics was an entertainment of universal interest. In a 1903 election meeting in Carman, R.P. spoke for almost three hours to general satisfaction. Figures and documents were freely quoted, opposition leaders and their press were castigated, and their doggerel verse ridiculed. The audience responded on cue and went home satisfied. The address was printed, opinions were swayed, and elections won. *O tempora o mores.*

One of the great issues of R.P.'s early premiership was transportation. Transportation was the key to development. There were, of course, no motor roads or trucks, there was just the railroad, and the railroad was everything. So a great deal of his early policy and effort was spent promoting the extension of a rail system with branch lines throughout the province to facilitate settlement, trade, and handling of the crops. He conducted a lively vendetta with the CPR, which he regarded as an unconscionable monopoly. One aim was to bring freight rates down. His successful tactic with the CPR involved shipping grain east to the Lakehead. Duluth in Minnesota is a lot closer to Winnipeg than is Port Arthur in Ontario. We could ship to Duluth and save money on freight. That forced the CPR to make a counter-offer, "If you ship to Port Arthur, we will only charge the lower Duluth rate." It was called a constructive mileage rate. This was quite a coup and saved freight costs for Manitoba farmers. When I came along and sat in the opposition 40 years later, the question of freight rates was still the subject of endless inquiries and royal commissions. At that time, the constructive mileage to Port Arthur was given up, and I reacted with horror. I pointed out it was a privilege won long ago and shouldn't be abandoned lightly, but to no avail.

Even though he came from Ontario, which dominated the national scene economically and politically, R.P. was a strong voice for western provincial rights. In fact, he attended the first meeting of provincial premiers ever held to promote provincial rights in dealing with the federal government. He was a Disraeli conservative, not a dogmatic or reactionary one. He was ready to respect and protect the traditions of the past, but equally ready to recognize new responsibilities and do something about them.

R.P. was an imperialist, and the British Empire suited him very well. Queen Victoria had just disappeared from the scene, a quarter of the globe was coloured red, our trade links with the United Kingdom were strong, and the whole rationale for the imperial system was powerful. As Rudyard Kipling said, empires come and go, and so it was with the British Empire, but in those days, it was an intelligent thing to be an imperialist because being part of the Empire gave Canada status in the world. In fact, R.P. was invited to tour Britain speaking on that subject, which he did with great success. But his view of the Empire never obscured his respect for the rights of others. He never allowed himself to think that it overrode the recognition that should be given to new Canadian settlers from wherever they came. That view was reflected in his school language policy where, in accordance with the Manitoba School Question compromise of 1897, a place was made in the school system for French and several immigrant languages. But in order to make sure that immigrants understood their loyalty to their new country, he arranged to have every school in Manitoba fly the Union Jack. The symbolism was plain.

I'm a bit of a flag man myself. In the 1960s, the legislature adopted the Manitoba flag that we have today as our provincial emblem. Flags have an important psychological and symbolic impact. When the Canadian Maple Leaf flag was introduced in 1964, I was premier, and I regretted that the new flag of the country had no trace whatever of our historical connection. I would have been happy if it had, but since that flag was the will of Parliament, I determined we would respect that will. So the day the new flag was proclaimed, I attended a parade in front of the Legislative Building where two flagpoles stand on Broadway, and we had a ceremony of respect to run up the new flag. At the time of the flag debate, Lester Pearson was prime minister. Ever the diplomat, Pearson sometimes seemed to value the achievement of the diplomatic solution over the realistic satisfaction of the interests at stake, but not always. Pearson came to state his case for the Maple Leaf flag at a convention of the Royal Canadian Legion in Winnipeg. It was a rough meeting. The legionnaires were ready to defend the old Canadian ensign to the last boo. Amid a welter of noise, cat-calls and general uproar, Pearson began to speak. I was on the platform with him, and saw him brace himself for the storm. There was no wavering there. He faced them down and he prevailed. Respect, however grudging, was offered in the end, and I take my hat off to him. The diplomat wore armour.

Duff Roblin

The episode of 1915 was traumatic, but R.P.'s reaction told something of the temper of the man. At 65 years of age, he was broke financially because he and three others had signed a very large promissory note to fight the 1914 election. The three others disappeared—through death or bankruptcy—and he was left to make good the debt. His reputation was in ruins, and his life seemed to be coming to a very unhappy conclusion, but he faced up to it all. His friends were still with him and he decided to re-enter the business world. He continued to be interested in a grain exchange firm but, being farsighted and enterprising, he saw in 1917 the potential of the automobile. He saw the opportunity and resolved to be part of it. So he set up a car dealership in a former retail store on Portage Avenue East with a big plate-glass window. He displayed a car in the window and sat himself beside it. Business came, and he was able to make enough money to pay off the bank loan and start anew. He refused to fade away, and he never looked back.

I remember as a child, visiting him in a new garage showroom the business then occupied. He would sit in an old wicker chair, and every day there would be people coming to see him, old retainers, old friends, who wanted to talk about things and see what R.P. thought. He had a place in the community which he never lost. When R.B. Bennett was active in politics, he came to Winnipeg and made a pilgrimage to R.P.'s house to visit him, which pleased the old man immensely—he was in his 70s or 80s. I was on tap, taking it all in, but I could tell he was pleased that Bennett had taken the trouble to come to see him. He was a strong personality. There's an Asiatic saying that nothing grows in the shade of the banyan tree. It's a great tree that spreads out its branches so widely that nothing grows underneath it. He was a banyan tree. Everyone felt that R.P. was a dominant and dominating personality, and so he was, but he could deal with the two sides of life. I dare say he didn't like it, but he could handle it.

I, of course, was blissfully unaware of any of his problems, but I did know that I was a pretty important part of his life. As his first grandchild, I received a great deal of attention. R.P. carried a walking stick, usually for decoration. We were visiting the buffalo enclosure at Assiniboine Park one day when R.P.

and I stepped up for a close look at the animals. In the spirit of enquiry, R.P. took a quick poke with his cane through the open meshwork stockade at the nearest bull. The savage reaction shook the fence, and it certainly shook me. Even the old man looked sheepish. Every Saturday as a small boy, I would go to visit him—he lived at 211 Garry St. which is now opposite the Winnipeg post office—and we would take a little expedition to Timothy Eaton's store where we would buy a book. In those days, it was Thornton W. Burgess's stories about animals or some other creatures. We would choose our book and then come back to his house and he would read it to me. This was a ritual, a new book every Saturday. When we ran through all the animals and got into the lives of insects, he drew the line. He wasn't interested in reading about insects! But when we ran out of books for him to read to me, he would read to himself, and if I was there, he would read aloud to the both of us. He was omnivorous—histories, biographies, all of literature, was his constant recreation. He sat in a big armchair. I would sit on its high back with my feet on his shoulders around his head, and he would read to me whatever happened to interest him. If it was *The War of the Roses*, or whatever, I got it!

My grandmother, Adelaide, was the homemaker—she had four sons and a husband to look after. Once when rebuked for misbehaviour, in a fit of infantile pique I called her that old woman, R.P. put that piece of impertinence and me in my place instanter. I would be very surprised if she was consulted much on his daily political activities, but she was certainly there with him in the difficult times. She was a dear old lady of whom I was very fond, but I have no means of knowing, really, what role she played in his life.

At home, my mother, Sophia May, was at the centre. She was the daughter of that old-style Scottish Grit previously mentioned, but to her, Roblin was a proud name, and I was left in no doubt about it. Her father, Andrew Murdoch, lived with us until he died. Grandfather Roblin would come over for dinner or lunch, and Grandfather Murdoch would start the political ball rolling, Grit versus Tory. He would address Grandfather Roblin as Gov'ner, and Grandfather Roblin would address him as Murdick. His name was, of course, Murdoch, but it soon got to be Murdick. So Murdick and Gov'ner would have at it until my mother would lower the boom. That would be the end of the politics and peace would be restored. Recollection does not record the subjects of these brisk exchanges.

During the Great Depression, many hungry men needed to be fed. R.P. would hand out his calling card with a handwritten note on the back asking a convenient restaurant where his credit was good to "give this man all he can eat." This gesture was not lost on me. Although my mother had a proper family attitude toward my grandfather, R.P., I really didn't understand much about him until later when I began to reflect on his life and his reactions to the vicissitudes of fortune. The politics of the situation didn't impinge on me. The first time it did was when I went to the University of Manitoba. I took first year there with a French language professor named W.F. Osborne[1]. He had run against my grandfather in 1910 in the constituency of Dufferin and had never got over it. When another Roblin appeared on the scene, there was no lack of oblique references from Osborne. He had a good time with me. The little political jibes he gave me from time to time didn't really hurt—they distinguished me in the class. When I made my first tentative political steps, it's true that sometimes these echoes of the past were directed at me and occasionally there were squalid rumbles in some corners about this grandson of old Roblin now appearing on the scene, but they never amounted to much. I dealt with this in my maiden speech in the legislature, when I made it quite clear that I was not backing away from the name of Roblin and that I was proud of my grandfather, regardless of what anyone else might think, and no more was heard on the subject.

My going into politics was thus no whim. I was determined from the beginning, even if subconsciously, to be premier of Manitoba. No doubt the memory of my grandfather was buried in my psyche, but it expressed itself in my actions. I know that R.P. did set some goals for me. The currents of life run deep, and we hardly know how they move us. I took much pleasure in August

---

1 W.F. Osborne came to Winnipeg in 1893 to be the head of the English Department at Wesley College. He was an eloquent lecturer both at the front of a classroom or in a public forum. Extensive travel in Europe prior to 1914 was fodder for an extremely popular series of lectures outlining the harbinger of war. Osborne was a leading light in the Liberal Party of Manitoba between 1908-1915. In 1910 he challenged Premier Rodmond Roblin in the Dufferin constituency but failed to unseat the Tory leader. Osborne moved over to the University of Manitoba in 1913 where he headed up the French Department until his retirement in 1942.

of 1963 in going to Ontario, at the invitation of Premier John Robarts, a friend of mine, to unveil a plaque at R.P.'s Quinte birthplace. It was a beautiful sunny day. There we were: the Premier of Ontario, the Premier of Manitoba, plus local nabobs, standing up on a hayrick, looking out on a sea of eastern Ontario faces, many of whom were somehow or other related to me, unveiling this plaque to my grandfather. It was a very satisfying afternoon.

two

FINDING MYSELF

◆

MY FATHER, CHARLES DUFFERIN ROBLIN, WAS THE YOUNGEST OF FOUR sons of R.P. and Adelaide Roblin, and was born a healthy but not a robust child. All his life he had to be careful with his health. He went to Tuckwell's boys' school in Winnipeg, was educated at the University of Manitoba, and graduated from Osgoode Hall Law School. When World War I broke out, he joined an infantry regiment. He married my mother in 1916. Mother was a strikingly handsome woman, with a beautiful head of auburn hair. She was born Sophia May Murdoch in Hamilton, Ontario, and came west with her father in the early part of the century. She was one of the first women to graduate from a college in this part of the world, and might have been called a feminist in today's reckoning. She was a very independent character. After she left university, she earned her living as a librarian, and I recall her as a spirited personality indeed. After their wedding, by Archdeacon Fortin at Holy Trinity Church, featuring an arch of swords supplied by fellow officers, my father was posted overseas.

I was born in Winnipeg on June 17, 1917, during his overseas duty. He had three older brothers, all of whom eventually married, but none of them produced any children. I was followed in my family by two sisters and a brother, Cynthia, Marcia, and then Rodmond II. It was an exceedingly happy home and a happy upbringing. My parents were most attentive, they were encouraging, they gave lots of freedom for self-expression, and as a corollary, they expected a degree of personal responsibility, so I count myself fortunate in that beginning.

The first home I remember was the end house in a five-house tenement, now called townhouses, at 48 Smith Street. It has since disappeared under a street relocation. Mother never appeared at breakfast, but I was allowed to go down to stand beside my father's chair to keep him company. My reward was to enjoy the top of his soft-boiled egg and a segment of his grapefruit. In good weather, I could also ride my tricycle with him to the end of the block as he set off for work in the morning. Unbeknownst to all, sitting in his little study, my resident grandfather Murdoch would give me a sip of his elevenses beer. I loved the bitter taste. The fire brigade station was on our street. When the horse-drawn hook and ladder section thundered by, all the world came to a halt.

My schooling was unremarkable, though a little varied perhaps from the ordinary run of things. I have been described as an "old girl" of Rupertsland Ladies' College, having attended kindergarten at that place. I remember well my first day. My mother took me, and when I found out that she was going to leave me in this circle of barbarians I put on a terrible tantrum. I can close my eyes and see myself standing on the chair in the lobby of the school, bawling my eyes out because my mother was going to leave me alone with all these strange folk. But that didn't last long. Public school followed, and then St. John's College School, where I was entered as a day boy. I remember the long streetcar journeys from Stradbrook Avenue down to the north end of the city to go to school each day. I found St. John's a happy experience. It was a traditional English-type boys' school. There were really two kinds of boys there: those who were sent by their families to be made into little gentlemen, and those who were sent by their families because nobody else could do anything with them. Both kinds of boys profited greatly by that admixture. As a putative little gentleman—I preferred the ruffians! The whole was moderated by several clergymen's sons who were sent there gratis, as no clergyman in the Anglican Church ever got enough money to pay school fees.

The routine was regular. It was a classical type of education, with the usual curriculum—Latin, history, English, scripture, with French and mathematics. There was a daily service in the chapel where I first got a taste of the beauty of the English language displayed in the Anglican Prayerbook. Its Elizabethan

Duff Roblin

ABOVE: MOTHER SOPHIA MAY AT THE
TIME OF HER WEDDING, 1916

BELOW: DUFF, FIRST OF THE SEVEN AGES

ABOVE: FATHER CHARLES ON BEING
POSTED OVERSEAS, 1916

RIGHT: DUFF, MODELING HIS
NEW WINTER OUTFIT

cadences linger in the memory. There was an annual prize-giving. I usually got a prize, but I never came in first, much to my chagrin. I joined the school in 1926, in what was called the lower first form, which is Grade 5. At that time I didn't know any Latin, and less mathematics, so when I got home at night my mother used to drill me in all these esoteric lines of instruction so I would catch up with the class. I remember well having that stuff pounded into my head. She did it well, and she also gave me good advice. "If you are familiar with Shakespeare, know Milton, Pope and the Bible, you will have the best in the English language." I found it to be so.

Four years later, the Great Depression became a concern in our family. Money was not so plentiful, so it was back to public school for me, and I went to Kelvin Technical High School for Grades 10 and 11. I was no more than a respectable scholar, but I flourished in that co-educational atmosphere. The big moment at Kelvin was when we decided to produce a play of John Drinkwater's called *Oliver Cromwell*. Of course, I wanted to be Cromwell. I didn't get the part, but I did play King Charles and had to be satisfied with losing my head.

Somewhere along the line after high school, I stumbled across an organization called the Winnipeg Youth Council: youths who had been stranded by the Great Depression and were determined to get something done to put their lives back on the rails. It was a catholic organization, in the "universal" sense. The Communists, both open and crypto, provided the intellectual leadership, and there was a group of young people from the CCF, the Liberal Party, church groups, ethnic groups, trade unions and, just for the laughs, one or two Conservatives. I was one of that latter number. It was an exhilarating, stimulating experience that exposed me to a view of life that was outside my cosy circle. It gave me a new perspective on the world. I learned a lot and made some interesting friends of all political stripes at Youth Council. Ken Woodsworth, Alistair Stewart, Donna Aiken, Laurier Regnier, Ann Ross, Emily Johnson, David Bowman, Ken McAskill and Dyson Carter come to mind. Jim Cowan, who was afterwards a colleague of mine in the legislature, appeared. So it was quite a group, and it was worthwhile. I mention another

member: Bill Ross. Joe Zuken, his brother, was a long-time elected municipal office holder, and Communist leader. I watched Bill's tactics at council
meetings. He would always wait until everybody else had their say. Then he
would wind up and, in the course of that winding up, successfully insinuate his
own views into the decision. It was a very effective technique, and I must say
I used it myself in the days that were to come. You learn little things as you go
through life about how to manage yourself and how to manage affairs.

In 1935, I was unexpectedly involved in the federal election. I got a phone
call from a Conservative organizer in Toronto named Denton Massey, who had
been given the job of mobilizing the youth vote in Manitoba. I was 18 at the
time, without either a vote or influence. Just the same, I got a free airplane trip
to Toronto, was loaded up with a lot of propaganda material to take back home.
I suppose I distributed the propaganda in the proper places, to no noticeable
effect—but it was fun. Massey fared better: in 1935, he was elected to the
House of Commons, representing the Greenwood riding in Toronto. He later
became the Reverend Denton Massey. I regret I only met him once.

Following the custom of the time, after high school I went to the University
of Manitoba. A number of interesting people taught us there, including history professor Joseph Howe. He had the distinction of being the grandson of
Joseph Howe, the Father of Confederation from Nova Scotia. He had the sin-
gular talent of being able to draw a map of Canada on the blackboard without
looking at it. He would face the class, lecturing, and then draw the map with
one hand on the board behind him. Latin was my best subject, higher mathematics the worst. My highlight was to appear in a one-act arts faculty play
opposite Brian Dickson who became a chief justice of Canada. I played an old
man. He starred as the ghost of a World War I officer. The notices were mixed.
After one year at university, I decided to drop out, brash enough to think that
I could do just as well educating myself by my own reading and by rubbing
shoulders with the world. Momentarily, I had a notion to take up law. My
father had long since given up his law practice for business. When I asked his
advice, he pointed to his legal diploma on the wall and offered it to me for
$50—nuff said. So, off I went and shortly afterwards, at the suggestion of my

grandfather—who else?—entered the Success Business College where I mastered bookkeeping, shorthand and typing. Only bookkeeping stuck with me and I found it to be very handy business asset as life went by.

After Success Business College, while I was working in our family's car dealership founded by R.P., some distant American relations came to Winnipeg from Chicago in order to shake hands with a real live "Sir." They considered my grandfather, who had been made a Knight Commander of the Order of St. Michael and St. George in 1912, to be a prestige relation, so they came up to get acquainted. In the course of the visit, I mused about further education. They mentioned the University of Chicago as a school with a high reputation. That started a 12-month adventure in Chicago in 1936, living in the student residence and taking various courses in the School of Business. Going to that university opened another new door for me because it put me in touch with the great American republic, and I learned to appreciate something of the various values of that society. In an inter-university debate, I supported public ownership of public utilities with Manitoba Hydro in mind. Broadcast on the powerful WGN Chicago radio station, it was heard in Winnipeg. I won a low-level athletic award in gymnastics and played squash in what became the famous Atomic Energy Squash Courts. Later on at that site, and after I had safely returned to Manitoba, the squash courts became the place where university scientists secretly conducted some of the critical experiments leading to the development of the atomic bomb.

At Easter in Chicago, a post graduate friend, Donald Smith, and I took a break to go to New York City by train, coach class. It was a long miserable overnight trip. Once arrived, we registered at the YMCA and got seats to see Maurice Evans, the Olivier of his day, play in Shakespeare's *Richard II*—great show. After a night on the town, we arrived back at the Y at dawn. Donald, much the worse for wear, threw up in the communal bathroom. I was in better shape for which I have no excuse. Nevertheless, both of us, the doctoral student and the junior, were both chucked out by the teetotal Y. One up for me.

My decision to go to the University of Chicago was much reprobated by R.P., who thought I would do better to stay home and get down to business and earn a living. In defiance of the patriarch's wishes, I went anyway. It was while I was in Chicago that he died—in Hot Springs, Arkansas, where he regularly spent the winters. Why anyone would go to Hot Springs for any reason always escaped me, but he seemed to find it congenial. I remember one story he told me of going to church there. It was an African-American church, where the singing was beautiful. He would attend with his wife, until one day he was visited by a delegation of the white citizens of the town. They told him that this was a white man's no-no in Arkansas, and he had better not go to a black church again.

I went to St. Louis to meet his body coming up by train from Hot Springs and escorted it into Winnipeg. It was at that time that I first entered the office of the Premier of Manitoba. My father took me with him to see Premier John Bracken to discuss the details of my grandfather's lying-in-state at the Legislative Building. I had a first-hand view of Mr. Bracken and the office. I have to admit that, at that time, neither moved me very much—a rather jejune reaction. They buried R.P. in Elmwood Cemetery on a desolate and cold winter day, and the day certainly matched my feelings. Losing my grandfather who had stood between me and the outside world was a disturbing experience. It made me feel that that great world was coming a little bit closer, and the shelter my family offered was reduced by the loss of his generation.

After my return from my 12-month term at the University of Chicago, it seemed that it would be a good thing if I were more informed about the ins and outs of farming. Agriculture was still the major economic activity in the province of Manitoba in those days, and Manitobans ought to know something about that part of our life. I was not a stranger to farming because the family homestead was near a little town called Homewood, six miles east of Carman. It was called Maplewood Farm, a beautiful place. There were great cottonwood trees my grandfather had planted, and a fine stable filled with cows and horses, run by my uncle Arthur who was a very good farmer. As a child, my great joy in life, whatever the season, whenever there was time off— was to be shipped off to the farm. I loved the farm and farming life. Even little boys could work at farmyard chores like cleaning stables, weeding gardens, and hobnobbing with the hired hands. In the winter I would be put on the train for the 40-mile trip: Homewood was the fifth stop from Winnipeg. In the station, everyone closed in on the pot-bellied stove, keeping warm until the grain-box sleigh arrived from the farm 1 1/2 cold miles away. The two-horse team, Chummy and Darkie, pulled us along, and looking back we could see the long dark train moving majestically onward over the snow-covered prairie with its plume of smoke rising from the engine and sounding its poignant whistle.

A special diversion was to drive in a closed cutter over the snow-bound road, the six miles to Carman. Even under a buffalo robe it was bone chilling. The one-room Homewood school always held a Christmas party where the local Santa Claus gave the children presents. Though I was not on the roll, my aunt Iona took me to join the fun. I had a hard time understanding how Santa could also have a present for me. In those hard times on the prairies, neighbours helped out. Being relatively a big farmer with a section and a half in land, my uncle Arthur and aunt Iona were the last resort of some of their struggling neighbours who needed cash or kind. Even a small child could sense the depth of the Depression. Friends with more good will than political sense once talked Arthur into running for the legislature. He was quite lost on the platform. No doubt he was glad to lose. The only memorable event of the campaign was that R.P. appeared to make one speech for him. More votes were lost than gained.

Later on, my father, in an ill-advised move, bought a farm near Dufrost, Manitoba, which was being managed for him by a Russian émigré called Michael Schramchenko. Schramchenko's father had been an official in Chernigov province in Ukraine and was a refugee from Communism. He had married a Scottish woman and these two lost souls, God save them, were trying to make a living on this farm. Their Franco-Manitoban neighbours watched with some surprise as their European-type agriculture was introduced to this Manitoba farm. I went out to help Michael. His skill was not with tractors or farming but in the breeding of Brabançons, a type of heavy draft horse that his farming neighbours had long since traded in for tractors.

Duff Roblin

I was pretty good at stooking sweet clover where the stooks stick together, but try stooking slippery wheat sheaves—that's a horse of another colour. The farm did produce country cream and fresh pork which it was my job to peddle in our Winnipeg neighbourhood in the wintertime. Anyway, I worked on the farm but no good came of it all, and my father decided to abandon the operation. This foray into agriculture led me to the University of Manitoba in 1937 where then, as now, an agricultural diploma course was offered as an introduction into the practical aspects of modern farming. Field crops, livestock, weed and insect control, and farm management were included in a wide variety of very practical topics for young men who were going into farming. Thus another door opened for me, giving a taste of Manitoba agriculture. This broadened perspective turned out to help significantly in the political arena later on.

This educational progression, focusing on my special interests, was all very well. But what did I have to show for it? Could it add up to a degree? To explore this possibility, I solicited an interview with the president of the University of Manitoba, Dr. Sidney Smith, to outline my academic achievements and to suggest that these odds and ends would be an interesting basis for academic recognition. Well, he heard me out and then ushered me out. I was confirmed as a university dropout. The four university degrees I now hold were bestowed *honoris causa*.

In 1938, I went to work for the Manitoba Blue Cross. The Blue Cross is based on an American idea that people could join together in voluntary groups to insure hospital expenses. Premiums would be collected through free payroll deduction by employers, and the members would then have the assurance of hospital treatment when needed. It was good for them as a health insurance project. It was good for hospitals because it was a way of making sure their bills were paid. This idea was picked up by a remarkable Winnipeg woman named Margaret McWilliams[2]. She was an outstanding personality, very active in civic affairs, who has left a good reputation and fine name behind her. She was the wife of R.F. McWilliams who served as Lieutenant Governor of Manitoba from 1940 to 1953.

Mrs. McWilliams decided that the Blue Cross idea was something we needed in Manitoba. She lived across the street from us, and one day, walking down to catch the streetcar, I met her. She wasted no time in telling me I had been selected—by her, of course—to help start the Blue Cross system in Manitoba. I'd never heard of Blue Cross, but if you had ever met Margaret McWilliams, you knew very well that it was no use arguing with her. To demur didn't count. If she had decided this was to be done, the sooner you got busy and did it, the better for all concerned, so I found myself an employee of the Manitoba Blue Cross. There were three sales agents—I was one of them—$70 a month and car expenses, and off we went.

I remember vividly my first sally as a salesman. I was sent out to break the ice at the Dominion Envelope Company. I walked up and down in front of their plant for at least 30 minutes before working up the courage to open their door. But I did. I went in to present myself to the management, to explain the Blue Cross idea that for the welfare of their employees and the hospitals, they should give us access to their staff to sell the Blue Cross principle to them, and as a community service collect our premiums for us without charge.

One of my more challenging calls was the CNR Shops in south Winnipeg. I was entrusted to an elderly, shop-steward type, obviously from somewhere in the United Kingdom who had, to put it mildly, a rather skeptical view of the proposition I was putting forward. He was given the job of taking me around to the various craftsmen as they worked at their sites so I could make the pitch for Blue Cross and to sign up members. He took me under his wing, made sure the craftsmen I was talking to knew who I was and why I was there, and in the end, he signed up himself. Signed Blue Cross cards came in by the score. I told myself I was a top producer. The truth, of course, was that it was an easy sell.

---

2 Margaret Stovel graduated from the University of Toronto in 1898 with a degree in political science. She spent four years in Detroit working for a newspaper before returning to Canada in 1903 to wed Roland Fairbairn McWilliams. The couple moved to Winnipeg in 1910 where Roland practised law. Margaret took an active interest in the public and educational affairs in the city. She conducted a current affairs course for women that continued for more than 30 years. A delegate to the International Labour Office Conference in Geneva in 1930, she attended the Institute of Pacific Affairs conference in Shanghai the following year. Mrs. McWilliams was the first President of the Canadian Federation of University Women. In 1933, she became the second woman ever elected to the Winnipeg City Council, a position she left in 1940 to become the Chatelaine of Government House upon her husband's appointment as Lieutenant-Governor. During the war, she served as a member of a bureau of speakers for the wartime Information Board in Washington.

Duff Roblin

Then something much more important happened. The Second World War was declared. I was at our Whytewold cottage on Lake Winnipeg, about 64 kilometres north of Winnipeg. It was a wonderful September day—sunny and warm—when we got the news. What followed was a rush to enlist. For some time the local militia units had, of course, been steadily recruiting, but I was too smart to bother to enlist. When the war actually came along, those in the militia went on active service, and I scrambled to catch up. Believe it or not, you couldn't find a place to enlist in September 1939. Every rank was filled. I finally found a spot as a private in the First Cavalry Division of the Royal Canadian Army Service Corps and went out to save my country by drilling once a week in the Minto Armory. At the same time, however, I decided to hedge my bets a little and put in a second application to join the air force. This produced a letter saying, "Nice to hear from you, but don't call us, we'll call you." My efforts to enlist took me to Ottawa where, for some queer reason, I thought my chances would be better. Much lobbying produced nothing. The YMCA where I bedded down had a coffee shop. Every day the new recruits in a highland regiment came stomping in for morning coffee break in their military boots and tartan kilt. Roll Out the Barrel was the jukebox selection of choice. All I could do was to sigh as I watched their military satisfactions.

That was during the period known as the phoney war, and the phoney war came to an abrupt end in the spring of 1940. The air force came to life at that time, and I received their notice to report full-time. Meanwhile, I had been getting ready to fly. At the Winnipeg Flying Club at Stevenson Field, I found Charlie Graffo, the flying instructor at the club, and asked him to take me on. I soloed in a Tiger Moth and also learned to pilot a Piper Cub. So I felt I was ready for the air force when the air force was ready for me. When the call came, I didn't know I was signing up for almost six long years of life in uniform, with all that would mean. They were six extraordinary years. Wartime service for some men is the best part of their lives. They look back at it with satisfaction, and I know why that is so. In the services, everyone has a clear purpose in life. There is responsibility, yes, but it's within an ordered and orderly structure.

Your daily bread is provided. The shared lives and the comradeship formed with the men with whom you serve become poignant memories as life goes by. Retrospection dulls the horror and the terror and the pure boredom of military life. The most accurate description of much of it is the old cliché, "hurry up and wait." But to have served is a significant part of one's life.

I found out, however, that I was not to fly. They told me that I had a serious physical defect, namely shortsightedness—I couldn't see far enough. I had successfully fudged the eye test chart at the start, but they soon caught up to me. The policy of the RCAF was that the perfect physical specimens got first crack at death, and the rest were saved for later. I happened to belong to the rest, and they gave me a number C2218. I became what was known as an equipment officer, dealing with supply and logistics. I went to training school at St. Thomas, Ontario, where I learned absolutely nothing. But at St. Thomas the radio delivered Winston Churchill's great speeches of defiance to Hitler and the Nazis that summoned up the blood and stamped us all. After the St. Thomas school, the new pilot officers were asked to nominate their next posting of choice. I put down Newfoundland and Tofino, British Columbia, in that order. Naturally I was sent to Winnipeg instead. I was then posted to No. 7 Services Flying Training School, British Commonwealth Air Training Plan, at Fort Macleod, Alberta, to help open it up. There, pilots for twin-engine aircraft were trained, and our first group of trainees came in from Australia and New Zealand. When our first squadron of rather tatty and well-used Anson aircraft, retired from the Battle of Britain, landed on our airstrip, we felt somehow closer to the fighting front.

Fort Macleod is a delightful little place about 160 kilometres south of Calgary right in the path of the Chinook winds coming through the mountain passes, and a typical pioneer prairie town. I liked it so well that I planned that when the war was over, I was coming back to Alberta to stay. So much for plans. One of my comrades there was Angus MacLean. Angus and I were the only two acknowledged Tories in the place, and we used to walk over the aerodrome field from time to time, commenting upon the vagaries of life under William Lyon Mackenzie King. Angus later became the premier of Prince Edward

Island and a federal cabinet minister. He has written an enthralling story of his own life experiences. By chance, a fellow Winnipegger, E.B. Osler, was a trainee at No. 7 SFTS. I recall one occasion when E.B. wanted to get out of the camp but didn't have a pass. I fitted him in the trunk of my car and smuggled him through the sentry post into Fort Macleod so he could savour the flesh-pots of the town, which consisted mainly of eating beefsteak at the Chinese restaurant. Afterwards, E.B. and I were reacquainted when he soundly trounced me in the federal election of 1968.

I was next summoned to Ottawa, where the powers that be had decided that I would make a good personal assistant to a high-ranking officer called the Air Member for Supply. My job was to sit in front of his office and act as a doorkeeper, making sure that only the right people got in and the others were diverted. Significantly, all communications and paper also came across my desk, and I had first look at it before it was taken in to be shown to the great man. Though I found this paper-pushing a pretty unsatisfactory occupation, it proved to have an advantage. One day early in 1942, a cable came in from England saying they wanted a junior officer for liaison duties in the United Kingdom. I wasted no time in recommending myself for the job and was promptly on my way overseas.

The ocean crossing was in mid-winter in a 13-knot convoy. My ship was the SS *Bayano* which was usually on the Jamaica banana trade run—not really suited for cold weather around Iceland. There was the usual flurry of U-boat alarms and that kind of thing, but we arrived safely at Greenock, Scotland, one cold winter's day. Our vital cargo was rum of the dark brown Demerara kind with an alcohol content of lethal proof. Taking a few bottles ashore boosted my welcome, as well as the war effort among the liquor rationed islanders. We took an overnight train to London. The train had been through the bombings and, being without windows, the bitter wind blew in and out. I don't think I've ever been so paralysed by damp cold as I was in that overnight trip from Greenock to London, trying to keep warm in my greatcoat. It was too much even for a prairie boy.

Reports of the blitz of London coloured every expectation. The first thing I did was check out Trafalgar Square to see if it was still really there. It was very early in the morning. There had been a slight rain. The sun had come up. The pavement was sparkling. No one in sight, no traffic, even the pigeons seemed to have disappeared. I thought of Wordsworth's *Lines Composed Upon Westminster Bridge*, in which he describes his vision of London at dawn— "Dear God! the very houses seem asleep;/And all that mighty heart is lying still!" And so it seemed. But then, of course, soon afterwards I became acquainted with the terrible damage that the air raids had done to the fabric of the city, saw buildings and houses split open, insides spilling out and abandoned to the world. The women and children were sleeping in the tube stations at night as you stepped over and around them. It was an eerie adventure trying to make your way on foot through this blackout to find your destination. Fortunately the early saturation bombing of London had passed, but the less concentrated attacks, duly advertised by the banshee wails of air raid sirens, put life on hold until they subsided and the menace of near miss- es could be shrugged off.

But my job was not in London, it was up in Harrogate, in the west riding of Yorkshire, where I worked to expedite the supply of aircraft spare parts to Canada for use in the British Commonwealth Air Training Plan. I had a small unit, a dozen people. As a squadron leader, I was grandiosely described as commander of this little group, and I made myself quite at home there.

One of the advantages of fighting in a war is that you get plenty of time to read in the moments when action is a little slow, and I took advantage of this opportunity during those years leading up to the D-Day invasion. My job in Harrogate meant that I was a frequent traveller, and I had access to the wonderful bookstores in the major railway stations in the United Kingdom. There I would pick up Penguin books on any number of subjects. In addition to that, I was exposed to the extraordinary variety of British weekly and daily newspapers that covered every aspect of life. *The Economist* newspaper was a favourite, and I'm still reading it today. I spent a lot of my time, too, reading the volumes then published of Arnold Toynbee's *A Study of History* in the unabridged edition. In order to make sure I had the right balance, I then turned to Oswald Spengler's diatribe in *The Decline of the West*. More constructive reading, perhaps, was contained in the Beveridge Report which came out toward the end of the war and which presented an attractive set of plans to improve the social welfare of the nation. Beveridge's three principles registered with me: society has a responsibility to help people in genuine need who are unable to look after themselves; individuals have a responsibility to provide for themselves when they can do so; and work is the best route out of poverty for people who are able to work. I remembered Beveridge when bringing in new social policy in Manitoba later on.

My father had a volume of the complete works of Shakespeare. They were printed on rice paper in a beautiful red leather cover stamped with R.P.'s monogram, and included in portable form everything Shakespeare wrote. My father carried that volume with him during his wartime service overseas in World War I, and I did the same in World War II. I go back often to *Richard III*, not because it's the best play, but because as a child it's the first one I ever saw. My grandfather took me to see it in the Walker Theatre in Winnipeg. I remember it well because when the Duke of Clarence was murdered and stuffed into the butt of malmsey wine, the axe descending on his back, I shrank under the seat in horror. For me, *Hamlet* is the pick, but the sonnets are not to be neglected.

When visiting London on leave, I found there was a Canadian Officers' Club, right across from Canada House in Cockspur Street on Trafalgar Square. This club provided a sandwich and soup lunch for Canadians and was very welcome in days of austerity and rationing. It was run by two interesting ladies. One was Mrs. Neville Chamberlain and the other was Mrs. Vincent Massey. On occasion I was invited to tea—I think it was to the Masseys—and that was a special event. At Harrogate, I bought a second-hand bicycle and cruised all around the Yorkshire Dales. There wasn't a pub in the area I wasn't acquainted with. It was fine, except that it was still a very long way from the scene of action and I soon began to chafe.

As it happened, preparations were in hand for an Allied landing somewhere in France. Nobody knew at that time where. The army was getting ready to go, and a mobile air-force formation was to give close fighter support to the army operations, operating at the front line with the army as it moved forward. This air-force formation was supposed to be very secret and, like everything in those days, it was more secret in name than in fact. It was originally described as Z Group just to preserve the mystery, and then it was transmuted into Blue Group, and finally it became 83 Group, 2nd TAF, RAF, with the task of providing close air support to the 2nd British army as the army landed in Normandy and made its way across Europe. Half of the 83 Group was Canadian and half was British, and the RCAF headquarters in London was casting around for people to man the Canadian positions.

I applied at once for one such job and was much disappointed to find out I was not chosen. Someone else was selected, and I was sent back to Harrogate to brood over my failure. Then the happy news arrived that the original selection had proved to be less than satisfactory and, as second choice, would I mind going to take his place? Hallelujah! 83 Group was commanded by Air Vice Marshall Harry Broadhurst. He had been the commander of the Desert Air Force that had fought the North African battle with General Bernard Montgomery from El Alamein to Tunis. He knew his business.

Our group mobilized, formed, and trained on RAF fighter command airfields in south-east England near the Channel. 83 Group headquarters, where I was posted, operated from the control and airport building at Gatwick aerodrome. We called it the Beehive, though any resemblance was moot. We slept in a deserted mansion on the perimeter which we shared with numberless rats. There was no heating, of course, but surprisingly great quantities of hot water. I remembered this with regret when we left the Beehive to live in tents in the countryside. No hot water there. Being a Canadian in an RAF group had pecuniary advantages. The Brits paid a shilling a day for "hard lying allowance" because we were living under canvas, and the Canadians paid 25 cents a day for being on staff. I collected both these rewards, though other

Duff Roblin

ABOVE: NEWLY MINTED
PILOT OFFICER

BELOW: SQUADRON LEADER ROBLIN, CENTRE, MIDDLE ROW, WITH CREW,
RCAF LIAISON SECTION – HARROGATE

Canadians or Brits serving in other posts could only collect one but not the other. There is something to be said for cockeyed regulations after all.

Working with the British was an interesting experience because they had two attitudes. One was a hearty welcome to these patriotic colonial volunteers who had come to help the mother country. The other half was rather wondering what on earth to do with these awkwardly not-quite-real Brits with whom they were expected to co-operate. There were rough spots, but I found that time and training and propinquity brought all of us up or down to the same level, and the camaraderie was complete by the time we were ready to cross the Channel. So over to Normandy I went.

Not surprisingly, I remember D-Day of June 6, 1944, very well. We were in a concentration area—horrors, what a name—a concentration area where the people who were destined to go to Normandy were sequestered so they wouldn't communicate with the locals and let the great secret out of the bag. Our concentration area was on Salisbury Plain, in sight of Stonehenge. Against all rules I sneaked out of camp to inspect that marvellous historic relic close up. Then we went on to our hard standing beach on the Channel and down to the landing craft. I had a jeep to drive. It was waterproofed and snorkelled so that if it landed in a runnel of water when we got to the other side, it wouldn't cut out, but would keep on going and get us ashore. Happily, we ran right up on the sand at Courseulles-sur-Mer on the Normandy beach with no trouble at all—June 30 was our day—and made our way inland to a place called Creuilly which had the romantic advantage of being a castle of William the Conqueror's from Norman times, or so it was alleged. Our principal recreation was furious games of poker—twenty-one or bust. Enormous bets in Allied invasion currency—phony French francs—were won and lost, worthless money but exhilarating.

The battle proceeded. A visit to a Royal Navy destroyer docked at the Mulberry prefabricated harbour was organized one day. The attraction was a good supply of naval gin available at 6 pence a tot. Navigating our return to our dry camp was a feat of no small proportions. Our contact with U.S. troops was equally basic. Our aim there was to trade rations and clothing—each side thought the other's was superior.

In August of 1944, the armies broke out of the Normandy bridgehead. \The 2nd British army with its attached Canadians moved down through the thoroughly fought-over rubble of the city of Caen to meet American armies coming up from the west to close the Falaise pocket through which retreating Germans were struggling to escape towards Paris. In a thunderous battle, the gap was sealed with terrible destruction to the enemy. The Typhoon fighter bombers of 83 Group RAF aided from the air in the deadly kill. Our group then moved through the battleground, centered around the village of Chambois. Carnage and devastation marked the spot. Dead enemy, dead horses, burned-out and smoking tanks, shattered guns—all the impedimenta of disaster and defeat lay with its stinking horror across the path of the advance. But the way ahead was open. We crossed the Seine, going through Brussels in a tremendous rush forward, trying to keep up with the army.

The speed of movement was stunning. On this passage through France to Belgium, I found myself at dusk within sight of Vimy Ridge. In World War I, the ridge, then behind German lines, long resisted capture until a Canadian assault finally carried the day in a remarkable feat of arms. Part of the ridge has been eternally dedicated by France to Canada and to the Canadians who died there. The spare, tall, white, sombre Canadian monument on this former battlefield is raised high from the top of the escarpment. In the twilight, its two great columns cast long shadows out over the fields of Artois. A system of trenches, sandbags and barbed wire was preserved so that the impressions of the battlefield were intense. Our advance had passed on; the place was deserted and I was alone. The air was calm, the sun was sinking, the silence was profound. And yet the presence of the soldiers who struggled there was almost palpable.

Later on, I drove through the gently swelling landscape of Passchendaele in Belgium where I thought I could discern a remaining pill box, sunk in the ground, bearing witness to the past. War is no stranger in the Low Countries. Passchendaele was the epitome of the stupifyingly fruitless trench warfare of World War I. There a water-logged zone of suffocating mud swallowed up all comers, where nothing was accomplished though thousands died. My father was badly wounded here in 1917, with a metal shaving kit pierced by shrapnel to show for it. Later on, invalided home, he toured Texas as part of an American War Bond campaign. The appearance of a wounded veteran, fresh from the trenches, was calculated to improve sales.

When we got to Brussels, everyone was out in the street to give us fruit and flowers and cheers. We kept right on going, through Brussels, and finally wound up at a little town called Lier, where the lace comes from—on the Albert Canal, not far from Antwerp which was blockaded by the Germans at the time. We bivouacked there for a short while, and then after the great parachute drop at the Arnhem Bridges—which didn't work, but which helped move us out across the border of Belgium into Holland—we settled down for the winter at a little place called Valkenswaard. Philip Campbell, my RAF counterpart, and I were billeted with a Dutch family named Wolters who were in the cigar manufacturing business. Hofnar was their brand. To celebrate our arrival, cigars they had carefully hidden during the German occupation were exhumed and handed around. Of course, I had to smoke one. After this initiation, the habit stuck. It was on this drive north that we liberated, meaning appropriated, an intact German supply dump. Part of the booty was several truckloads of a sweet red French aperitif called Du Bonnet. It took our liquor-rationed men several weeks to work their way through this bonanza, but it was enough Du Bonnet to last me a lifetime.

As we fanned out from the narrow Normandy bridgehead over the considerable territory of France and the Low Countries, communications with our units became stretched. In our formation were several Auster squadrons. Auster was an army term for Piper Cubs which were used as low-flying air observation posts for the military. As they could take off and land from almost any field, they were just the thing to help us to maintain contact with our own units. My pilot was Denis LeBlanc, a very young New Brunswicker who, it soon became apparent, flew by the seat of his pants and visual ground contact only. Flying with me over south-east Holland, Denis became uncertain about exactly where to locate the battle line. Spotting an artillery group on the ground, he attempted to drop in and confirm his bearings. Suddenly, instead of landing, he pulled up and veered away. Sorry, he said, not one of ours. The guns were pointing the wrong way. The logic was curious, but it was not the time to argue. His next adventure involved landing in a heavily plowed field where the Piper Cub nosed right over into the mud. We crawled out. Awkward, but no personal harm done. Tragically, after Denis left me, word came that he had been killed. The loss of this young life brought home poignantly my own good fortune.

On New Year's Day, 1945, our headquarters in Valkenswaard occupied a schoolhouse. About 10 kilometres away was the Eindhoven Airport, which was an 83 Group RAF base. I walked out of my little schoolhouse early in the morning on that New Year's Day attracted by a sweep of low-flying aircraft coming over fast. I wondered what in the name of God our people were doing in our particular part of the battlefield on that particular morning. Well, when I took a good look I discovered the planes had iron crosses on the wings. This was the Luftwaffe. They had come to the rather sensible conclusion that the Canadians may very well be suffering from a good New Year's Eve and this was a good time to get at them. So bright and early New Year's Day, the Luftwaffe strafed our air base at Eindhoven among others and did great damage to our aircraft on the ground.

One of my jobs was to report every day to London on the state of the aircraft: how many we had, how many could fly, how many needed repair, and that sort of thing. God knows what they did with the information when Broadhurst was running our show, but anyway, they got it. It was intimated to me from on high, and not too subtly, that it might be a good idea if this morning I fudged my report a little bit and downplayed the amount of damage. Accustomed to obeying orders, that's what I did. By the dispensation of providence, after that attack we had several days of very heavy fog. Nothing much flew. During that time, our excellent maintenance people got many aircraft back into good shape so they could fly again. Soon I could give the real facts that we were ready to go.

In the spring of 1945 the Rhine was breached. I crossed it at a place called Wavel, and eventually wound up just down the Elbe River from Hamburg in a little town called Altona, a familiar Manitoba name to me. Altona had been a headquarters of the Luftwaffe, so we moved in as they moved out. Central Hamburg was an eerie burned-out shell. On a riverside dock was a jumble of hundreds of church bells carrying the names of their many European places of origin. These names, molded or etched in Latin or the languages of conquered Europe, were names of places, most of which I had scarcely heard of. We arrived in time to spare them from the armament scrap metal furnace. I wonder if any got home again to call the faithful and ring the hours.

I came back to Canada a little while later, in early 1946; I actually crossed the ocean four times during the war. The first was in the *SS Bayano*, as I previously reported. The second time, I came back on special duty (read a visit home) on the *Queen Mary*, landing in New York. I don't know how many thousand men were on the ship, but I do know it was unbelievably crowded. As a senior officer, I was put in charge of a lifeboat crew. Fortunately my talents for that assignment went untested. We had a swift unchallenged crossing.

I then flew back to England in the empty belly of a Liberator. This third cold trip was painfully slow by modern reckoning, but it was then a real adventure to fly over. Then I finally returned to Canada in a ship called the *Lady Nelson* in deluxe style. So I had four interesting ocean experiences. Flying beats sailing. For years after, I carried around a dollar bill, endorsed as a "short snorter"[3] to confirm my trans-Atlantic airborne prowess.

One thing I recall vividly about the return home is my pleasure at seeing the blue western sky. Although I had been overseas for almost four years, I was never homesick except for the blue sky of Manitoba, and it was a great thing to see it again. Also, curiously enough, the Canadian accent struck me as unusual, after four years of listening to plummy English voices. When I landed in Halifax, I phoned my family. My mother answered the call, and I couldn't believe that this tinny Canadian voice was really my mother. To hear her flat Canadian accent once again was something I had to get used to, but it didn't take long.

A recital of my experience during World War II might strike one as a rather pleasant canter through six earth-shaking years, and perhaps it's best to leave it that way. But the war was undoubtedly a critical event in my life. I entered it as a callow, rather self-centred 22-year-old, and I emerged from it much improved because war matures as very few other human activities can do. The experience of command—I was a Wing Commander when the war ended—with responsibility for results and outcomes, and indeed for lives, is something that moulds the personality. I took a small part in preparing for the D-Day expedition, that miracle of organization, in which the use and disposition of every item was so carefully devised, even down to which kit you would take on your back when you went over the Channel. Critical management of things like fuel, ammunition and supplies is not the exciting part of war but is certainly complex. Because 83 Group RAF was a mobile group, whole aerodromes and all support units were completely transportable. Everything was on wheels to keep up with the movements of the 2nd British Army. In 83 Group RAF, scores

3 A dollar bill endorsed by fellow crew members was a rite of passage.

of aircraft, hundreds of vehicles, and thousands of airmen had to be at the right places at the right time with what they needed to fight the battle. Organization and planning were of the essence, and miraculously most of the time everything worked. Snafus could be expected to produce inevitable panic excitement from time to time, but in the end, amateur enthusiasm grew into a rough professionalism.

All those things were full of challenge to the inexperience of most of us. It's remarkable that things worked as well as they did. Of course, we had to deal with the natural succession of events and the prospect of death and disaster which was always present, if ignored. You're seasoned by a life of that sort and you're enlivened and developed by the comradeship that is all part of those enormous undertakings. I do not record any of my brushes with fear or with loss or with death. They pale into insignificance when compared with the experience and trials of so many others. I'm grateful that the workings of fate favoured me in the course of that great cataclysm, and in the end, the RAF awarded me a "mention in despatches," a significant military honour.

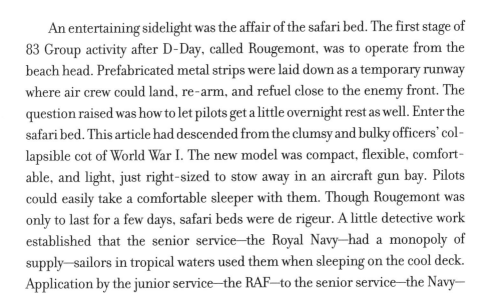

An entertaining sidelight was the affair of the safari bed. The first stage of 83 Group activity after D-Day, called Rougemont, was to operate from the beach head. Prefabricated metal strips were laid down as a temporary runway where air crew could land, re-arm, and refuel close to the enemy front. The question raised was how to let pilots get a little overnight rest as well. Enter the safari bed. This article had descended from the clumsy and bulky officers' collapsible cot of World War I. The new model was compact, flexible, comfortable, and light, just right-sized to stow away in an aircraft gun bay. Pilots could easily take a comfortable sleeper with them. Though Rougemont was only to last for a few days, safari beds were de rigeur. A little detective work established that the senior service—the Royal Navy—had a monopoly of supply—sailors in tropical waters used them when sleeping on the cool deck. Application by the junior service—the RAF—to the senior service—the Navy—

for a small supply through regular channels received a dusty answer. None could be spared. Queen Anne's Gate in London is not far from Birdcage Walk, and there the naval safari bed monopolists held forth. A personal reconnaissance seemed called for. The access to their upper floor office led to a curious elevator that looked like an elegant dumb waiter. Once inside, muscular force applied to a convenient rope powered a majestic ascent to the target floor. Two grey-headed controllers in mufti heard my dramatic plea for the comfort of gallant airmen, delivered in a Canadian accent. Thus stimulated, they consented to "start a paper" which meant I got my beds. Whether any airmen ever used them in Rougemont is not reported. But I used the one I appropriated as we progressed across Europe and good it was, too. I still have it as my one souvenir of the campaign.

When I was a teenager, I had a job sweeping floors and running errands in my father's business. Arthur G. Lush was my boss. In those days, there were no driving schools—you learned to drive by doing—and he took me out on the highway for my first experience driving in traffic. When I came back from the war, Arthur Lush was still on the job. He had found the Masonic Lodge to have been very helpful in his life and was determined that I should have the same experience. Under his guidance, I went through the various stages of the Masonic system. I wound up with the Shriners, and in the Shriners, everyone is supposed to volunteer for some particular activity that promotes the Shrine's charitable activities in child health care. When I looked over the scene, the idea of playing the bagpipes appealed quite strongly, so I volunteered for the bagpipe band. While no one ever accused me of being an expert at playing that instrument, nevertheless I was considered suitable to play in the band. Later on, I also played in the Air Force Reserve Bagpipe Band, so I got to wear two different kinds of tartans. Because I played the bagpipes, it seemed that I should be a member of the musicians' union, so I applied. This created a problem because they had really no convincing evidence that the bagpipe was a musical instrument, and it took some degree of persuasion to make the point. Fortunately, they didn't ask James Caesar Petrillo, who was then the president of the American Federation of Musicians, for permission, because he probably would have balked. Anyway, I got in and as a result, I attended union meetings from time to time. I still count myself an honorary member.

Soon after returning from overseas, I joined the Manitoba No. 1 Branch of the Royal Canadian Legion, and I never regretted it. Veterans are a very special kind of citizen in this country, and I found myself to be pleasantly compatible with the legion. No. 1 Branch was unusual because it contained a high proportion of old sweats who had come in after World War I. They frequently discussed politics, and their comments about politics and politicians were both direct and pungent. I found it advisable to be a listener in those surroundings. The legion did much good work, particularly in No. 1 Branch which took a special interest in housing for returned veterans. James Cowan, who as I have mentioned was later a colleague of mine in the legislature, led the charge on Legion housing agitation, and I helped out as best I could. One of the results of being a legionnaire was I was often called upon to make the address on Remembrance Day celebrations which I did, it seemed, in every nook and cranny in Manitoba. That gave me much pleasure and led to many new contacts and experiences. The Legion then and now is the salt of the earth. What particularly pleased me was that at one time there was a motion to nominate me for president of the Manitoba and Northwest Ontario Command Royal Canadian Legion. This was a gratifying compliment by my comrades. It seemed to me, however, that as I was at the time an active party politician, it would not be in the best interests of the Legion for me to accept the honour, enticing as it was. They sensibly agreed to seek someone who did not carry such obvious political baggage.

Just after the war, I was a very junior delegate at the 1948 Conservative convention when George Drew was elected leader. George Hees, strikingly identified in his officer's uniform, made an impressive debut. During the course of the proceedings, I heard Arthur Meighen[4] speak. Indeed that was a voice from the past, but he presented us with a patriotic topic so eloquently that I, for one, was swept away. I recall finding myself standing on my chair, cheering this veteran of the political wars and a former prime minister. His voice represented only a minority view in the intellectual climate of the party in those days, but his eloquence was hard to beat. Not only in what he had to say, but the way in which he said it. It was wonderful. Voices like Meighen's are missing today. After that, all was quiet on the political front, particularly in the provincial field, where the system of government by coalition was still in full swing after the long war.

During the war, my father had decided to make himself useful and had set up a company called Western Tools and Industries Ltd., a fine, magniloquent name. It undertook small wartime contracts for airplane parts and things of that sort, and had been quite useful as a source of supply for military requirements. Of course when the war was over, there were no military supplies required, but this company still existed. So my father suggested that I should see what I could do with it. I took on the oversight of Western Tools and Industries Ltd., depending very heavily on a partner, W.E. Schick, who was an experienced and skilled operator and who had been the soul of the wartime operation. We began building agricultural equipment of various kinds, wagons, parts of spraying equipment, garden furniture, metal structures for building activities, licence plates, all kinds of small metal products. Though the rate of return scarcely justified the risk, it was that business that occupied my time up until 1954, when I became the leader of the Opposition.

---

4 Much later I made a courtesy call on Arthur Meighen in Toronto, out of respect for his Manitoba roots which were strong (Portage la Prairie) and his public service. In those days he was old and bed-ridden and near the end of his life. We exchanged only a few pleasant words. I had no idea that some day I was to follow him as Leader of the Senate and indeed to be a colleague of his grandson, Senator Michael Meighen. During my time in Montreal, Michael ran for the Progressive Conservative Party in Westmount. He and I rode in a horse-drawn carriage through the constituency to advertise his candidacy. Nice try, but no cigar.

three

LIFE *on the* BACK BENCH

---◆---

THE YEAR 1948 WAS NOT A PARTICULARLY GOOD ONE FOR THE operations of the traditional parliamentary system in the Manitoba legislature. Most of the MLAs were resting quietly in a self-induced lethargy arising from the fact that a hoary coalition was governing the province. The genesis of this situation is interesting. The 1936 election had brought a stiff rebuke to John Bracken's government. The province was in the throes of deep economic depression and the premier's taxation policy was thoroughly unpopular. The Liberal-Progressives managed to keep 22 seats out of 57 and held a precarious minority government.

The Conservatives, under their new leader, Errick Willis, captured 16 seats. Two minor political parties, CCF and Social Credit, held six and five seats respectively, plus four others. Bracken pushed to form a coalition government. The Conservatives flatly refused his offer, but Social Crediters lent their slender support to the Liberal Progressives. This experience proved so agreeable that at the outbreak of World War II, it seemed like a good idea to expand the coalition. It was suggested that partisan provincial politics were an unnecessary distraction when the people were engaged in strenuous efforts to win the war. All party support for the Rowell-Sirois Report on dominion-provincial relations would also be consolidated. On that basis, Bracken extended his coalition to include all the political parties and members in the legislature, with the one personal exception of Lewis St. George Stubbs. You had the Liberal Progressives, the Conservatives, the CCF and Social Credit all in this new arrangement. The cabinet posts were shared out, and a grand coalition was arranged. The idea of a parliamentary opposition was abandoned for the duration.

Lewis St. George Stubbs, who was elected as an Independent candidate, the People's Tribune, in 1936, was the sole holdout. He did himself much credit, rejecting the possibility of a cabinet post in Bracken's coalition to sit as the lone member on the opposition bench. He was joined later by Salome Halldorson, the Social Credit member for St. George. In time, other parties withdrew from the coalition—the CCF in particular—but as the Conservatives and the Liberal Progressives remained together in the coalition, they formed a force that dominated the legislature. Public opinion, to the extent that it paid any attention to what was going on in the House in those days, seemed to support this arrangement. It is of interest to note here that for some 23 years, one of the government's supporters didn't open his mouth once in the legislature.

When the war ended, drawbacks of the coalition system became clear. It gave a strong tendency to reinforce the status quo in the legislature and in the constituencies. Coalition nominations were seldom contested, and a nomination in that system was the equivalent of election. The Progressive Conservative and Liberal Progressive party organizations generally co-operated in supporting whoever happened to be the sitting member of the time, so this was pretty much a closed system. In the legislature, the government proceeded serenely, not much disturbed by the views of the few members who were in the opposition. All the features of the traditional parliamentary system—the clash of ideas, debates about policy, vigorous criticism, sustained review of government record—were sadly curtailed. With the government's position so strong, the opposition was muted.

Thus there was a stately maintenance of things as they were, or at best a glacial response to changing times. The practice, which in wartime seemed to be acceptable, proved to be less attractive when the war was over. After V-E Day, the nation, including Manitoba, took a new lease on life. There was a strong feeling that we were in a period of catch-up and change. A new order of the day was emerging. Who can now recall how hard life was in Manitoba in the years leading up to World War II? The promise of our beginnings had faded. The Great Depression of the thirties descended with full force on a province of farmers. Agricultural prices fell to unimagined low numbers, reducing producers to a subsistence life. Then several years of bitter prairie drought, with poor crops all round, compounded the misery. City dwellers escaped the worst, but the total economy steeply declined. Opportunity seemed to have disappeared, and want was acute. Even the resources of the government seemed to be exhausted. But all things pass—prices bottomed, better weather returned, and the World War II superseded all. So it was in the immediate post-war period that Manitoba was a province of survivors, first of that Great Depression—which had been reinforced by the bitter prairie droughts of that period—and later of the war. The austerity of those times as we dedicated ourselves to achieving a victory had stretched the province pretty thin. But we came through it, strengthened and revitalized, ready to slough off the past. We could see better days ahead and wanted to be part of it. Manitoba was ready to move.

The coalition government responded, but poorly, to the hopes of the public. It had outworn its welcome. The coalition would no longer do. Good government required a good opposition. These comments were running through the public discourse at the time, but nothing very much was happening. One day as I was lamenting our stick-in-the-mud state of affairs, Jim Cowan's wife, Dorothy, raised her voice to say, "Well, if you don't like it, why don't you do something about it?" Her timing was excellent because a provincial election had just been called for December 1949, and as far as one could see, only the usual coalition policy was to be on offer.[5]

Winnipeg was then divided into three large provincial constituencies, each of which elected four members. South Winnipeg was one of these constituencies. The ballot might list anywhere from 10 to 12 names, and

5 During my earlier days in politics, I occasionally took morning coffee with Horace Everett (father of senator-to-be, Douglas Everett). As a political observer, he advised me to defect to the provincial Social Credit Party to improve my electoral chances. If that was a temptation, I resisted it.

voters would mark their choices, numbering them from one to 10 or 12 as the case might be. The four top candidates were the ones elected, but there was a proviso that they each had to obtain a minimum quota before they crossed into the elected column. If the quota was not reached on the first count, then the names on the bottom of the list of candidates were examined and the second choices recorded on those ballots were allotted to those still in contention. This process went on until four candidates reached the quota.

My constituency was Winnipeg South, and there were thus four seats to be filled. Each party had its nomination meeting. The South Winnipeg Progressive Conservatives had their convention and decided they would run a slate of two candidates only. My name was put forward in a rousing nomination speech by a boyhood friend, Gordon Chown, who later was elected to Parliament from South Winnipeg. In my nomination speech, I laid it on the line that I was running against the government and the coalition. Indeed, I was running against my own party, which was part of that coalition, and I explained to the meeting why good government required a return to traditional parliamentary operations in our legislature. One of the other candidates was Alec Stringer, formerly a naval service MLA, who offered himself as a straight-line establishment man and a coalition supporter. Marvellous to relate, we were both accepted by the convention, even though we were running on diametrically opposed principles. Either the South Winnipeg Progressive Conservatives were hedging their bets, or they didn't know which way they really did want to go.

The campaign was relatively low-key. I attacked the coalition as might be expected, while Alec spoke for the coalition arrangement. As the election proceeded, I found I was not alone in the anti-coalition camp. Edmond Prefontaine, who had been a Liberal backbencher in the legislature, and whose father was in my grandfather's cabinet in 1914, had come to the same conclusion that I had: the coalition had to go. He, too, thought the coalition system was destructive of the basic values of Parliament, and he certainly was able to say why, because his command of the practice and theory of British parliamentary democracy was complete. He was remarkably eloquent and well-informed on this subject. I thought it unusual that this Franco-Manitoban was better instructed than his colleagues. I found Edmond to be a very good colleague, but he did not stay as an independent in the opposition benches very long. Premier Douglas Campbell soon recognized it was much better to have Prefontaine inside the cabinet than outside. After he became a minister, our association became attenuated.

When the votes were counted in Winnipeg South, the poll was led by J.S. McDiarmid, later lieutenant-governor of the province, a Liberal coalitionist. He was followed by Ron Turner of the same description, Lloyd Stinson of the CCF who was against the coalition, and then finally myself, an independent anti-coalitionist. I have to admit that it took the counting of many second, third, fourth, and fifth choices to get me elected, and I only scraped in over the quota by the skin of my teeth. This was the first of seven successful provincial elections for me. It's hard to recall how you feel election night—so long ago. Undoubtedly, I was elated. I must admit my performance did not exceed my expectations. I thought it was going to be a very hard slog and indeed it was, and when you consider the sort of independent position I had adopted, it's really quite surprising that so many people decided to vote for me. That, of course, was an encouragement.

The election returned six independent members, all more or less agreed on an anti-coalition position, but otherwise rather a mixed bag. They consisted of Edmond Prefontaine, Harry Shewman, George Renouf, John McDowell, Duff Roblin, and Hugh B. Morrison. When the legislature opened in the winter of 1950, I naturally made my maiden speech. I took pains to set out my principles with respect to the parliamentary process, and I quote what I said: "The people are served, and only served, when the government has a daily reminder that they are not indispensable, that there is an alternative group able and ready to take their place." The records of the day suggest that I did my best to supply that daily reminder.

In the same maiden speech, I referred to an earlier day when another Roblin had sat in the Manitoba legislature.

"This is all the more memorable an occasion for me because I remember one whose name I bear who stood in this place before me, many years ago, and whose achievements and memories are one of the dearest possessions of my heart. In this land and in this life, men are not judged by the names they bear or from whence they come, but from what they themselves are. I hope, however, that when I meet with those triumphs and disasters which are the lot of every mortal man, I shall meet them with the same serene and tranquil mind that he displayed and which stems from a true conscience of the knowledge of a duty done." That laid down the gauntlet about the 1915 controversy, and to the credit of the legislature, no one ever picked it up.

My position as an independent member of the opposition was, of course, in the back row, and my seat-mate was another loner, Bill Kardash, the sole representative of the Labour Progressive Party in the House. Bill Kardash, a Mackenzie-Papineau Battalion veteran, who lost a leg to the Spanish conflict, was first elected in 1941. The Communist Party of Canada had been declared illegal, forcing its members to seek office under another name. As a single voice, he found it difficult to present resolutions for debate in the house because any resolution would require a seconder. I made myself available to second Bill Kardash's resolutions, much to the chagrin of the front bench of the other side, who considered this some form of treason. Nevertheless, Kardash, whose opinions I never shared, was able to make interesting contributions to legislative debates.

I had done my best to make sure the debate about the coalition would be introduced into public discussion and form an important element of the 1949 election. To my surprise, it did not take long for this initiative to bear fruit within the Progressive Conservative Party because shortly afterwards, on October 30, 1950, at the recommendation of the party leader, Errick Willis, a party convention resolved by a vote of 215 to 17 to withdraw from the coalition government. The lamentable failure of the coalition government in confronting the 1950 flood helped to bring the party together in this vote.

The party had previously held four cabinet positions in the coalition. One of these was the post of attorney general held by James McLenaghen, who was devoted to the coalition status quo, and whose influence in caucus was weighty. McLenaghen had studied law in the Portage la Prairie law office of former prime minister Rt. Hon. Arthur Meighen. He first entered the Manitoba legislature in 1927, representing the constituency of Kildonan-St. Andrews. On one occasion when an opposition backbencher, I trespassed on the attorney general's authority in an enthusiastically critical speech on highway safety. There was an ominous delay of a day or two until Jim made a major response leaving me lying in little pieces on the Legislature floor. Chalk that one up to experience! He died on June 23, 1950, and thus released a heavy constraint on Willis's drive to pull out of the coalition.

At the convention, the Progressive Conservative Party split. Charles E. Greenlay, the MLA for Portage la Prairie, rejected the decision of the party, and decided to remain on as labour minister in the Campbell cabinet. He was joined by the former Speaker of the legislature, Wallace C. Miller, who became the minister of education. Two other MLAs, J.O. Argue, the member for Deloraine-Glenwood, and J.C. Donaldson of Brandon, opted to sit as independents. Donaldson resigned his seat on April 18, 1951. Thomas Seens of Lansdowne did not join the Progressive-Conservative ranks immediately following the convention but sat with the party in the next legislature. Willis and the rest accepted the vote of the convention to leave the coalition.

At the same convention, there were rumblings in the ranks over the question of provincial leadership. Ill-advised dissidents put forward my name as a leadership candidate, but I soon made it clear I would not consent to this proposal. It seemed to me that it would have been a very poor reward for Willis, who had just agreed to do what we wanted him to do, namely, leave the coalition. To then say we also wanted him to leave the leadership as well was wrong. I was not willing to lend myself to that combination. On a less lofty note, my prospects of success at that time, deservedly so, were not bright. I was certainly an unseasoned legislator.

Work in the opposition under Willis's leadership resumed in the legislature. I took up routine duties, acting as party spokesman in the budget debate, and was

active in discussions on the staple topics of education, roads, municipal government, and social welfare. One proposal of interest at the time was a resolution to
let women sit on juries in the province. Strange as it may seem, this was not
provided for in the law. I can report that I voted "yes" on the motion, which
unfortunately lost 31 to 17. R.P. Roblin had been a strong opponent of extending the franchise to women, and for his pains he was very hotly attacked at the
time. I doubt he would have confirmed my vote, but I was certain that my
mother would—and did.

I became briefly notorious in December 1953 when I took the opportunity, while appearing before a national party meeting in Winnipeg, to deliver a
jeremiad on the state of the Progressive Conservative Party in Canada. Most of
the time, the ties that link the federal and provincial branches of the
Progressive Conservative Party are tenuous, whether in government or opposition. But in 1953, they certainly had one thing in common—they were both
losers—and that situation attracted my notice. I was rather free with my advice
about shortfalls I discerned in ideas, policies and organization, to say nothing
of personnel. If the party was to serve the country, it needed to tackle issues,
rather than assiduously avoiding them. The Progressive Conservative establishment did not take this speech well. They made it clear they did not welcome advice from a provincial neophyte. Nevertheless, some of the press
across the nation took notice.[6]

The 1954 election was then upon us. In the course of that campaign, I had
great difficulty addressing the electorate in any convincing fashion because
basically our main platform was simply that we were not the government. We
were not conspicuously offering new or fresh notions as to how provincial
business should be conducted. On the day of the election, this appeal, limited
though it was, moved us somewhat forward but not much. Our numbers in the
legislature were increased from nine to 12. In the constituency of Winnipeg
South, which still elected four members, the successful candidates were Ron

---

6 An editorial in the *Vancouver Sun* acknowledged the wisdom of the young Tory from Manitoba and advised the party brass
to take his advice, but it was not hopeful.

Turner, Lloyd Stinson, myself and Gurney Evans, a new Progressive Conservative face.

Gurney was my first recruit in my goal to obtain quality candidates to stand in the various seats in the province. Gurney had been the chairman of the Public Service Commission of Manitoba, which managed recruitment to the public service and other personnel matters of that kind. One day I found myself sitting next to Gurney at an unattractive lunch counter in the legislative basement, where you sat on a stool as you ate your soup. It occurred to me that he would be an ideal candidate for one of our seats in Winnipeg, particularly as a running-mate for me in Winnipeg South. When I proposed the notion to him, I have to say he didn't exactly jump up to accept, because my prospects were hardly first-class at that moment. But it turned out he was willing to be a candidate, and I'm glad to say a successful one. Later he was a colleague of mine in the cabinet, as minister of natural resources and industry and later treasurer. Gurney was dignity personified, and a good companion. I remember one occasion when he and I were campaigning in a by-election in the Mountain constituency, which had a large French and Belgian population. I decided we would sing "O Canada" in French at the opening of the meeting and he joined in nobly. The only trouble, as I found later, was that that particular audience was Belgian alright, but Flemish-speaking, so our contribution to national unity went unappreciated.

Something happened in the course of the very first session of the new legislature which, in retrospect, affected me more profoundly than I would ever have thought. Perhaps the incident may be described as the Ross Revolt.

Arthur Ross was a farmer from southwestern Manitoba. He was affable, able, experienced and vigorous. He had been the Progressive Conservative member of Parliament for Souris for some time and gained a reputation for presenting a very effective voice for western Canada. In 1954, for reasons which were not clear, he switched from federal politics to the provincial arena and was elected in the constituency of Arthur. I regarded him as an asset to our cause. It appears, however, that Ross nourished a deep conviction that the leadership of

Errick Willis was going nowhere. He found friends in the caucus who agreed with him, and he determined to do something about it. At a caucus during the session of 1954, Ross raised the subject of the leadership of the party and made, to my astonishment, the extraordinary proposition that those who questioned Willis's leadership, as he did, would resign from caucus, but not from their seats. They would then move across the floor of the House in open revolt against their leader, with the clear expectation of bringing him down.

I found this idea profoundly misguided. After all, we had just finished running a provincial election as a Progressive Conservative Party under the leadership of Willis. We had given no notice to the voters that there was any inclination to question his position. We had all been elected under his banner. It seemed to me nothing short of a breach of trust with the public so soon after the election that we should now be asked to repudiate his leadership. I did my very best to convince the caucus that some other method than a walkout must be found to resolve their differences. In that discussion, which was hot and heavy, it seemed pretty clear that Ross had the support of the majority of the caucus. My position was unclear. Nobody knew what I was going to do. I didn't know myself at the time. Anyway, I tried to broker some kind of a solution. In the end, Ross and his friends agreed to stay their hand and remain with Willis, provided there was a public announcement that a leadership convention would be called at a fixed date in the near future. On that basis, we resumed our activities in the legislature.

Up until that moment, the thought of the leadership of the party had not been an active consideration. That had always been a goal, but any action in that respect was certainly not imminent, as far as I was concerned. I had no reason not to wait until Willis's own views and the confluence of events might call for a change in the leadership. I was not promoting it, but when the issue was raised and the leadership convention was declared, I then had to make a decision. If the Ross faction prevailed and a leadership convention was to be held, I decided it was a good idea to make it a three-man race.

In the caucus of the 13 members, I think Gurney Evans was the only one who was urging me to run. I believe George Renouf would have favoured the idea, but I could claim at the most only two members of caucus in my camp. At that particular time, I don't think I brought into my confidence any great number of people outside the caucus. However, once it was noised abroad that I was a possible candidate, support began to come in; but I made the initial decision myself, with very little outside consultation .

Why did I make that decision? For the same reason I was against the coalition: I wanted a better deal in Manitoba. I had known perfectly well the coalition was not going to provide it, and I had some real concerns about whether the Progressive Conservative Party was going to do any better because in the election of 1954, they failed to impress. They had simply said, "We're not the government. Vote for us." I found that exceedingly difficult to handle because that was not my temperament. I wanted a policy, I wanted a plan, I wanted a goal to work for. It seemed to me this was an opportunity to set the stage for something new.

In the provincial leadership campaign, we arranged to have joint candidate meetings in which the three of us appeared on the same platform to present ourselves and our ideas throughout the province. One early meeting I recall was in the Brandon constituency. The popular local member of the legislature, Reg Lissaman, took part, and his contribution consisted of an excoriating attack on Willis, raising an *ad hominem* invective by several levels. This seemed to me to be a very poor business. I was of the view that the process was best served if we restricted ourselves to dealing in the main with matters of policy and public business rather than personalities. Although it is perfectly true that personalities cannot be left out of the political equation, personal rancour can. I resolved after that meeting I would have no harsh words with either Ross or Willis during the course of that campaign, nor did I, and I think I may fairly say that we remained on good terms through the campaign, and indeed after.

Meanwhile, we were scuttling around Manitoba like mad, trying to line up delegates. To my chagrin, I found I could not even command support in my own constituency of South Winnipeg. The Willis team had taken over, and there was no room left for me and for my delegates. Of course, that made me run all the harder in areas where my welcome was a little warmer. The convention was held June 19, 1954, in the old Royal Alexandra Hotel. After the usual preliminaries, we got down to business. The guest speaker was a newly minted federal MP named George Hees, who took great care not to be seen hobnobbing with any of the candidates, including me.

From the political point of view, it seemed to me the Ross candidature had fatal tactical drawbacks, leaving aside the question of policy altogether. His area in southwestern Manitoba was a minority force in the province. It provided far too narrow a base for a successful political party in Manitoba, and he had entirely left out the city of Winnipeg in his appeal, although two local politicians in Winnipeg, Hank Scott (Winnipeg Centre) and Stan Carrick, a city alderman, came out solidly for Ross and were rather uncomplimentary about my prospects. The Ross candidature was a recipe for continued marginalization of the party, while Willis had to carry the record of umpteen difficult years of somewhat limited success. In such a context, I rated my prospects as promising.

On my election, I was carried up to the podium by two enthusiasts, one of whom was Louis D. Morosnick. Morosnick was a friend of my father's. In fact, there had previously been a legal firm in Winnipeg called Shinbane Morosnick and Roblin of which my father was a member before he went into business. Interestingly, both Shinbane and Morosnick were present at my christening. Shinbane was a leading Liberal, but Morosnick was a staunch Conservative who went so far as to offer himself up as a "dark horse" candidate in 1954. When it became clear at the leadership convention no one would either nominate or second him, he threw his support to me. I might say that he was not well regarded by the legal fraternity as belonging to the prim and proper branch of that profession. He was a criminal lawyer and delighted in courtroom pyrotechnics at which he excelled—in fact, he was dubbed the John Barrymore of the courtroom for his often theatrical outbursts. This, of course, was not looked upon with favour by the establishment. Consequently, he was never made a QC.

I had always cherished the thought that if ever I became premier, I would have the pleasure of recommending Louis to be a QC. Unfortunately he died November 7, 1956, before that happy event could take place.

Nevertheless, as expected, Willis led on the first ballot. The question was who was going to come second, and with what kind of a margin. On that first count, Willis got 118 votes, I got 114, Ross got 55. My 114, it was afterwards calculated, included 99 votes from rural Manitoba and 15 votes from Winnipeg. On the second ballot, Willis got 123 votes, I got 160, with 137 rural, 23 Winnipeg votes. It was pretty clear I was the choice of the rural opinion in the province. Notably it was the first time in the history of the Progressive Conservative Party in Manitoba that a city member was selected as party leader. It was considered up to then an unbreakable rule that the leader had to come from rural Manitoba, but times were changing and this was the change. Willis's response to the change in leadership was typical. He declared his complete loyalty to the new leader, which he meant, and which he delivered. As a political leader, he had been perhaps a trifle laid-back for the times and indeed for the taste of some of the party. He was, nevertheless, a capable and experienced colleague on whom I could always rely. Art Ross, unfortunately, didn't live much longer. He died before that particular legislature had expired. But I had a new job, and I had a *tabla rasa* before me.

While I was struggling to bring the Progressive Conservative Party in Manitoba into the post-war era, the national Progressive Conservative Party was undergoing its own evolution. When the war was over, the federal Progressive Conservative Party examined the question of its leadership, and it became apparent John Bracken was not providing the kind the party expected from him, although I may say he was a man I was later to appreciate. At that time, in 1948, the leading candidates for his replacement were George Drew and the newcomer, John Diefenbaker. Diefenbaker, the prairie evangel, was an attractive personality, and I took an early opportunity to make his acquaintance. As the convention drew nearer, I did my best to organize a pro-Diefenbaker group in Manitoba which was greatly outnumbered by the establishment, which favoured Drew. I went to that convention and though Drew won, I gladly cast my vote for Diefenbaker, for whom I had developed an esteem and rapport.

George Drew then had the problem of leading a dispirited and unorganized party, particularly in the West. He struggled manfully with it. Drew suffered slings and arrows in the opinion of western Canadians. He was branded in this province as being a Bay Street man, which I guess he was, and being an Ontario man, which I guess he also was, and therefore quite incapable of appreciating any of our interests, which is another question. He did appear to great advantage in the great pipeline debate. Drew's condemnation of the vacillation of the Speaker, in the course of that debate[7], is a parliamentary masterpiece, a splendid effort, displaying a clear grasp of the principle of the parliamentary system which seemed to elude the St. Laurent government. Soon after, Drew's health forced him to relinquish the leadership, and in 1956 Diefenbaker was a candidate again.

John Diefenbaker was one of the most compelling politicians to grace our public life. Against all the odds, he emerged from the then Tory desert of Saskatchewan to party leadership, propelled by the gifts of oratory and a spirit of prairie populism. Humour and story-telling were part of his appeal. He brought Canadians of every origin and kind to his side. He did not so much deal in policy or principle as he dealt in people, both en masse and one by one. He demanded and received a fierce and unquestioning loyalty. In fact, he looked at politics and life through the prism of people and personalities. Issues often resolved themselves through that prism. "Who is for me—who is against me?" was a touchstone. On one of my visits to Ottawa in the sixties, he ruminated to me about the dismissal of Donald Gordon, then running the CNR. Gordon's capacity as a competent railroader was not the issue, but his suspected insufficient loyalty was. Happily, nothing happened. Whatever the

---

7 The debate was the climax of the "pipeline" political crisis and the disgrace of speaker Beaudoin.

substantial justification, the dismissal of James Coyne from the Bank of Canada when he was within a few months of the end of his regular appointment allowed personal animosity to expose the prime minister to unnecessary political attack. His relations with his cabinet colleagues and, indeed, with other party supporters like me all carried the demand for unquestioned followership. To fail that test risked being cast into oblivion. But for those over whom he cast his spell, Dief was the authentic tribune of the people and that is how he saw himself. As a result, though his prime ministership faded, in elections after 1958 he rallied the troops against the forces of darkness to prove on election day the continuing loyalty of thousands, if sadly not of majorities of "my fellow Canadians."

"Over the years," to use his favourite opening line, I watched his course. Under Drew he was a freelancer in Parliament, not the best of team players. I was fervent for him at the Drew leadership convention. At the next convention, he was still the best man running and carried my enthusiastic support, but I knew he was not the Galahad of the early days. In 1957 and after, I appeared on the election platform with him in Manitoba in every federal campaign. Whatever human shortcoming that hubris identified, he gave one immeasurable gift to his party and to the nation. In particular, he made western Canadians feel welcome and at home within the Progressive Conservative Party, and by extension within the charmed mainstream of the Canadian psyche. In his One Canada appeal, no one was to be left out—old Canadians, new Canadians of whatever name or origin. He made the Progressive Conservative Party a new vehicle for the aspirations of many. That was why I stood up when John Diefenbaker came to Manitoba.

four

LEADER *of the* OPPOSITION

◆

THE LEADERSHIP CAMPAIGN OF 1954 HAD EXPOSED ONE HAPPY fact: There was a solid core of faithful party supporters, people who were present through thick and thin and through good times and bad. They were to be counted upon. Marvellously, some were survivors from the days of my grandfather. A group of die-hards, calling themselves the Winnipeg Conservative Club, had kept a feeble flame alive during the long years in political wilderness. The supercilious observer might be ready to dismiss these party faithful as so much background noise. That would be a mistake. In our system of representative parliamentary government, it is through political parties that the public is offered a choice of policies and personalities, both in Parliament and in the legislatures. Parties are a necessary part of the mechanism in our style of political democracy. The party faithful stand firm amid ebb and flow of public opinion and political vicissitudes, and without them we would forfeit that basic foundation, that sense of continuity, that is the key to life and effectiveness of any social structure.

My first impulse after the convention was to pay my respects to those who had kept the faith. While that was by no means sufficient, it gave me a place to start and I found I could always depend on their stalwart support whatever the fates unfolded. My concern was to regain party unity. It is natural in the course of a vigorous and sometimes bitter leadership struggle that emotions are aroused and personal feelings are sharpened among the contending factions.

Duff Roblin

After a decision, it is necessary to promptly seize the moment and begin the process of healing and reconciliation, to soothe the disappointed and calm the victorious. It greatly helped in this task that Willis and Ross set good examples. I made it known to my critics, especially the disaffected, that they were welcome within the charmed circle of a newly reunited party. In fact, I sought to bind them to me with hoops of steel. Nobody would be excluded because of previous views. Inevitably there were some intransigents.

When the legislature next met, Willis remained undisturbed in the chair that he had formerly occupied as leader of the Opposition. I took my place beside him. This gesture was not lost on the other parties, which might have been expecting a split in our party. In other respects, however, the prospects of success for the party were distinctly questionable. We had survived, but for what purpose? We had barely recovered from the atrophy and deadening influence of the long coalition years when normal political activity was suspended. Our organization was mostly non-existent. There was no process of policy formulation to speak of. In certain areas of the province, and among certain important parts of the population, there was little or no representation or recognition of the Progressive Conservative Party. To add to the state of affairs, there was no money, and consequently no headquarters, no office, no staff. These were the days when public funds were not provided to political parties.

These considerations set my agenda and did not then seem to present an impossible task to me. It was simply necessary to make a start, and that's what I did. The office was easily found, in dusty quarters over a Portage Avenue fur store. A telephone and a secretary, salary to be determined—and taken from the corps of political junkies—was provided. Shirley Gibbons was an early and effective one-woman band in the office. She was a steady point of contact during my absences, satisfying the curious, giving work to the volunteer, and keeping me in touch with the party. In my new position as leader of the Opposition, my legislative salary went up. The stipend now became $5,500 per annum. In those days, the only public support parties received was the salaries given to members of the legislature. No other funds or services were provided. Consequently, the system of raising money in those days was straightforward. You had to canvass those people who had said they would support you and were willing to put up their money to prove it. That was the sole source of financing. It was limited, and when I consider the money we spent running an election campaign in those days and compare it to what is spent these days, I can hardly realize the extent of the difference—it's so great.

Doing something about our finances became a matter of some priority, so to bridge the cash-flow gap, I went to where the money was and called on the Ontario party for help. I paid a visit to Beverley Matthews, who then controlled the party purse in that province. He gave me a courteous hearing while I outlined my problems and my plans, and then, with no hesitation whatsoever, he drew out a cheque-book from the drawer and gave me a cheque for $5,000. I had crossed the financial bridge. This was the sole occasion on which I asked anybody for money. Thereafter, a financial committee was structured, and never again was financial constraint a problem to me in my political life. Understandably, I have a soft spot in my heart for the political bagmen who are now often unfairly denigrated. Our style of democracy calls for political parties. Without some cash, the operation of parties is crippled. The question is how much cash is enough, and how can it be kept in its place. There is no perfect answer, but a ceiling on election spending and full disclosure of significant contributions are a reasonable protection of the public interest.

I have to admit that on one occasion somebody offered to give me money in a questionable way. The out-of-province gentleman concerned came to my office in the legislature when I was premier and we had a pleasant conversation about matters of mutual interest. Then, as he was about to depart, he tried to give me an envelope which appeared to be stuffed with a wad of cash. I hustled him out the door in pretty quick fashion. He didn't ask for any return on his investment, but the conclusion is that he expected there might be one. In my case, it was strictly understood by fund raisers that no promises could be entertained to or from anybody. In fact, the names of contributors were never disclosed to me. The authorized sales pitch was to present an opportunity to contribute to good government in Manitoba through the Progressive

Duff Roblin

Conservative Party, and if that proposition failed to sell, end of solicitation. The appeal to the public spirit of the donor worked well enough, and if there were violations of the rules, none was ever reported to me.

To establish a party organization was harder. Too much of the province was *terra incognita* to the Progressive Conservative Party. Often there was no effective constituency organization. Often there were no Progressive Conservatives at all. In some ridings, only the old-timers had ever had an opportunity to vote for a Progressive Conservative candidate. In one area, wiseacres advised me to visit the graveyard because there I would find the only known Progressive Conservative supporters. An exaggeration, I trusted. So I stopped limiting myself to Progressive Conservative partisans, and started looking for good people and worrying about their politics later. The plan was straightforward: go there, be seen, shake hands. Any place where two or three were together, for whatever reason, was a good place for me. Church teas, ethnic gatherings, picnics, fall suppers, fraternal meetings, farm fairs, even funerals—in the city or in the country, at any time. I had friendly helpers who would bird-dog for me, telling me about the various occasions as they arose. If I was lucky, some local would be willing to introduce me to the crowd. If it was just a friendly visit, I never talked politics. I didn't have to. They knew why I was there. It gave the people a chance to size up the new boy, and when they heard about me later on, they could at least put a face to the name. This was hard work, but the system of visitations, as I called it, rigorously pursued, had a number of uncovenanted advantages. It gave me an opportunity to seek out and identify leading local citizens on their home territory, and to make friendly contact with them. It put me in touch with the hopes and the aspirations of the developing communities, cities, and towns around the province, and I became on friendly terms with the movers and shakers in those areas. At the beginning, I drove my own car. Later, a willing core of volunteer drivers presented themselves, mostly young people interested in the party. I made many new friends in this way.

Meanwhile, the sessions of the legislature proceeded. They gave me a bully pulpit to present my views and I did my best to take advantage of it. We then had 13 members of the legislative assembly and naturally they were a group of mixed talents. Every one of them received a special assignment in the legislature: to lead in debates, to examine estimates, and to propose resolutions when required. I hoped they would develop a reputation and recognition, not only as parliamentarians but as good representatives of the voters who had sent them there and thus expand the image of the party. Of course, the quality was mixed, but the spirit was at all times willing. There was one exception, and that was Jack McDowell, the MLA for Iberville He was a Progressive Conservative all right, but he was not a Roblin Progressive Conservative. Whenever I made a speech in the legislature, setting out our party position, I could be fairly sure the next person on his feet would be Jack, and I could be equally sure he would vigorously dissent from whatever I had to say. This became a habit with him. Later on, when our Red River Floodway plan was up before the legislature, he still was at odds with the policy of the government. He would have none of it.

One day, Joe Martin appeared in my office to make himself known, introducing himself as the president of the Young Progressive Conservative organization at United College, now the University of Winnipeg. That was good news as I thought the student body there was so heavily CCF that few YPCs were to be seen. But Joe came through with Sterling Lyon and Heath MacQuarrie. I took this initiative to be a hopeful sign of the times.

The first real public test outside the house came soon. In the summer of 1955, I was confronted with two rural by-elections. The first was called in the constituency of Mountain, which was a curious name for the gentle landscape of the Pembina escarpment in which this constituency was to be found. But figuratively, it was a mountain to climb. We hadn't run a candidate there for 23 years and we were dealing with a constituency in which there was a large population of Franco-Manitobans and of Belgians, none of whom had previously shown much enthusiasm for the party. Fortunately for me, the last Progressive Conservative MLA in Mountain was still on the scene. Peter Lusignan might have been elderly and frail, but he was my eyes and ears in the constituency.

One day, under Pete's instruction, I attended a funeral in Notre-Dame-de-Lourdes for his old friend, Marc Moreau, who was thought to have been a

Duff Roblin

Progressive Conservative supporter at some time in the past. At the community gathering which followed the funeral mass, a number of people spoke. One was a man called Marcel Boulic, the reeve of the municipality and operator of the local creamery. He was a man in his forties, open-faced, well set-up, of diffident manner, but clearly a leader. His politics were in doubt but I got to know him just the same. When the by-election came, I had my man. Marcel agreed to run. His vote was good, but he did not win. He did, however, lay the foundations for victory in 1958. Before 1958 the constituency changed. Redistribution eliminated the Mountain riding and added it to a territory further west. Marcel was apprehensive lest this shift in geography have political consequences, because it was known that many of the new voters had a background in the Orange Order. How would they welcome a Franco-Catholic candidate? My counsel to Marcel was direct: present yourself at every door, put out your hand and say, "I'm Marcel Boulic running for Duff Roblin and the Tories and I need your vote and your help." There was nothing to fear; he won handsomely in 1958.

The second test was in Deloraine-Glenwood. This was long-time Progressive Conservative territory, and the local association found its own candidate, Earl Draper, a man with extensive local connections who had not yet distinguished himself. He remedied that defect during the election, proving to be a formidable candidate who won easily. His opponent, too, was a formidable choice. Bob Moffat was an able former aide to Premier Campbell. He was born locally but had been living in Winnipeg, and for that reason was labelled a parachute candidate. The dangers of being a political parachutist were demonstrated in this by-election. Too bad I conveniently overlooked this irritating fact when I presented myself to the constituency of Peterborough, Ontario, in 1974.

The third by-election came about in the constituency of St. George, a riding in the Interlake country, in a very cold December in 1956. Here again, the prospects were poor. The area had long been a Progressive Conservative desert. Just the same, we had an eager candidate. Marlin Magnusson was the editor, proprietor, and printer of the Lundar Weekly—his personal political broadsheet of uncertain circulation. Marlin delivered his decided opinions under gigantic headlines while other views got short shrift. We fought hard. We had meetings at every crossroad and in every school, whether or not there was anybody to attend. The cold was severe and the snowdrifts, on the back roads particularly, were a constant threat. It was a miserable experience. Driving home in the middle of the night after a meeting, I turned on the car radio and heard the voice of a popular singer named Guy Mitchell. The song he was crooning had one mournful sentence which resonated with me, and it went like this: "I never felt more like running away." My sentiments exactly. In the end, we lost, but we saved face and our deposit.

All told, during the period when I was leader of the Opposition, no seats changed hands, but our share of the popular vote increased. I gained hands-on experience in local politics, and local politics teaches valuable lessons in the arts of democracy. It may well have been that my success in becoming leader in 1954 had repercussions outside the province. There were newspaper observations that the change of the guard in Manitoba presaged a change in the guard in the federal party, in Ottawa. I didn't agree with that analysis. My election as leader in Manitoba, as far as the nation was concerned, was a nine-day wonder, and had little lasting effect on the federal scene.

Meanwhile, I had several interesting excursions outside the province. In 1956, the national party was having its leadership convention to replace George Drew. John Diefenbaker was a candidate once again. I was not the unqualified supporter I had been on the previous occasion when he ran against Drew in 1948, but he was still the best man running and I supported him. Every convention has its doldrums, when delegates mill around rather aimlessly waiting for something interesting to happen. Very often to fill the time, somebody is pitched into the gap to make a speech. At the Diefenbaker convention, I was put up to speak on such an occasion. My theme was French-English relations—a topic which I have pursued all through my political experience—and how those relations contributed to nation-building. I spoke in both English and French. My reward was a standing ovation, with the francophone delegation leading the applause. I am often reminded of that experience when the unity question arises from time to time, particularly in a form which taxes our faith. My motto is *nil desperandum*.

When the Manitoba party emerged from coalition, to all outward appearances it seemed to be the political preserve of white Anglo-Saxon Protestant Manitobans. There were individual exceptions, but by and large, the charge rang true. The need to broaden this base was obvious. Manitoba began as a province of immigrants. Regardless of who came first, important ethnic communities had been established in this province. Not only that, the newcomers had made their way to the top in every field. Though the aboriginal citizens of this country were here before any of the folk I mentioned, I regret to say they were pretty well confined to the reserve system, particularly in northern Manitoba. They were wards of the federal government, they had no right to vote, and they made little impact on the lives of their fellow citizens. That is the situation we are now trying to change. It is a long and difficult task, but we must believe we will succeed. In no small sense, the immigrant communities were the making of modern Manitoba, and yet at that time they saw little place for themselves within our ranks.

It was clear to me that action was called for to recognize the role of the so-called ethnic groups, not only on political grounds but on philosophic grounds. The party could hardly claim to speak for Manitoba when part of the population felt excluded: Franco-Manitobans, Ukrainians, Mennonites, Jews, Icelanders, and many others. They were at the heart of our provincial life, yet many of them scarcely felt welcome within the Progressive Conservative ranks. That feeling of a lukewarm acceptance had to be changed. But how? Personal contact was my choice. For example, there was a vibrant ethnic press at work in several languages in Manitoba, of which *La Liberté* for French speakers was a very important example. The editors of these language journals had seldom, if ever, seen a Progressive Conservative leader. That shortcoming had to be remedied. Then, just as I had done with other communities, I canvassed ethnic, religious, cultural, and social occasions to demonstrate a recognition on our part of their unique interests and their place in the province. To undo accepted perceptions of political uninterest is a hard thing to achieve, but simple and sincere human contact began to make a change. And I had help. Maurice Arpin, a Franco-Manitoban lawyer, via St. Boniface College, was my French-speaking interlocutor. He deftly steered me through the politics of his suspicious community though the going was tough. A Polish Catholic grandmother, Mrs. Elias Grabowsky, inveigled a place for me at the head table at the various functions of organizations of her community. These friendly promotions were heaven sent.

Then in 1956, I had one significant if unexpected breakthrough. The election of John Diefenbaker as the national leader heralded a sea change in the image of our party among ethnic Canadians. His background, his personality, his political sensitivity—all brought about a reorientation of the federal Progressive Conservative Party. He made it attractive and welcoming to the so-called ethnic Canadians, and he aroused in them an unprecedented interest, participation, and support, a near miraculous transformation. This was a great help to me. Manitobans of every origin began to see themselves as part of everything we did. Thus the influence of one man was significant, and I pay my respects to him.

In 1957, Diefenbaker led his party to an unexpected victory over the Liberal government of Louis St. Laurent and, a year later, was returned to power with 208 seats, the most ever held by a party up to that time. His series of gigantic election meetings across Manitoba aroused an almost apocalyptic fervour. He carried all before him, including me. Just as Diefenbaker had opened up the Canadian scene to all talents, so the same groups of people in Manitoba who formerly had not considered our provincial party realized we were part of the same team. From that time onward, we had no difficulty securing support, not only in the constituencies but in the recruiting of candidates. So Ottawa made a big difference.

But Diefenbaker's victory in 1958 was so sweeping and so complete it cast a shadow on the Progressive Conservative Party in the province. This was not because of what was commonly said—"Duff will do what Dief did"—which is a stupid slogan, but because people also said, "These Conservatives are getting too high and mighty. We don't really need so many of them around in our legislatures." His majority, his great success, was a handicap to me, and I was aware of it.

It is rightly said that the first duty of the Opposition is to oppose, and we surely fulfilled that function in the legislature. In fact, as I review some of the press clippings of our activities in those days, I come to the conclusion that we were a decided nuisance to the Campbell government. Departmental estimates, operations and outcomes were carefully scrutinized. Legislation was examined. Suggestions for improvements were proposed but never accepted. We launched debates on important issues. As I look back over the record of this period, prior to the 1958 election, subjects such as beer pricing, oil royalties, municipal assessment problems, and of course the ever-present question of education and the social network, were subjects of significant interest. More importantly, they served to establish the image of an effective and innovative opposition on the trail of an administration too satisfied with things as they were.

It was at this time I first met Walter Kucharczyk. He picked me up, so to speak, when I was leader of the Opposition to tell me how drilling rights on the small oil patch in the province should be allotted. His term 'checker-boarding' meant nothing to me, but I soon discovered the principle was really quite simple. When the government is giving out oil drilling rights on Crown lands, it should do so as if it were disposing of a checker board. Every other square would be kept for the Crown. This would enable the Crown to benefit from the discovery of oil in the square owned by its neighbour, the private operator. The government of the day negligently omitted to do this. Under the checker-board system, if oil is found in the private area, the government's area was right next door and the public interest gained. Walter educated me on this topic, and I tried to educate the government. In the end, checker boarding was a success. Walter's Polish accent remained unimpaired, but his citizenship was distinctly Canadian. Fortunately my political world was full of Walter Kucharczyks. I remember another brouhaha with the government, this time between me and Premier Campbell. I was attacking his agricultural research policy, and in rebuttal he alleged I was guilty of half truths. This semi-unparliamentary expression struck a nerve and became a rare personal bone of contention. Over several exchanges, neither of us would let go. Finally, the *Winnipeg Free Press* grew bored with our disputes and pontificated in my favour, or so I thought. At best, a petty triumph. The role of the Opposition gave us broad experience from which we gradually uncovered ideas for new and better policies. We watched the operation of the governmental machine at work so we could detect some of the ways in which it could be made to work better.

Thus, a coherent plan for an alternative government became our next objective. In the last session before the 1958 election, we began to set out important election planks, a process that exposed us to a tactical political danger. Premature disclosure of our plans would make it possible for a lively government to steal our clothes. The fact is, no one has all the good ideas by himself. It is important, therefore, to recognize a good idea when it comes along and whatever the source was, never to hesitate to make it one's own. That was my rule. I felt that I had the measure of the mindset of the government of the day. Proposals from the opposition were ignored. In any case, it was unlikely that they would make changes fast enough or sufficiently to matter. So, as we unveiled our party proposals, we put our own stamp on these ideas when the time came to discuss them in the election campaign.

This technique only took us so far. The final job of filling out our election manifesto was done elsewhere. As a first step, I established the major topics with which we wished to deal. They included education, agriculture, highways, social welfare, northern development, and waste and mismanagement. We put together special task forces, small groups of political people, technical experts and private citizens, to consider each one of these subjects in the light of the needs of Manitoba. I recall particularly that Ralph Hedlin, a newspaperman and a friend, helped put these task forces together so we could bring to bear the best minds we could find on the problems we wanted to solve. We accepted this help wherever we could find it. Some of our people volunteered, others were co-opted. We drew on the wide experience of some, on the expertise of specialists, and on the skill of experienced political observers and public figures. The result was a series of six small books arranged as speaking notes, setting out our policies, suitable for easy presentation by our neophyte candidates and easily digestible by party organizations. When the election writ was dropped, our platform was ready and so were we.

With my name and history, it might seem unnecessary to locate my place in the Manitoba political spectrum. Indeed, I did look to such political icons as Macdonald, Burke, Shaftesbury, Wilberforce, and Disraeli for inspiration and I read with satisfaction such classics as Quinton Hogg's *The Case for Conservatism*. In the beginning, this was philosophy enough. But when I entered the 1949 Manitoba election, I saw on one side—and to the far right, beyond Burke and the rest—a Liberal-Progressive/Progressive-Conservative coalition—in spite of its double progressives—standing for a very small "c" conservatism, intent on preserving things as they had been. On the left I saw an urban-based Social Democratic trade union party in the style of British Labour, with nothing in between, that is unless I count myself.

Classified as an Independent, I was running a single issue campaign, to disrupt the coalition and return to a normal democratic party parliamentary system in the provincial legislature. As it turned out, that goal was achieved in 1950, sooner than I had expected, allowing me to give up my Independent status and join the Progressive Conservative caucus. That re-united caucus was then exposed to the political vacuum between the far right wing views of the so-called Liberal-Progressive government and the muted radicalism of the minority CCF. In 1950, as an opposition backbencher, I had only a vague idea of how that vacuum should be filled, but the opportunity—indeed, the need to occupy that space was compelling. Ideological purity was not an issue. In my supporting role in the opposition, I could observe, mark and learn as the sessions of the legislature displayed the working of the governmental machine and find myself and, hopefully, an interested public, exposed to the challenging opportunities to frame a better alternative. Nevertheless, we fought the next election in 1954 mainly on a simple anti-government platform. We got the result we deserved. That failure was a factor in the Ross revolt which I describe elsewhere, leading to the subsequent party leadership struggle. My success in that contest faced me squarely with the responsibility to find those better policy alternatives that the public interest demanded. As was the case in re-organization of the party, I again had a clean slate to write on. My previous four years on the opposition bench had been an educational introductory course in Political Science 101. Now I faced the examination. No new deal manifesto sprang fully formed into being. But the direction was set and the goal was marked out.

As a conservative, I found it natural to accept and build on the goodly inheritance of the past. As a progressive, I found it natural to seek out the promising opportunities of the coming day and to align both old and new with the welfare of the community. We would fill the political vacuum and take up a strong position at the centre. It was uncertain how the supporters of the more traditional wing of the party would react to change. Fortunately they had no place else they were willing to go, so I could safely stand on their broad shoulders. During my four years as Opposition leader, one by one, and gradually, the various aspects of provincial policy and public need were examined, both during legislative debates and in private consultations. There was no preconceived dogma to restrict us. Tradition was respected while practicality and pragmatism were guidelines to public utility, all within the bounds of a robust respect for civility and the human equation. If, in moments of euphoria, I may have claimed to have made over our public persona in my own image, I was brought up short by the devoted labours of my colleagues in the political arena and the seminal inputs of supporting friends outside. It is enough to be permitted to conduct the orchestra without trying to play all the instruments. So with the help of many hands, by the time of the crucial election of 1958, we could tell the electorate what we wanted to do and why we wanted to do it and how the public interest would be served. The vacuum was filled and the progressive-conservative centre was our own.

But the 1958 campaign was still, in a sense, amateur night. It was transforming a bunch of amateurs, both in terms of candidates and organizational leaders, into professionals to fight the election. This was done in two ways. First of all, a two-day meeting was held of all the candidates to discuss our booklets and speaking notes. They were prepared in such a way that if a candidate would follow them closely, he would not only have a reasonable speech, but could also outline the policy of the Progressive Conservative Party. This process brought all these candidates together, strangers to one another who didn't know much about being politicians, and were not quite sure what the party would do if it got into office. This was a deliberate effort to make them feel comfortable in their political skins and to give them knowledge of the platform they would support. It went well. We solicited any views the members had, but I think they were preoccupied digesting what had been presented. I suppose the main impact of the meeting was psychological. It brought the candidates together as a team, introduced them to each other, inspired them with some confidence in the policies they were to espouse, and gave them the means to present that policy to the population.

The second area where we were transforming amateurs into professionals was in the field of organization. We did the same thing with the candidates' agents and one or perhaps two leaders of their constituency organizations. They were bought together in the same way, only the subject of their agenda was not so much policy as it was procedures, programs and methods of dealing with the electorate. Organizations, publicity, getting out the vote, canvassing the constituency were grist to their mill. It produced the same satisfactory result with these people as with the candidates, for the same reasons. They found themselves members of an intelligent, organized, focused approach to the business of getting elected. They were part of the team, and the team was going to help them perform their job.

Elections nowadays are much more densely organized performances than were our efforts in 1958. Television debates are all image and little substance; speech writers, spin doctors, press liaisons, pollsters, focus groups, advance men, and all the rest are called into play at great cost. Television saturates our attention. Still, there is really very little new in modern election methods, except for the intensified influence of the media. We did much the same things, but only in embryonic scope and on a lesser scale. In our case, the leader carried the flag, but volunteers carried the day.

In a sense, Dalton Camp was our secret weapon in that first campaign. He had been successful in elections in Nova Scotia and in New Brunswick, and had been brought in to see what he could do for us. In those days the idea of bringing in any foreigner, that is non-Manitoban, to a provincial election was anathema—you just didn't do that—and we had to go to some pains to conceal Dalton's whereabouts. He was not advertised as being among those present. His function was to prepare material for the press on our behalf. We could not expect to get a highly favourable press, although I think we got a pretty square deal, all things being told. In order to get our message across, we decided to put in a series of small mini-editorials as advertisements carrying our logo. Dalton wrote these. They were designed to be eye-catching, attention-getting, and amusing, and they were all those things. One that always appealed to me had to do with a candidate in Seven Oaks, Morris Gutnick. Morris Gutnick was an interesting young man who threw his hat in the ring at my earnest request in a constituency where the chances were not very bright. But he was brave and he took it on. Somewhere along the line he gave an undertaking that if a certain something didn't happen, he was going to jump out of an airplane—with a parachute, mind you, but he was going to do something dramatic. As events turned out, for one reason or another, the jump didn't come off, but Dalton produced a wonderful little vignette on this issue which bore the intriguing title, "Why Gutnick didn't jump." No matter how the newspapers ruffled us from time to time—and they did—Dalton's daily paid minitorial restored the balance and, better still, made us laugh.

The bulk of the campaign was fought in rural Manitoba. I had a car and some of the eager young beavers would drive me. I'm very grateful to those people who helped so much because they enabled me to sleep in the back of the car while we were driving around so I could arrive refreshed. When we arrived at a town, the procedure was to take a sidewalk stroll. Some of these places weren't very big, and it was quite possible to cover the business district in an hour or so and call on all the stores and shops and professional people and shake their hands. It was an opportunity to canvass the business district, drum up a little attention for our meeting that evening, and to meet the local press, who always had something they wanted to talk to me about. The meetings, usually consisting of one or two hundred people, were mainly to showcase the candidate. They would give the candidate a chance to present himself to the public, and gave me a chance also to deal with the major issues of party policy. My custom in rural campaigns was to enter the room from the back. Never appear on the stage. Enter the room from the back and from the back, shake hands with every person in that room. I would make my way to the front, and if anyone escaped a handshake with me he could count himself lucky because I made it a point to make a personal contact with every person in that room and to inject a little human warmth into what might otherwise be a dull proceeding. That system gave me a chance to see who it was I was talking to, and who had come to our meeting, what they looked like, and sometimes what they thought, because they would tell me. Getting acquainted with my audience was important and I enjoyed it. It was fun.

The need to find good candidates was paramount. The best ideas, the best platforms, the best programs, the best proposals—all depend on the calibre of the men and women who put them into effect. Without good candidates, platforms don't count, and the leader works in vain. I made it my first priority to find those good people and, more to the point, get them to run as our candidates. Our members of the legislature were few—only 13 out of 57 seats. But that apparent shortfall transformed itself into a great advantage when it came to recruiting new candidates. It was an opportunity which was available to me only once. I never afterwards had the same freedom of action. This meant that there were potentially 44 places to fill with new talents and new capacities. The leader, in my view, should seldom attempt to usurp the right of constituencies to select their own candidates. That is their privilege and responsibility. But the leader can try to get good men or women to agree to appear before a nomination meeting and offer themselves for selection. This procedure I found almost invariably successful because when my patently suitable candidate was proposed to a nomination meeting, delegates had no difficulty coming to the right conclusion. It occasionally failed, and on those occasions, often the judgment of the convention was better than mine. So above all else, I made the identification and nomination of good candidates a principal responsibility. It is obvious that the quality of the persons who are elected has a significant impact on the long-term strength, life and usefulness of a government. It is also not a bad thing to have a few men and women around who are smarter than oneself. It keeps the game honest. Not all of my recruits succeeded in 1958. Some of them had to wait for the next election, but most of the members of my first cabinet came from the new boys.

In the candidate search, for obvious reasons, I did not limit myself to known Progressive Conservative supporters. This made it possible for me to canvass a community widely to identify the local leaders. That done, the task was to show such a person the reasons why he should run with me in the coming election. Only the unusual state of the Progressive Conservative Party at this time made such a search necessary, and my success ratio in finding good recruits was encouraging. By election day, we had a superior slate of 57 candidates for 57 seats. I did not make any promises to candidates that they would be eligible for cabinet posts. Of course they were eligible for consideration, but one could never be sure of who the other possibilities would be, or whether indeed the candidate himself would be returned. Anyway, it's usually bad policy to offer that kind of inducement in most circumstances. I think, however, it would be fair to say I left the thought in their minds that the possibility of being a cabinet minister was not out of the question, and it was really up to them to justify the choice.

One of the successes of my candidate search was the wooing of Dr. George Johnson. Earlier, at one of my "get-acquainted" visits at Gimli, which, incidentally, had not returned a Conservative member since 1914, I heard George Johnson speaking. It was at a Chamber of Commerce meeting, and he was outlining the needs of his town and community, which he felt were not being met. We did not meet then but, for me, he was a marked man. Shortly thereafter, the 1957 federal election was called, and Gordon Churchill asked me to appear on the platform in Gimli in support of our candidate, Eric Stefanson. It was a warm, sunny summer day. There were almost more people on the platform than in the scanty audience, and it was clear that my presence was somewhat superfluous. It occurred to me, on the spur of the moment, that

Duff Roblin

I could improve the shining hour, so I slipped away from the meeting to track down George. His wife Doris greeted me at the door and told me the doctor was occupied. I was invited to wait, and wait I did. It was obvious the name Roblin meant nothing at all to her. In fact, she thought I was a drug salesman come to canvass her husband for business. When George appeared, I explained my presence and put the idea in his mind that he should consider entering politics. This was the beginning of a life-long friendship, both with him and his wife. As he had said at the community meeting, he wanted to see improvements such as sewer and water, old folks' homes, better schools and good roads to Winnipeg. He had tried to interest the Campbell government in a program of this sort, but without much encouragement. My suggestion was that he should try a new man, a new party, and new ideas. Our thoughts coincided. I challenged him, if he was seriously concerned about the situation, to come and help me do something about it. That, in essence, was the simple message I offered to other prospective candidates on other occasions and in other areas. The same message of challenge and response that attracted George Johnson was the means by which other promising candidates were convinced to stand. Manitoba needed a new politics. Only new men and new ideas would secure it. Rise to the challenge, come with me, and join a happy band of brothers in our political wars. That was my pitch.

Although I pride myself on having visited almost every nook and cranny in the province of Manitoba over my years in provincial politics, I have to admit the one constituency in which I rarely set foot was Rupertsland. That's the enormous swatch of territory running from the Winnipeg River up the east side of Lake Winnipeg and encompassing in those days a great chunk of Manitoba's great northern forest. It was inaccessible in many respects, but one day before the 1958 election, a Rupertslandian turned up in my office. His name was Joe Jeannotte, and he announced to me that he was recommending himself as the candidate for Rupertsland. I was overjoyed because that was one of the few blank spots in my table of candidates. Joe turned out to be perfect. If I had to design a member of the legislature for a remote wilderness area, I would have picked Joe Jeannotte. He was a wiry little frontiersman. He was interested in cattle, he traded and did all kinds of interesting things. He proved to be eminently electable. He flew his own plane. That little plane during the summertime would visit every nook and corner of his inaccessible frontier constituency—mostly comprising aboriginal Canadians where regular local government was non-existent—to fly the government flag, to establish government presence. As a result of these trips, he knew exactly what each locality required, in the way of a small road or landing strip or some betterment, which was completely beyond the ken of anyone in the bureaucracy in Winnipeg. So Joe would come to me after one of his expeditions with a shopping list of things that ought to be done to help the people of his area. They were never anything more than modest improvements, which municipalities provided elsewhere, things that local government—had there been one—could do and should do to make life a little easier. Joe's problem as an MLA was to get the bureaucracy to pay any attention to him. Well, we fixed that. So Joe was an ideal MLA for that territory, and I very greatly valued his confidence and support.

The North is full of interesting characters. Later our candidate in Thompson was Gordon Beard. Gordon was a very large man. In fact, he was a little bit self-conscious about his size. This was demonstrated one day when his seat in the legislature collapsed and set him down on the floor. He never quite got over this unfortunate incident, but he also was a great man to understand his people and his area. I remember on one occasion when I was in Thompson campaigning with Gordon, I could see the town was in pretty good shape, but the hinterland was different. The hinterland consisted of a number of reserves and other isolated settlements. So I said to Gordon, "Get the hell out of Thompson and go and look after these people. I don't want to see you back here until voting day." I knew perfectly well that if he could make his mark with the people in these isolated communities, the town of Thompson would support him as well. He was a very successful MLA. He empathized with the people of this area and they had a strong voice in the government when he was their member of the legislature.

In fact, we held all the northern seats from 1959 to 1967: Churchill, Flin Flon, The Pas, Rupertsland, and later Thompson. In my opinion, that's the strongest team ever that has come out of northern Manitoba. Their influence on the caucus and on the conduct of the government was noticeable because our policies with respect to building roads in the North and in developing a hydro-electric system and matters of that sort of course had their enthusiastic support. I think the North probably received more attention from the government during those days than before or perhaps since.

Preparing for the 1958 election, one area which was a particularly barren prospect for us was the district around the town of Russell. They had had no Progressive Conservative candidate in sight. I did find one and I found him at the summer fair. The master of ceremonies at the harness racing event, in charge of the loudspeaker, invited me to mount the podium with him so he could introduce me to the crowd. That was a good idea because I'm sure none of them knew who I was by looking at me. One of the big events of the fair was a beard-growing contest, and as a special privilege I was invited to judge who had the best beard. My credentials were limited, but my choice was inspired because the man I chose was a gentleman unknown to me by the name of George Smellie, head of the leading Liberal family in that area and a prominent local businessman. He and his brother ran the creamery in Russell. I learned he had a son Robert, and of all the people I met in the area during that visit, Bob impressed me as being a self-starter, one likely to be of use to the community, and a good candidate for the legislature. Bob was a lawyer in town and a leading figure in the Royal Canadian Legion. Eventually, after a good deal of to-and-froing, Bob decided to throw his hat into the ring. On the second election, in 1959, he was successful, and not long after that he entered the cabinet. That's a good way to find candidate material. I later found out the Smellie family were distantly related to my mother.

I met another solid candidate at dusk at a farmhouse just outside Winnipeg. George Hutton had just come in from the harvest field and was covered with the dust and chaff of action. Elmer Ridge, an old faithful, had identified George as candidate material for the 1958 election, and nothing would do but that I should drop everything at once and come out to Lilyfield and inspect him. That was good advice. George was ready for politics, and I was ready for George. Hutton was a successful farmer, well-educated and with wide interests. Agriculture was his occupation, but his mind ranged over the whole of the provincial scene. Elected in 1959, he became minister of agriculture. His assignment later to supervise construction of the floodway gave him a valuable urban connection. Had he continued in politics, I have no doubt he would have been a strong and welcome candidate to succeed me. He left the government to resume a life of service with the United Nations Food and Agricultural Organization where he served until his death.

One beautiful summer afternoon in June, the eponymous Roblin riding was having a nomination meeting in the town of Roblin. Before the meeting, and in order to calm my nerves, I retired alone to a quiet clearing in the nearby beautiful Assiniboine River valley. I had brought with me my bagpipes and began to play. The local response was immediate. Out of the bush appeared the heads of a herd of dairy cows who had poked their ears out in order to hear and to see what this noisy wonder might be. Still, the meeting was a success. We had a good candidate in Keith Alexander.

When I became leader in 1954, I speculated on a one-two election punch. I thought the 1958 election would be one in which I would strengthen the opposition, but I would have to wait for a second opportunity in order to dislodge the government. However, as the 1958 campaign proceeded, I revised that timetable and came to the conclusion that one knockout punch was certainly a possibility. In that hope, no seat went conceded. We fought one campaign against the Liberals on the right, strange as it may seem, and in the country, and another campaign against the CCF on the left in the city. We made the progressive centre our own.

In my progress toward the 1958 election, Tom Kent deserves honourable mention. He became editor of the *Winnipeg Free Press* from a Manchester Liberal background via *The Economist* newspaper. He found little to approve of in the small "c" conservative policies of the Campbell government and raised critical concern in his editorial pieces. This gave unexpected and independent weight to my own views and did good things to morale. Though the *Free Press* was the Liberal journal of record and was unlikely to endorse me, Tom brought a new eye to the Manitoba scene.

Duff Roblin

During the campaign, as a rule, the press followed me closely. As we toured the province, they awarded points after each meeting, providing a sort of hands-on polling method. But to make sure that we had the right balance in the press, Ralph Hedlin, then a freelance journalist, went with me on many occasions, and he took advantage of the opportunity to write up the meeting. Sometimes the meeting was written up and telephoned into the *Free Press* and the *Tribune* in advance of the actual event. Ralph felt he not only knew what I was going to say—and of course he was right—but also what the reaction of the audience was going to be, and that's a little more speculative. Thus we filled in the gaps when the regular reporters failed to appear.

The 1958 election was the first under a new system of constituency redistribution. The old four-member Winnipeg seats were done away with, and the city was divided into single-member constituencies as the rest of the province had been. Wolseley was one of these. It was situated almost in the downtown residential centre of Winnipeg, populated mostly by middle- to lower-income respectable self-supporting citizens—the backbone of our society. There were also a large number of apartment blocks around the area with a fluctuating population. So it was a centre seat, an urban seat, and largely an owner-occupied seat—and it was completely unknown territory to me. Wolseley, however, became my seat of choice, although I did not live there. I knew it was not naturally a Tory area and that I had my work cut out for me. I made up my mind, however, that rather than seek a relatively safer seat in River Heights or the Tuxedo area, I as leader ought to take this seat on. It would indicate I had a real interest in the central urban questions, and not those of the rural areas only. Anyway, if I couldn't win that seat, well, tough luck. So I decided to run there, and my instincts proved to be reliable, thank goodness. A leader, sadly, can seldom focus on his own riding, as a regular candidate would do. The demands of a province-wide responsibility forbid it. I spoke at my nomination meeting and not much more. Fortunately, a good organization of men and women soon formed itself, but the backbone was made up of a group of ladies of uncertain age and of argumentative disposition. They took me to their hearts, and in every election provided a satisfactory majority. God bless them. Hugh

John Macleod, Graham Haig, Douglas Leatherdale, Harry Sibbald, Leonard Claydon, Lorne Tuman, and Ernie Enns were some of the male stalwarts. But the political powerhouse consisted of the women who in every election provided a satisfactory majority. The MacPhails, mother and daughter, Ethel Johnson, Jenny MacDonald, Edna Ginkel, Irene Kerr, Ann Tansany, Nita Nixon, Lottie Penner, Myrtle Sutherland, Sonya Roeder, Ida Volume, and Irene Enns were among the faithful who kept home base secure. With their basic political skills organizing teas, setting up the polls, canvassing and getting out the vote, they carried me along. Democracy and party politics flourished in Wolseley.

We voted on June 16, the day before my 41st birthday, and when the vote was in, Manitobans had elected 26 PCs, 19 Liberals, and 11 CCF. In Wolseley, where I had barely been able to campaign at all, I won my seat with 3,988 votes. My two opponents lost their deposits.

five

THE PERILS
of MINORITY GOVERNMENT

WHEN ALL THE BALLOTS WERE COUNTED, IT APPEARED WE HAD won the election...sort of. At least, we were the largest party, though we did not have a clear majority. The old government, however, felt no pressing need to resign. They resolved to consider their position, and to general surprise, they considered it in consultation with the CCF. Those two parties, one over on the right and the other on the left, parlayed in secret. There seemed to me no doubt that the issue was another coalition to share power and office. Several days passed while rumours flew. In the midst of the confusion, I decided to leave town to visit my sister, Marcia, in Ontario, because I was confident nothing would come of these manoeuvres and I would hear about the future in due course. The wriggling soon came to an end, however, and the government did resign. The lieutenant-governor, the Honourable J.S. McDiarmid, reached me by telephone. I felt a personal interview was called for in this important matter so I attended His Honour's office to accept the seals and the responsibility of office. It was a profound-ly sobering act. But I had one condition. The Liberal/CCF bargaining for power, in the aftermath of the election over the last few days, delivered its own warning. If they bargained then, they could do it again. They could join forces to defeat a minority government at any time and to resume office together, and all without having a new election. This consideration made me request an assurance in advance that, if we were defeated in the House, His Honour would grant a dissolution to us and a new election. A purist might say that such a request was of doubtful constitutionality. It engages the royal prerogative and, in a sense, forecloses a future alternative but, of course, that was my aim. In any case, His Honour consented. I must frankly say that when the constitutional expert Eugene Forsey became my friend in the Senate many years later, I forbore to get his opinion on this issue.

On June 30, 1958, we formed the government. When governments change in some jurisdictions, formal handovers are arranged from the old to the new. This certainly wasn't my experience when I took over in Manitoba in 1958. There was no contact whatsoever with the outgoing government, except in one respect. The day that I was sworn in, early that morning, I took over the pre-mier's office. Sterling Lyon was with me going over the orders-in-council to appoint the new cabinet. I heard a little scratching noise at an outside door. As Sterling went to investigate, a key was turned, the door opened, and the former Premier, Douglas Campbell, appeared. He seemed rather nonplussed to find us already, so soon, behind his former desk and, with a muttered remark, "Oh, you're here already," disappeared. That was the handover between govern-ments in the province of Manitoba.

My first move was to select a cabinet so we could take the oath of office as a government. Eight men—we had no female MLAs—were summoned on a Sunday to convene with me in my little Portage Avenue office to receive their assignments. Errick Willis was to be Deputy Premier, with Agriculture and Highways, Sterling Lyon was to be Attorney General, George Johnson was to be Minister of Health, Stewart McLean was to be Minister of Education, Marcel Boulic was to be Provincial Secretary, Gurney Evans was to be Minister of Industry and Commerce, John Thompson was to be Minister of Labour, Jack Carroll was to head Public Utilities, and Duff Roblin was to be Premier and Provincial Treasurer. Nine in all.

There is no cabinet like the first cabinet. There were nine of us: one veter-an, Errick, and eight tyros, including the premier. The principal criterion for selection was ability. Regional or social representation or response to other pressure groups was secondary. We were a happy band, exploring an adventure in government together, and we became close companions, knowing we would

Duff Roblin

ABOVE: A FRIENDLY WORD FROM DEPARTING PREMIER DOUGLAS CAMPBELL UPON TAKING THE OATH OF OFFICE

BELOW: THE QUEEN'S FIRST VISIT TO MANITOBA, WITH PRINCE PHILIP AND WIFE MARY'S HAT

sink or swim together. Around the cabinet table, regardless of portfolio, all voices are equal and all take part and agree on the decisions arrived at. Admittedly, my voice was more equal than the others, but nevertheless, it was a collegial operation. Each member of the cabinet was now trying to find his new office and to master his new role. The cabinet is officially described as the Lieutenant-Governor-in-Council. In practice, of course, the lieutenant-governor never personally appears. But to mark what was for us a rather special occasion—the first Progressive Conservative government in 43 years—we asked the lieutenant-governor to preside in person over our first cabinet meeting. This was a one-time event, and he graciously agreed to accommodate us. J.S. McDiarmid was a tall, grave, handsome gentleman. A former cabinet colleague of Douglas Campbell, he conducted his office with dignity and aplomb. As a first item of business, we assigned ourselves to our several portfolios, and he signed the validating order-in-council on the spot.

But we had no Clerk of the Council at this time to record our proceedings and to bring order to the decisions of the cabinet. Our predecessors had made other arrangements, but we felt the lack of such a post, and a candidate soon suggested himself—Derek Bedson. He had been an aide to George Drew and John Diefenbaker in Ottawa, but he was an ardent Manitoban and wanted to come home. Derek was strong on protocol and political propriety. In his role, he kept the gate at the cabinet and did so with a degree of hauteur which did not exactly ingratiate himself with some members of the civil service. Derek managed all the council business with efficiency and panache. While his relations with the civil service establishment were occasionally frosty, his loyalty to the government and his office was complete. Our judgment of his qualities was confirmed when, after the Progressive Conservative party under Walter Weir left office, Derek continued as Clerk of the Executive Council to future administrations, including the New Democratic government of Ed Schreyer. It wasn't until 1981, when Howard Pawley became premier, that he was asked to leave. Claudette Lavack later came in to become my secretary in the Premier's office. Her keen mind and taste for politics served both of us well.

Another early innovation was to bring in a Manitoba Hansard to provide a verbatim record of legislative proceedings. Previously, press reports were the principal record of debates. But our Hansard was to be completely unedited and unrevised—just as the words came off a tape with their imperfections intact. This avoided the self-serving pitfalls of the Ottawa system where speakers can edit, refine and surreptitiously improve their contributions. Posterity would get the undiluted milk of the word just as it was uttered. And besides, it was economical.

During the election, we had promised to meet the legislature as soon as possible, so work on a new throne speech was the order of the day. We knew that when the house opened, our minority position would be exposed, so we determined on a short speech, showcasing some of the more important propositions we had placed before the electorate, and for which we might reasonably claim had received electoral approval. If defeat came, we could look to the voters for vindication. During the election, rumours were spread that if a Progressive Conservative government were elected, it would bring in wholesale changes to the higher civil service. This counter-productive stupidity was not on our agenda.

Duff Roblin

Nevertheless, I thought it wise to let the civil service know where it stood. Almost as a first move after taking over, I invited all the deputy ministers to meet as a group alone with me in the cabinet room. My only demand of them was that they should give loyal and non-political support to the new management. If that were the case, we would get along very well, indeed.

The response was gratifying. They seemed almost to welcome the change in the direction of the government. We drew on their immense reserves of experience and expertise. They made it possible to translate our policies into action. They saved us from egregious errors of enthusiasm and inexperience. Indeed, we made a pretty good fit. I had the highest respect for the integrity of the civil service in the province of Manitoba. They adhered to the classic principle of a non-political but active partner in the processes of government, and it was not our view that we needed political partisans of our administration occupying the controlling heights of the civil service organization. In fact, I cannot recall that more than one senior civil servant was replaced when we came into office. This speaks well of the policy of our predecessors and is certainly one we endorsed. Later, it became fashionable to think you had to ensure the civil service was sympathetic to the political leadership. The fear was that the civil service would be prejudiced against the new administration, and only by putting your own people in place could you be sure your policies would be faithfully followed. This certainly wasn't necessary in my experience. It corrupts the classical position of the civil service in the parliamentary system to suggest this is necessary. The question of the role of public servants in the political process needs to be examined. My own view is that it is unwise to encourage civil servants while in office to associate themselves with a political party. If they do so, they bring upon themselves the justified suspicion they are partisan. Although it might be considered their political right to take part in politics like anyone else, common sense suggests it's a bad idea.

When a new legislature meets, it requires a new Speaker. I proposed Abraham Harrison, veteran member for Rock Lake, for discussion with Douglas Campbell and CCF leader Lloyd Stinson. Usually, opposition leaders freely approve the government's nominee. In this case Campbell demurred.

The procedure I followed had been good in the past, but at the present time it was not good enough for him. On the Legislature's opening day, he launched a full-fledged debate on the speakership lasting some four hours. The opening-day crowd was bemused, the Speaker in question was cooling his heels, and nothing could be done until the matter was settled. Finally, when all and more than all had been said, and with the support of the CCF, Harrison was enthroned in the Speaker's chair.

This contretemps set the pattern both for the Liberals and the CCF for the rest of this session. For reasons which no doubt they could explain to themselves, the CCF voted to keep us in power, while the Liberals voted to get us out. Our aim was to set down public markers, attesting to our willingness and capacity to perform, despite opposition in the chamber. The government would propose, the Liberals would condemn, the CCF would waffle but, in the end, would vote with us. As a result, we got our programs accepted. Creating larger rural high school divisions was the highlight of the session. Its benefit for students across rural Manitoba was widely acknowledged, and it proved to be a good springboard for the coming election.

At first, it is a great temptation to bury oneself in the detail of administration. But on my visits to members of the cabinet in their offices, I would say that the only thing I wanted to see on the minister's desk was his feet. Let the deputy minister worry about the paper chase. In contrast, the job of the minister is to think ahead and to plan, and every now and then to tell the civil service what the public won't stand for. My chief aim in dealing with my cabinet was to ensure it was well-organized, did not waste its time, and concentrated on the issues before it. The way I accomplished this was to say to the ministers that work takes the time allotted to do it. You set a time for the meeting to conclude and you have an agenda in front of you. There is a great stimulus to get that agenda properly dealt with within the time allotted; otherwise any gathering of politicians is likely to wander off into the wild blue yonder, discussing all kinds of issues and matters that are not strictly relevant to the issues at hand. So, we had our rule. I have to be candid enough to say that one reason I wanted the meeting to end at 5 p.m. was so I could appear on the squash court at 5:30 and get my ration of

Duff Roblin

ABOVE: FIRST CABINET, 1958– LEFT TO RIGHT: MARCEL BOULIC, GEORGE JOHNSON, STERLING LYON, JOHN THOMPSON, JACK CARROLL, ERRICK WILLIS, DUFF ROBLIN, GURNEY EVANS, STEWART MCLEAN

ABOVE: WORKING CABINET, 1965

exercise in.[8] I didn't tell my colleagues too much about that, but it was very helpful to me to be able to break away with the knowledge the work had been done, and I could have an hour off to enjoy the game. Later on, after the frustrations of night sittings of the legislature, I found playing the bagpipes in my office to be a sovereign relaxation. The cleaning staff soon got used to it.

Later on, after the election of 1959, we instituted such things as cabinet retreats. The full cabinet would leave its legislative offices in the city, get away from the daily grind, and meet in an isolated rural setting, free from all distractions. There, colleagues would reflect upon the state of affairs in the province. I convinced myself I had invented this idea—maybe yes, maybe no—but since then it has become quite a common event, and I think with good reason. During these retreats of two or three days, financial allocations were reviewed and agreed on, and the co-operation between ministries was sketched out—those things which get lost in the hurly-burly of public administration. Regular retreats were features of our cabinet system. Personal relations were strengthened among colleagues, the government was reinvigorated, and policy was redefined and strengthened.

The question of gifts or hospitality arose. Our rule was that if well-meaning friends wished to offer gifts to us, we would accept only those things which a single young lady under strict family discipline could accept from her admirers. This meant flowers, books, and candy were in, and almost everything else was a no-no. We determined that ministers should have an open attitude, both to the press and to the public at large. We also came to the conclusion it was no use making just one speech on any particular topic and then considering the job done and the press and public informed. The fact is, you can make the same speech a hundred times on the same topic and still find there are gaps in the public attention.

---

8 I played squash twice a week until I was 75. After that, I decided that I'd damaged my right wrist by waving the racquet a little too strenuously. The Winnipeg Squash Club was an interesting institution, quite unlike some squash clubs elsewhere in the country which are apt to be a bit cliquish. It welcomed all sorts and conditions of men—I'm afraid men only, except in wartime when women, including my sister Marcia, took over. Consequently, the conversation covered the waterfront, and I always found it to be an interesting and informal sounding board. The high point of my squash career was to win the club's novice doubles championship. I owe my triumph to careful selection of the right squash doubles partners. Ross Parke carried me through to victory.

Duff Roblin

Cabinet ministers occupy the high ground in the political arena. Their conduct in their office will make or mar the fortunes of government. But behind the cabinet is the caucus. Ours had 26 members in 1958. The care and feeding of the caucus is a skill every party badly needs. It is a basic political requirement. The caucus is the place where confidence in the government is established. The caucus is the place where backbenchers have their say, and in our caucus, they said a lot. Every proposed bill, except budgets, was examined in that caucus clause by clause, and I used to tell ministers that if they could get their bills through the caucus, they were pretty well-positioned to tackle the legislature. The caucus was tough. Caucus members mediate local opinion. They bring shrewd judgments to bear on government proposals.

The caucus can be difficult, sometimes over small matters, sometimes over great ones. Believe it or not, some of the most serious disputes in our caucus took place over mundane problems, such as the introduction of daylight saving time or how we should colour our margarine. These issues provoked almost unbridgeable differences between country and city members, and it took skill and good luck to arrive at solutions which all could accept. Similarly, there were varied opinions on more serious matters such as public schools and shared services in education with private, separate schools, and the use of French as a teaching language in the public schools of which more later. They aroused sincerely held passions. In the end, the confidence of the caucus in the leadership can make or break a policy.

Occasionally, members of the caucus would grapple with matters of conscience, feeling compelled not only to oppose a government policy, but also to declare their opposition in public, namely by voting against it in the legislature. I was sensitive to these personal issues and took the view, even on votes of confidence, that provided we knew what the member intended—that there would be no surprises when he spoke in the house—we could honour this kind of freedom. So, on occasion, members might bolt the party line with no danger of automatic expulsion from the caucus. This happened at least once. Fred Groves, one of my backbenchers, tested this tolerance to the limit when he voted against legislation to permit separate schools to share facilities and services with schools in the public system. Other members of the caucus grumbled because they felt Groves was permitted to take an action that was not, in a practical sense, available to all of them. My attitude toward this matter was simple. Party discipline in our system was already too strict, and there had to be some safety valve, some way in which members could express themselves, even if it was not in conformity with the party line. Not everything is a matter of confidence. This proposition cannot be carried to extremes—it's limited, because otherwise, governments would fall prey to faction and an unmanageable caucus. It is clear this liberty can be extended farther than is now the practice. I elaborate on this theme elsewhere. In the case of Fred Groves, the mood in the caucus was to throw the member out, but I resisted the idea. But the caucus does respond to fair treatment. The leadership must be careful not to be too far out of step with the mood of the caucus because trust is a basic consideration. Discussion in the caucus must be uninhibited. Each member of the caucus must have elbow room to reconsider his position as discussions proceed. Peer pressure often leads toward consensus. You don't win them all, but on the whole, we had a happy caucus. My door was open to any caucus member who wanted to see me. I was there to listen to any discontents, to reassure the doubtful and to stiffen the faint-hearted. The frank one-on-one touch was good medicine in caucus management.

Cabinet ministers were thrust into new responsibilities. Errick Willis, the gentleman farmer, was the only exception. Willis, minister of public works and agriculture, was a skilled parliamentarian with a long political background both in Ottawa and in Manitoba. He was a good friend, whose word was his bond. Sometimes his languid air irritated the enthusiasts in the party and probably had something to do with the Ross revolt. At least he had actually been in a cabinet room before. The remaining ministers, new to the job, displayed deep application and a broad range of talents. The civil service, however, would provide a measure of ballast for the ship of state.

The previous administration's budget was still in effect, so no budgetary proposals were required from us during that first session of 1958. But the cabinet needed a system to provide coherence and discipline and direction in our financial and administrative proceedings. The Treasury Board provided the means to effect this. At the beginning, I took the chair of the Treasury Board in order to give personal attention and focus to our overall strategy. The operation was straightforward. The estimates of revenue were before us. Keeping in mind the major policy goals of the administration, departments presented their plans, and resources were then allocated. Deputy ministers usually wanted more money for their departments, as indeed did their ministers. Deputy ministers and the higher civil service, with their expertise, could be very convincing. In my air force days, that was called "blinding with science."

How, then, was a new administration to deal with the experts? I'm afraid we employed the bloody-minded tactic. If any department complained its funding was inadequate, the first move was to devise a list of priorities for the operation. The task was to list in order of importance all the activities that would be proposed for the departmental expenditure. The department would then report which of those priorities could be covered by the money that had been allocated, and which would have to be left out. It was the political function to rule on the suitability of the priorities thus proposed, and to accept the public opprobrium for any items which would be left out. It did give us a rough and ready system of making sure that first things came first. Setting priorities was the key to this system, and ultimately we got along very well using it as a guide.

Generally, costs were met from current revenues. When the Red River diversion came along later on, we decided to finance this very large project from current revenue as well. Hydro and telephones were self-supporting public utilities and, therefore, they could borrow the money they required without any strain on the provincial treasury, save for the provincial guarantee. Highways fell somewhere in between. Sometimes these were financed by current revenue, sometimes we borrowed for them. Our view was that they were long-term fixed assets and, therefore, were appropriately subject to this approach. But when we borrowed funds for roads, we arranged to pay for them by raising the gasoline tax to cover the carrying charge so, in one sense, we regarded them as self-supporting activities as well. Happily, most taxpayers saw the logic. Thus, we proceeded to operate in our first year. Later on, after the election in 1959, and when our experience was sufficiently mature, I left the

Treasury Board to others, and we returned to a more traditional system of financial management. So much for 1958.

It was in the next session, 1959, that the crunch duly arrived. A new budget was required, and it was a trigger for a heated debate in the legislature. The fiscal year ended on March 31, 1959, and as that date approached, the pressure to pass the budget became more and more intense. We struggled hard to get our budget statement presented to the house in good time, but when we moved to do this, Douglas Campbell proposed an ingenious amendment to our budget resolution. We would be allowed to proceed, according to him, but only on his terms and conditions. Stripping aside the wording, Campbell's amendment removed our power to guide the house and was, in effect, a clear expression of lack of confidence in the government. I doubt if the annals of any British parliamentary body could furnish a precedent for this interesting device. For us, it was at once unacceptable and, at the same time, transparent, because no one in opposition really expected us to accept it. We made it clear that if the amendment was carried, it amounted to a vote of non-confidence, and the government would be compelled to resign. As matters turned out, the CCF decided to support the Liberal amendment, so on March 30, 1959, the day before the financial year expired, the amendment was carried and the government lost the confidence of the legislature.

The next day, the lieutenant-governor attended the house to give royal assent to an interim emergency supply bill. Until this took place, we were still in office, but on notice to quit. Without advertising my intention, I had taken the opportunity of preparing an order-in-council authorizing the dissolution of the house, and kept this document concealed in my desk in the chamber until the very last moment. At that time, I held a quick huddle with the ministers who were seated around me in the chamber. They signified their formal consent to dissolution. When the lieutenant-governor left the chamber that evening, I followed him out to his office. As he had been informed in advance of our intention, he was able to give his signature and approval on the spot. Thus authorized, I returned to the house to announce the dissolution and call the new election. I doubt that many were surprised. My satisfaction was obvious.

Duff Roblin

So began the election of June 1959. We had our record, we were honouring our program, government finances were in good order, and the momentum was with us. The opposition parties—the Liberals to the right, as usual, and the CCF to the left—were short of new ideas. As a result, the verdict at the polls was decisive. The returns showed the Progressive Conservatives with 36 seats, the Liberals with 11, the CCF with 10. Our majority was satisfactory.[9]

With the achievement of a majority, the threat to the fate of the government was lifted, and the world changed. After 12 months, there were no new boys any more. The apprentices had mastered their trade, the ministers had a firm grip on their portfolios, and the caucus had its feet on the ground. A new style of management was called for, and my role was changed to that of policy maker, public relations oversight, and occasionally, trouble-shooter, and so our world expanded and fulfilled itself.

Election night, 1959, afforded me an opportunity to say two things, one wise and one stupid. In response to a query posed by the press as to how long a period of office I would seek, I replied off the cuff that 10 years would give me a good run for my money. This turned out to be a wiser remark than I knew at the time because near the end of the 10-year period, it was clear to me I not only had done all the things I set out to do, but was physically drained by a very high-tension job. Later on, I discussed this matter with John Robarts, who became a warm friend of mine, and we both agreed that 10 years was a sensible target. Both of us adopted it.

The foolish response, also off the cuff, had to do with the question of a provincial sales tax. When asked whether I intended to introduce one, I gave the flip reply that the sales tax was as dead as a dodo. Later on, it was little use to explain the remark was made in the context of 1959 and the election manifesto of that day, and that it really did not apply to circumstances that might arise in a future election fought on a different manifesto. Two elections later, this argument carried no weight whatsoever. The voters remembered the remark and ignored the changed circumstances. When I contested a federal seat in

9 We were successful again in 1962 and 1966, making it four in a row, the last three with majorities.

Winnipeg South Centre in 1968, shortly after the actual provincial sales tax had been brought in, public memory helped to bring me down.

No leader can accomplish goals without the support of a strong team, and I was blessed with an array of impressive and talented ministers. I have spoken of some already. Sterling Lyon was a born politician in many ways. He was a natural to be leader of the house. His quick wit, clever tongue, and restrained pugnacity helped maintain the house in good order, although he never suffered fools gladly. He kept the house moving and got business done. At the age of 31, he was said to be the youngest attorney general at the time in the Commonwealth, and he exercised that office with great discretion, with a firm grip of legal and political principles. When he became premier himself, and the Charter of Rights and Freedoms was proposed, his concern for the supremacy of Parliament gave him a leading interest in the "notwithstanding clause." I am sufficiently traditional myself to agree with that provision. This brilliant constitutional innovation attempted to balance the large new powers being given to the courts with the ultimate power of the elected democracy to hold back the judges for a time. Later, as premier himself, he earned a reputation as a hard-line right-winger, which was hardly deserved. In my day, Sterling was an active supporter of the progressive measures that we proposed from time to time and certainly was a full partner in the operations of the government. It's perfectly true that sometimes Sterling talked the right-wing talk, but he didn't always walk the walk, even as premier. I think he should be credited with being far more flexible and open-minded than some would be later inclined to suggest.

Stewart McLean, minister of education, was a Scottish Presbyterian lawyer and former mayor of Dauphin. He had all the qualities, good and bad, of that background. He involved himself heart and soul in his job. Hard work was a stimulus to him and it inspired his colleagues. During the time when we were running the campaign for larger high school districts in rural Manitoba, he performed prodigies in securing a favourable vote. He was not so keen about some of the other educational policies the government pursued; for example, shared services. Stewart was the focus of the small-c conservative opinion in the caucus. His views were a good litmus test as to the sentiment of that section.

Duff Roblin

For no apparent reason, George Johnson christened him 'Skuli' McLean and made him a sort of honorary Icelandic Canadian. His distinguishing characteristic as a politician was the careful way in which he nursed his constituents. I don't think any constituency in Manitoba received the attention from its member that Dauphin received from Stewart McLean. It was always a sadness to me that, in the end, his constituents did not support him the way he had supported them.

Marcel Boulic, provincial secretary, was first and foremost a Franco-Manitoban, with that solid Norman temperament we often see in the province. His transition from rural reeve to provincial cabinet minister was difficult for him because it brought him into an entirely new circle of activity, both in government and indeed in city life. He was making a very good fist of things when unfortunately he died of a heart attack on September 22, 1959, at the age of 43, soon after he assumed office. This was a blow from which I never recovered because never again was I able to have Franco-Manitoban represen-tation in the cabinet. I tried very hard, but Marcel's loss was a tremendous grief to me in every way. He was literally irreplaceable. Life has its ways.

My search for a replacement was continuous but futile. In the course of events, however, I took notice of a young Franco-Manitoban named René Prefontaine who was making a name for himself. He was a leader in his community, and his special interest was in public school education. He was well-spoken, modest, and eager. But there was a drawback. He was the son of Edmond Prefontaine, my old colleague of anti-coalition days and a some-time Liberal cabinet minister. Interestingly, René's grandfather, Albert Prefontaine, had sat in my own grandfather's cabinet, so I really had no com-punction in speaking to him. I am sure that as we talked, he knew that, like his father and grandfather, he would obviously be of cabinet material. In the event, he agreed to run, and I agreed to a cabinet position. This is the one occasion in which I made such a commitment in advance. On announcement day, the press was alerted, and I stood by in my office waiting to attend the swearing-in cere-mony. Almost at the appointed hour, René appeared, clearly distraught, to tell me the deal was off and that he could not accept the challenge. His father, to my mind somewhat indifferent to his son's career, had besought him in tears not to bring down his grey hairs in sorrow to the grave by appearing in a Progressive Conservative government cabinet. Family loyalty prevailed. This was a blow, and I put the best public face on it that I could muster. I gave René my sympathy and understanding and faced the press. As things turned out, I was never to fill that francophone spot again.

At the by-election to replace Marcel Boulic, and without assistance from me—because I scarcely knew her at the time—Thelma Forbes came forward to win the Progressive Conservative nomination. She was a very interesting personality and a useful politician. After she had been in the legislature a little while, I was happy to suggest to her to accept the nomination for speakership; she turned out to be a very good Speaker, indeed. She succeeded veteran Abe Harrison who, as time would tell, was really not cut out for that job. Abe was promoted to the cabinet as a minister without portfolio and we experienced a little tighter procedural grip on the reins when Thelma was in the chair. Thelma was an excellent Speaker. The only thing was, she didn't like the job! Her natural political instincts were so well-developed she had an awful time maintaining a decent neutrality as Speakers were bound to do. Still, she was able to carry it off for some time, but with great personal chagrin. I finally agreed she should be relieved of that task. I asked her to become a member of the cabinet, and she did an excellent job as minister of urban development and municipal affairs. She was succeeded as Speaker by the member from Swan River, Jim Bilton, an ex-Mountie and local newspaper editor, and he carried on in a fine style. Thelma was the first woman Speaker in Manitoba and the first woman cabinet minister in Manitoba, so she has her place in history.[10]

John Thompson was a small-town country lawyer from Elkhorn in western Manitoba, a man of considerable capacity. His ability to speak well, convincingly, with a firm grasp of his subject was a great asset to us. His relaxed rural

---

10 We had another woman in the legislature at the time, Caroline Morrison. She came from the Manitou country and had succeeded her husband, Hughie Morrison, as MLA after his death. She, too, was a very good member, sensible and down-to-earth. She understood what her people wanted, yet was able to grapple with the larger issues that MLAs have to consider.

ways could be maddening, however. When he was scheduled to debate in the house, to declare some aspect of our policy, his seat would be empty until the very last minute. When the Speaker arose to put the question, he would miraculously appear and take his place just in time to speak before the vote was called. The effect of this on my anxiety level and blood pressure was visible, but he never failed to deliver a cogent and effective argument. When he was needed, John was always there, and when he was there, he delivered the goods. He was a born conciliator. As minister of labour, he had much success getting both sides to see the merit of an argument. At an early labour management confrontation, at my suggestion he summoned the disputants to an isolated location and, behind closed doors, made agreement the price of release. Harmony carried the day.

Jack Carroll, minister of public utilities, was from north of 53. He had been a merchant in The Pas. He looked something of a bantam, but in debate, he certainly punched far beyond his weight. He was a small man, quick-witted, a good study, unprepossessing perhaps, but when challenged in the legislature he never backed down. His exposure to the vicissitudes of frontier life made him sympathetic to the human condition. Later on, as minister of welfare, he understood the spirit of charity and had the firmness to understand its limitations.

I speak again of Dr. George Johnson, minister of health—the family physician with a latent talent for politics. The whole world was his friend. He had enormous sympathy for his patients and indeed for all society, and great understanding of people. He had a clear vision as to how the state could serve its people's needs for doctors and hospitals. He commanded the respect of health-care professionals and knew how to evoke their co-operation. George could carry out the most sensitive tasks. Later he was front and centre as minister of education in the introduction of shared services. His heart, of course, lay in the Department of Health and Welfare, and his vision in expanding the hospital system and his assistance in bringing in our health and welfare reforms were essential to their success. George was an interesting man to work with because he never came to conclusions lightly. He required the most intensive examination. Issues were revisited time and time again until he had satisfied himself that all aspects had been considered and he was happy to proceed. Part of this process consisted of visits to my office, and he would sit with me by the hour, explaining in a monologue the issues involved, outlining his concerns, offering me the alternatives, shyly proposing the solutions. In the end, he'd get the answer right. Dithering has its uses.

C.H. (Buck) Witney was the radio king of Flin Flon. Flin Flon had one radio station (CFAR), and Buck Witney was the centre of listener attraction. He had the most mellifluous and comforting voice, with a slight touch of an accent—I wasn't quite sure what it was. It seemed to me that with that contact with the public, he ought to be a candidate. I made it my business to ensure he allowed his name to go forward. He had a pretty tough fight. His competition, Bud Jobin, was a minister in the Campbell government, who later became lieutenant-governor of the province. But Buck was successful. He got himself adopted by Flin Flonners as if he were a twice-born northerner. He joined the cabinet in 1959.

Sidney Spivak arrived in the cabinet after his election in 1966. Malek Spivak, his father, had been among my earlier supporters in the Jewish community, and Sidney had followed suit. He came to the legislature and to his portfolio of industry and commerce with a fresh look and new enthusiasm marked by innovative ideas and energetic applications. He soon proved an engaging debater with a deceptively smiling demeanour. During my federal leadership run in 1967, Sidney was a key player in devising tactics and organization which displayed his talents to very good effect. He was later a strong and successful candidate to replace Walter Weir as leader of the party. He laboured manfully in that position for several difficult years before losing his post to Sterling Lyon. That he finally retired from active politics was a public loss.

Facing me across the floor of the legislature was Douglas Campbell. He was first elected in 1922 as a farmer's candidate, and he represented then, and always, that strain of social and political conservatism and of populism that runs through many of us on these western plains. His career was long and distinguished and moulded in large part by the very hard times which were imposed upon the province by events, both natural and man-made, in the '20s and '30s. He joined the Bracken cabinet in 1934. He had a capacious memory. Not only that, he was able, without a note, to make a long and involved statement involving many asides, but in the end would make his point. Though we were strong competitors and had many a clash in the legislature and on the platform, there was never on my part, and I suspect not on his, any feeling of personal animosity. Neither of us had any difficulty adopting a friendly relationship in later years. We had numerous contacts because we both attended the same public functions, and I was particularly pleased to be asked to attend his 95th birthday, celebrated at the Campbell farm at Flee Island. That was a pleasant occasion and a gesture I appreciated. Gildas Molgat later took over from Douglas Campbell as Liberal leader. He had been nurtured in the Campbell school so he seldom provided any surprises. In fact, with Campbell still at his side in the house and in their caucus for some time, I suspected his freedom of manoeuvre was not complete. He espoused the Campbell record and mostly did what oppositions are supposed to do, and that is to oppose the government. He preceded me into the Senate and reached the high post of Speaker.

Lloyd Stinson was a significant figure as leader of the CCF. I could always expect a cool reasoned critic of the government from a sincere believer in the welfare state. Our views parted when he wanted to enlarge the government role beyond the need and beyond a prudent use of our tax capabilities. His successor, Russell Pauley, preached the straight trade union line to the satisfaction of that constituency. In our parliamentary exchanges, he was straightforward and honest. Edward Schreyer served in the NDP ranks as a financial critic. Our budgets seemed to survive his assaults pretty well. After my time, he succeeded as provincial premier, to be followed by the royal appointment of Governor General.

Of course, life isn't just about politics. More important than elections was meeting my wife—Mary MacKay. I recall seeing Mary for the first time at a Tuxedo cocktail party. I remember how she disappeared under a very fashionable party hat with an enormous brim. It took a while for that encounter to ripen. Of course, Mary was not the first girl I knew. Wartime England was full of them, but they were moving targets. After the war, I did manage a brief engagement to an attractive young Winnipeg woman, but it did not stick. Happily, and to my great good fortune, what did stick was my engagement to Mary, but that was to come later.

Our next, more serious, encounter took place courtesy of the CBC after I became Leader of the Opposition. Mary was one of their talks producers; along with Sunday School of the Air, she was assigned the free-time provincial political broadcasts. The combination was interesting, if coincidental. I was a free-time politician. Inevitably she produced me and my gaggle of political hopefuls. We saw more of each other after that!

The 1958 election campaign created complications. I found I was waging two campaigns at the same time—one to get elected and one to get married. I hoped to keep public affairs and private affairs apart. In the end, success in politics financed success in the other when my stipend went from $6,000 as Leader of the Opposition to $13,000 as Premier. We were married August 30, 1958, in the Chapel of All Saints Church across from the Legislative Building. My brother, Rod, was my best man, and few beside the family were in attendance. Having just become Premier three months before, it was family only or include half the province. We had all of the Labour Day weekend to honeymoon. We found our first permanent home in our familiar Crescentwood district. Mary, much pregnant and in high good spirits, took to painting the walls. I pretended to look for second-hand furniture, but Mary called the shots. The birth of our son, Andrew, in 1959, followed by our daughter, Jennifer, in 1961, completed the charmed circle.

In the changes and chances of almost 40 years, Mary has been my helpmate. In politics she is superb. She improved my image, she attracted new friends, she performed the duties of a public person with grace and charm. Her open-hearted and sympathetic nature instructed me to offer a human face to the world. She does not allow me carelessly to take for granted the debt I owe to so many others I meet along the way. She puts a foot down on my thoughtless moves and on my

Duff Roblin

ABOVE: DUFF, MARY, OLIVE AND DIEF PREPARING TO HIT THE CAMPAIGN TRAIL IN 1962

ABOVE: WEDDING DAY,
AUGUST 30, 1958

ABOVE: ANDREW AND JENNIFER WITH SANTA CLAUS AT
LEGISLATIVE CHRISTMAS PARTY

egregious errors of neglect. When at times she is dismayed, she never allows it to show. She has an iron fortitude. For Mary, the children came first, but that did not prevent public duties such as appearances with me, opening teas and other such functions that required a degree of public speaking and an overcoming of public nerves. She had problems with both at first, but she conquered them most successfully. She took the children whenever she or we could, and when we went together, she was certainly a star attraction.

In those days, the house usually sat until late evening, and I could be sure that the makings of a hot toddy were always ready for me when I eventually got home. Things like a cottage at the lake, which seemed to be a natural move, were quite beyond us in those days with a husband who was at some public engagement almost every working weekend. So, as much as she liked Minaki, we were never able to satisfy the desire for a cottage there. She rounded out the public personality of the Roblin family. My image was certainly improved, and she had only friends, regardless of political views. She was a regular campaigner with me, particularly at the main events, and as Milton says, "The cynosure of neighbouring eyes."

Our son Andrew was born in 1959 at the Misericordia Hospital, courtesy of the good sisters. They were very helpful. Andrew's first exposure to the great public was at the age of about 12 months when I took him with me to a celebration at Lido Plage, a small resort on the Assiniboine River just outside Winnipeg, where they were holding an old-time fiddlers' and dancers' competition with Red River tunes and jigs, mostly to display the talents and the culture of Métis Manitobans. I suspect he remembers nothing about that, but certainly music seems to be a great part of his life. Politics in Manitoba, fortunately, had little impact on him because of his age. But when we moved to Montreal, we found he had to deal with other schoolboys who had something to say about the former politician's son who was in their midst. I am happy to say he was able to punch considerably above his weight. The Peterborough campaign, however, was his real introduction to the rough and tumble and dirty aspect of political life. He gamely—at the age of 12—canvassed for me and stuffed envelopes, but my defeat was a disillusioning experience for him. It left him with a permanent

Duff Roblin

dislike for politics, or indeed for many other conventional activities. That, assisted no doubt by his genes, made him an independent self-starter determined to make his own way in his own method. That turned out to be music. When we returned from Montreal to Winnipeg in 1975, high school had little charm for him, and he soon declared independence, leaving home to follow his bluegrass muse, but Mary kept a watchful eye. In a broken-down bus and as a member of a pickup band, he guitared his way across the West. He established himself in a musical career in the United States and married a charming young photographer, Patricia Rees, from Nashville, Tennessee. Their two little girls, Lily and Rachel, enliven and enchant my days.

Jennifer is one and a half years younger than Andrew. Manitoba politics were peripheral for her, but at some events she was not above stealing the limelight. When Diefenbaker came to town on one occasion, I brought her with me in my arms. This gave her an opportunity to retrieve his breast-pocket handkerchief which started a tug of war between the two of them. Later on, on an airplane trip, also with Diefenbaker, her chatter induced the Chief to say, "Little girl, don't interrupt your father and me when we're talking." Much good that did. Dief had no way with children. At Expo '67, Jennifer was along with us inspecting a United States warship tied up to the dock. This impressed her mightily, but could not deflect her from her decided purpose, to get a big stick of pink cotton candy floss. To keep her quiet, I said, "We'll stuff your face with it." And after the warship was inspected, we did.

The children did get into one provincial election campaign, when we set out for a tour of the North, going by plane to Thompson. The trip was enlivened by our unscheduled return to the Winnipeg airport, caused by some aircraft malfunction. This short hiatus back on the ground gave me time to make a frantic return trip to our house to secure a baby security blanket without which Jennifer could not live. On the second try, we made Thompson. On landing, Jennifer promptly vomited on the shoes of the mayor, while Andrew had a car door slammed on his hand. Jennifer went to bed. Andrew got to ride a pony and to see a movie. We won the seat—indeed, we had earned it. Princess Alexandra's visit to Winnipeg was also a test for Jennifer. She was instructed how to say

"Ma'am" when spoken to and to attempt a curtsey. No problem. Probably a stimulus for her later career on the stage. Nowadays with her Californian husband, Craig Lathrop, and our youngest grandchild, Siân, she has established her personality in the theatre. I subscribe to the view that fathers are allowed to believe that their children are exceptional.

At the time I became premier in 1958, I was still about three months away from being a married man, but I observed my colleagues in those early days as a bachelor, and I was moved to note how important the husband and wife relationship was in their lives. Political spouses complemented and fulfilled each other in a way I had not previously noticed. Political spouses have a very difficult role to fill. At that time, they were not usually in the limelight and yet they had a deep and profound influence on the political fortunes of their partner and, through the partner, on the province. The family relationship was vital to the impact the politician made on the community and his supporters, and the contribution of the spouse to that relationship is usually underestimated by far. Later on, my own personal experience emphasized the validity of these observations. Of course, there are occasions where, sadly, the reverse is true.

EDUCATION, *the* PRIORITY

WHEN WE CAME TO POWER IN 1958, THE STATE OF EDUCATION IN Manitoba could well be described as benighted. The best that could be said is that it might have met the educational needs of Manitoba students of the 1930s. Obviously, this would not do in the 1950s and '60s. During our days in opposition, we examined every level of the educational structure— elementary schools, high schools, and the university—and found they were sadly deficient for the times. As for community colleges, we had none. At every session, education was a topic of debate. We attempted to relate what was available to what students would need. Invidious comparisons were made with other provinces. Statistics were unearthed. Our per-capita spending on education was at the bottom of the provincial list. Local school taxes were highly unequal in different areas of the province. There were proportionally twice as many students in the urban high schools as there were in the high schools of rural Manitoba. It seemed that when discussion in the legislature moved past the little red schoolhouse, the attention of the Campbell government benches sagged. The demands of education in a changing economy were quite beyond the range of their interests. But public opinion had been stirred, and pressure for improvement began to grow.

Education headlined our 1958 election platform, so when the voters confirmed our mandate, we knew we had to move. For our first session, reform of the rural high school system took pride of place. Rural high schools in those days were too small to offer an adequate variety of instruction for the children they served and, understandably, attendance was low. The contrast with urban high schools was stark. Equality of educational opportunity in the province was an illusion. We did not discover this problem entirely by ourselves. A study in 1951 had investigated the subject, and its proposals for change had been placed before the legislature. Cowed by fears of alleged grassroots disapproval, the Campbell government consigned the report to the files. In opposition, we called for action, but fruitlessly.

Between the election of June 1958 and the session the following October, we scrambled to put our plan in place. The staff of the Department of Education, from Deputy Minister Scott Bateman on down, laboured day and night to be ready in time. The plan was to establish 36 larger high school divisions in rural Manitoba to bring rural high schools up to urban standards in quality, variety, and opportunities. A special financial regime was introduced to bear the extra costs involved in operating this new system. In order to preserve the integrity of their community, under the effective adjudication of Alfred Monnin we took special care to see that as far as possible, Franco-Manitoban areas were included in the same division. I confess this gave rise to some peculiar configurations in the system.

When we disclosed our plans to the legislature, the first public reactions were interesting. Peter Kuch, the cartoonist at the *Winnipeg Free Press*, devised a splendid cartoon which pictured me in a Boy Scout uniform driving my car, apparently on the way to school. The cartoon has me stopping and saying to a small boy standing by, "Do you want a lift, son?" I liked that, and I liked the Boy Scout image. After all, I had indeed been one. Kuch regularly identified me in this guise and I could hardly ask for anything better. A *Free Press* editorial at the time chimed in with the comment that the plan was "one of the best." Obscurantism, however, prevailed in the Liberal legislative ranks.

Making laws may not be easy, but implementing them can be much more difficult again. New ideas sometimes arouse fears, especially among minority groups—in this case, the Mennonites. They worried about students driving long distances to the new high schools. They were concerned about the mixing of students from strange communities, and perceived loss of local parental control. These issues were of real concern in some parts of the countryside. Real or not, we did not intend to ignore them. Grassroots anxiety about so local an issue as education and educational change called for the widest possible public participation. We decided to have a winter campaign of meetings to take the issue directly to the people in every proposed new high school division and then to call for a validating vote.

Every minister participated in the campaign. Public meetings attracted a good turnout, even though the winter was harsh. Some 600 local gatherings were held, and in each of them, plenty of time was allowed for questions from the audience and answers from the government. At the end of this intensive process, the vote was called. Thirty-two divisions approved, while four dissented. Happily, those four soon changed their minds and joined the plan, so the whole of the province was covered by the larger rural school divisions. This process was an exercise in direct democracy, but I would recommend it be reserved for special occasions such as this where local concerns were deeply involved. There is a place in our system for votes of this kind. This is particularly true when the issue is one of high local sensitivity where broad policies may conflict with legitimate local concerns. But, it should not be elevated into a fixed principle of our parliamentary democracy.

As the new, larger divisions were established, new high schools sprang up all over the province. They naturally were bigger than the previous buildings, which enabled them not only to accommodate a larger number of students, but to drastically enlarge and modernize courses, bringing them more in line with the needs of the time and the needs of rural people. To get students to the new schools, a substantial bus transportation system was established. While there were growing pains in putting it into place, students and families accommodated themselves to the longer trip. The best result of all was the dramatic increase in the numbers of students attending the new high schools, giving greater educational equality and opportunity to all young Manitobans.

We did other things to improve education in the session of 1958. We arranged for free textbooks for students, reinstating my grandfather's policy of 1908, and took steps to improve working conditions for teachers. Teachers had long felt themselves underpaid and unrecognized, and for once, they were right. The question of salaries had to be tackled. The province agreed to increase its contribution to the costs of running the public educational system to 60 percent. This was a sharp increase, and it gave school authorities the means to raise teachers' salaries to more realistic levels, which they did. We wanted a *quid pro quo* from the teachers in return for this improvement in their situation. We wanted them to accept the principle that merit rating should have some role in setting teachers' salaries. Minister of Education Stewart McLean negotiated long and hard with the teachers' union. They did agree that length of service and the level of academic qualifications should count in any pay settlement, but union solidarity would permit them to go no farther. The concept of merit rating was widely recognized elsewhere, and we did our best to convince the teachers this would enhance the reputation of their profession, to say nothing of the quality of teaching. Unfortunately, the teachers did not accept this point of view, and we had to reconcile ourselves to the fact that it was an idea whose time had not yet come. I now regret we did not push harder. We also wanted to increase the quality of teacher training. There was an undue number of permit teachers, underqualified and underpaid. The existing normal school, a specialist institute, left something to be desired. We decided to remove the normal school to the University of Manitoba and make it a university faculty. The period of teacher training was extended, and the syllabus was updated. The supply of fully trained teachers soon met the demand.

In 1958, another event took place which had considerable consequences. Dr. Robert McFarlane, a former deputy minister of education, had been commissioned by our predecessors to review outstanding educational issues. His report revived the central issue of the Manitoba Schools Question of 1890, namely that there should be public support for separate schools. In that instance, the separate schools were mostly Roman Catholic, and the religious, racial, and constitutional crisis created by the abolition of public support for those schools in 1890 had convulsed the province's political and social structure across the years and reverberated throughout the nation.

Duff Roblin

When the McFarlane report came out, it was clear that even after 70 years, the Manitoba Schools Question was not entirely dead. The old shibboleths appeared. To accept the report as it was threatened to revive old animosities. This was deeply troubling. We cast around for some time to devise a policy to grapple with this issue. The separate school supporters, mostly Roman Catholics, felt their position was vindicated, and demanded action. Other forces, including some within my own caucus, felt otherwise. I concluded that direct action was not possible, but something had to be done. Our solution was to institute a system of shared services. This concept was foreign to public discussion in Manitoba. I had stumbled across the idea in the United States, where it was associated with the quarrel over separation of state and church and had evolved as a partial answer to that conundrum. When I reviewed the issue, it was apparent this might be useful dealing with our problem here.

The current dogma laid it down that the public school system was all or nothing. Separate school students had to accept the full public school system, or have nothing at all. Shared services challenged this idea. It postulated that students outside the public school system should not be compelled to take all or nothing. If they found something they could accept in any part of the public school menu, they should be allowed to do so. A crude example would be the bus service. If the public school bus was going their way, why shouldn't separate school scholars be allowed to get aboard? Similarly, any other school service should be available. The "all or nothing" rule had to go. All or part of the public school offering, including textbooks and technical education, could be made available to separate school students.

This plan had two great disadvantages. Public school supporters would be dismayed, fearing the gradual dismantlement of their system, and separate school supporters would feel prevented from achieving their expectations. Still, the plan had, in my eyes, substantial merit. It would bring the separate school question back on the public agenda in a practical manner. It would break the hard crust of prejudice which had precluded consideration of this subject up to then, and it would open the door to other options when public opinion permitted. In any case, from a political point of view, we were pressing against the limits of our power. Even so, within the government, this proposition was not a done deal. Caucus was distinctly uneasy, if not hostile, to the proposal. The debate in caucus reflected public opinion. It was very difficult, indeed. There are strongly held opinions in Manitoba which can only be described as unenlightened in matters of language and religion and the constitutional framework of the province. The issues of 1890 still linger. That was evident in the caucus debates. A substantial group felt that the arrangements of 1890 should not be disturbed, that there should be no public support of any description to sectarian schools, that the public school was the means by which we reconcile the various streams of immigrants who had come into this province. They argued that to abandon this wholesome exercise in nation building would be a dangerous mistake. A lot of anti-Catholicism was expressed. The Orange Order had disappeared, but its philosophy lingered on. These issues all came to the surface in a very intense argument in the caucus. The old WASP Ontario-bred faction that led the charge in 1890 was still on the field, and its voice was heard.

I think that some of my Roman Catholic friends were very disappointed in me because I advocated shared services, and I could say equally that supporters of the public school system were very disappointed in me but for opposite reasons. What won the caucus over was the illustration I gave about the bus. We said the public school system remains. We're not asking the public school system to make any changes to accommodate separate schools. We're not asking separate schools to make any changes to accommodate public schools. However, if the bus comes by, how do you keep a Catholic kid off? And if free textbooks are available and a Catholic school wants some, how can you fairly say, "No, you can't."? The concept of sharing the service won the day. No one had to change—what they had to do was share.

When I first considered how to manage the shared-services issue, it was clear it would be difficult to ask Stewart McLean to abandon his public school views, which were somewhat rigid, and take on the responsibility of presenting the policy to the caucus, the legislature, and the country. I concluded that

Duff Roblin

George Johnson was suited, both by temperament and conviction, to hold the cabinet responsibility for this program, so I asked him to take over the education portfolio. One of the first things he had to do was prepare a statement for the House, which would explain what shared services was and why it was a good thing. The first draft he brought me was hopeless. Obviously, there had been some bureaucratic input: it was convoluted and difficult to follow. So I tried my own hand at drafting this statement and asked George to look it over. Well, we looked it over, all right. I dare say that statement crossed his desk and mine anywhere up to 20 times before we got the wording exactly right to express our purpose and conviction.

Public reaction was fierce. Separate school supporters were furious, feeling their expectations had been denied. Public school supporters were distraught, lest their system suffer. Obviously, we pleased few, but reaction in the legislature was more encouraging. Arthur Mauro, a constant personal friend, used his good offices to consult with the leaders of the Liberal and the CCF parties, and in the end, shared services received almost unanimous support in the legislature. It was quite different, however, when the public was consulted. A committee of the legislature provided an opportunity for people to present their views. As expected, protests on both sides were loud and long. Nevertheless, shared services served its purpose. It ultimately proved to be the catalyst by which we finally put the Manitoba Schools Question of 1890 behind us. In the end, both public and separate schools were well served. Much later, after I was out of office, I had an airplane encounter with Monsignor Baudoux, the former Archbishop of St. Boniface. At the time, he had been a vehement opponent of shared services, and I dare say he had not changed his mind. But he was kind enough to say that he now realized that it was the most that could be done at the time. The development of this policy, from idea to legislation, confirmed some of my prejudices. The first thing was that if I could secure the agreement of my cabinet colleagues, I was off to a good start. The real touchstone was to bring caucus on side because the considerations there would be as far-ranging as any in the public domain and would be just as difficult to conciliate.

Up until 1916, French was authorized as a teaching language in the schools of Manitoba. Then, in a spasm of educational change, the provincial government made English the sole language of instruction in the schools. From 1917 on, it was against the law to use French as a teaching language. Naturally, this imposition was thoroughly resented by the French-speaking community and many of their schools continued to teach in French despite the law. On those occasions when the school inspector was expected, French teaching materials were put away until he withdrew. I made sure the 1916 law was done away with. French was restored as a teaching language, with certain conditions. Here again, caucus debate was hot and heavy, but to my comfort, good will prevailed in the end.

The university system also attracted our attention. We were conscious of its role as the heart of Manitoba's intellectual and cultural life. We felt it not only lacked recognition, but the means to carry out its mission. It was clear the university had to be prepared for an increase in students. It had to be expanded and modernized to meet the needs of the time. This required more money. We found the funds and put in place a program to significantly expand the University of Manitoba's Fort Garry site. We also established scholarships and made arrangements to increase aid to students requiring financial assistance. We paid particular attention to the faculty of agriculture. The previous farmers' government was strangely neglectful of the agricultural research activities of the university. My grandfather established the Agricultural College in the first place, and it later became a part of the University of Manitoba. In any case, we did what we could to revive and rejuvenate the faculty because of its critical importance in agricultural farm practice and research to the thousands of farmers who were still the backbone of the economic life of Manitoba. Later on, I am happy to report that federal post-secondary grants became available and they reinforced the efforts we were able to make at the university. It is obscurantist that recent federal policy changes are reducing their contribution. In fact, before long, the cash grants from the federal government to the university will diminish almost to nothing. This is a sadly short-sighted action.

Duff Roblin

Other institutions of higher education also needed help. We rescued Brandon College, which was floundering in a financial morass, and we included United College in our own plans. Both of these institutions were promoted to university status in 1967. There were two small colleges situated in Winnipeg, both with very interesting historical pedigrees. One was St. John's College—Anglican—and the other was St. Paul's College—Roman Catholic. Both were in downtown Winnipeg. It seemed a good thing to provide them the means to join the University of Manitoba Fort Garry campus. By doing so, we would only enhance the university's diversity of activities, human colour and student resources. Within the university, we also provided for the establishment of University College.

Adding the two universities to complement the University of Manitoba raised interesting problems of administration and management. While government is an important sponsor of a university, it should not trespass on its autonomy. The government should provide funds, but the university should decide how those funds can best be spent. We were anxious to ensure this process was not politicized. We also had a problem with three institutions, of making sure they were well co-ordinated, keeping overlap and duplication to a minimum. In order to reconcile this question of political control, and also of co-ordination between the institutions, we decided to put a buffer in place called the University Grants Commission. Its role was to find out and monitor what the universities required and to consolidate these objectives into a request for government funding. So the government provided the money and the commission co-ordinated and supervised the universities' activities. But on the whole, the institutions were autonomous in their academic role.

There was at the time, however, one complete blank in our educational structure: a post-secondary community college system. Ontario and other provinces had long supported community colleges, and for very good reasons, because they were an essential part of the economic structure of the province, supplying the skilled people to make the economic machine work. The community college filled a vital gap in the post-secondary area. It prepared young men and women for entrance into the economic world. And the more the economic world evolved through the modern information revolution and other activities, the more the need for community colleges grew.

We had none, and we needed them very badly. In co-operation with the government of John Diefenbaker, we made plans to create three community colleges in the province: Red River Community College in Winnipeg, Assiniboine Community College in Brandon, and Keewatin Community College in The Pas. This distribution of services, we thought, would best serve both the urban, rural, and northern areas. My hopes for the effectiveness of community colleges were abundantly confirmed. They provided another practical option for students, both young and old. The solid relationship that community colleges have established with the local community, the strong university flavour that has been added to many of the courses, the up-to-date and wide-ranging community-oriented courses, all helped more young men and women—and some not so young—to find employment. A very high per- centage of their graduates find employment within the province of Manitoba. This high success rate confirms the essential role community colleges play in the province. The fact that most of their graduates are employed in Manitoba indicates how well articulated the community college system is with our local economic community.

Basic education in northern Manitoba also received a boost. We gathered together clutches of schools in the various settlements of the north and unit- ed them in an organization we called the Frontier School Division. This made it possible to improve standards and increase variety for students in that area.

It was in reference to education that I first became aware of Canada's leadership position in the Commonwealth of Nations. The link was the Commonwealth Parliamentary Association that, in its program of meet- ings, to which every legislature in its member states sends delegates, constitutes a bridge-building exercise among races, religions, languages and cultures superior, in my opinion, to many other international organi- zations. It derives from the days of the old British Empire and includes two score or so of countries that were formerly colonies or dominions in that system, but which now, free and independent, still recognize the Queen as head of the Commonwealth. Nothing holds it together but good will, fraternal association, and a common interest in the parliamentary democratic heritage. The British tradition, while strong, is only one of the several prominent in the association. English, in many and varied accents, is the language of communication. It has no powers but those of persuasion, a common interest, and the force of a good example. At its meetings, all the races of men with their several religions, in a rainbow of cultures and coming from economies sophisticated to undeveloped, take their places. Gathered on each occasion in a different host country, the delegates meet as strangers to one another, but the conference program provides that for their first week, divided into small groups, parties tour the host country together. Thus they get to know something of their host and, not coincidentally, they get to know something of each other. Strangeness begins to wear off and a certain camaraderie develops. During the second week, all meet in plenary session to debate the issues of the day. The liberating and humanizing effect of this process on such a group of parliamentarians is a powerful force for good in the world, opening up a new respect and understanding for the variety of humanity.

Early in the '6os, I attended a Commonwealth Parliamentary Association meeting in Malaysia at which the Columbo Plan was featured. The Columbo Plan was a post-war agreement between the members of the Commonwealth of Nations whereby the well-established and senior nations would help less favoured members of the Commonwealth to improve their lot. All kinds of facilities and programs were devised to transfer this support from the wealthy to the others. Education ranked prominently in the Columbo Plan concept. A number of good students from the lesser developed countries were invited to attend universities in other Commonwealth countries to learn what they could, and this was a very useful and helpful thing.

It struck me at the time, however, there was another education angle we might explore. It was all very well to have university students trained in England go back to Tanzania, for example, with university skills, but it was also important to help people at the local level master the mundane every-day business of living in a modern society. Somebody should know how to fix a car. Somebody should know how to design an electrical circuit. Somebody should know something about plumbing and house-building and all those journeyman skills which we take for granted in this country. And if we were to try to transfer these capacities to other places, it didn't make much sense to bring the people concerned, say, to Winnipeg to show them how we do it here, when the question was how they were going to do it at home.

Our solution was to send a cadre of teachers who were skilled in these technical trades and activities out to these countries—in our case it was Malaysia—to help local people get up to speed. This, of course, meant that when the local people graduated from the courses, they knew how to do things in terms of their home-base possibilities, rather than how it was done in other places. We sent a small group of our teachers to Kuala Lumpur, which was then struggling to find its feet, to transfer these rather mundane and elementary skills to the people of that part of the world. It was not a big operation, perhaps more symbolic than anything else, but it did serve a useful purpose. We called it rather grandiosely the Little Columbo Plan. Naturally we ran into some trouble in the legislature when we asked for monetary support because as then-Liberal MLA Larry Desjardins observed, quite properly, charity begins at home and, there-fore, we shouldn't spend this money abroad. My response was that charity does begin at home, but I didn't know that it ended there. In any case, the contribution was so small that we really should have been ashamed it was not larger. This did not satisfy Desjardins. I also recall that he voted against the Red River Floodway when that came up, so there wasn't very much I could do to please him.

Meanwhile, our tour of Malaysia proceeded. Sarawak, part of the island of Borneo, was formerly an independent entity ruled by the famous White Rajah, James Brook, an English adventurer. It had recently been trans-ferred by the United Kingdom to Malaysia, and I was one of a party of six to

Duff Roblin

Above: Laying the cornerstone for new R.B. Russell school with George Johnson and Mrs. R.B. Russell

Above: Presenting shared services policy to the legislature

visit it. There were two Australians, one Nigerian—a minister of Education who was murdered at the next military uprising—plus two West Indians and myself. I was given the honorific title of leader of this intriguing party. We flew from Kuala Lumpur to Kuching in Sarawak and made our way via Sibu to the Rajang River. As in pioneer Canada, in Sarawak rivers were the main arteries of travel. The Rajang River, streaming out of a tropical jungle, was the highway into a primitive interior. There, we were put into the hands of our guide who had formerly been a British District Officer, undoubtedly a holdover from the days of Rajah Brook. He was to take us by a large motor-ized dug-out canoe up the Rajang River to visit a Dyak village. A small war was going on in the island of Borneo between Malaysia and Indonesia. Indonesia thought Sarawak should belong to them. Consequently, we were escorted by a half-platoon of Gurkha soldiers. In the evening, making landfall at our destination, the Gurkhas jumped out and beat around the bushes, but to no one's surprise, the all-clear was given.

We found ourselves on the river bank, and there in the surrounding jungle was a Dyak long-house, made mostly of bamboo and raised up from the ground on stilts. Our party was invited to climb up steps that had been cut in a large tree trunk to gain the platform of the long house. I was the last one to mount, and as I climbed, I could hear some kind of commotion at the top, noises I didn't quite understand. Someone appeared to be saying, "Never mind. The leader's coming, wait for him." Well, they waited for him, all right.

When I reached the platform, a small pig, carefully bound up, was placed at my feet. Some sort of offering no doubt, to propitiate the gods on the arrival of these visitors. I was given a sharp spear and in sign language was told to dis-patch this unfortunate sacrificial animal. That was the leader's prerogative, and I did not shirk. The Dyak men were almost entirely covered with a deep blue tattoo and little else. Women were more modestly clad. A feast had been prepared, consisting of some rather small hard-boiled eggs and some rather small hard-boiled chicken. That was the toughest fowl I ever set my teeth into. As we feasted, I could not help looking around me to see several shrunken

Duff Roblin

human heads nodding from the wall; souvenirs, I was told, of a Japanese expedition in the Second World War. Entertainment soon followed. Our hosts gave us a shy warm welcome and a sample of traditional dancing and traditional song. Then it was our turn to perform. I gave an inspired rendition of a North American Indian war dance straight out of James Fennimore Cooper, accompanied by appropriate war whoops. I hope I may be forgiven for a well-meaning if ill-informed rendition of another culture's ceremony.

My repose that night on the bamboo floor was fitful. A delegate from the Caribbean, slightly inebriated no doubt, was trying to misconduct himself with one of the local ladies. The head man of the long house complained. Brisk action on my part restored order without delay. When dawn came and we began a new day, the culprit seemed to have no remorse whatsoever for his undiplomatic approach.

Many years after these events, I was asked to head up a review of higher education in the province of Manitoba. In 1993, the government of Manitoba appointed me, together with three able colleagues, Syd Gordon, Kathleen Richardson and Kevin Kavanagh, to review the position of higher education in the province of Manitoba. A principal target of our attention was the University of Manitoba, as it was the largest institution in the province. The 1960s were halcyon days for the universities. They had been neglected and were being recognized. They had been marginalized and were taking centre stage. Their connections with the community had been tenuous and now they were being strengthened. The number of students coming to them was increasing out of all proportion to past experience. At the same time, they were quite properly receiving the necessary funding to carry out this large task. The economy was favourable, public opinion was positive. Unfortunately, by 1993, the situation had changed.

In 1993, the main challenge at the university was the limitations of public funding and how to respond to the discipline and the changes imposed by fiscal restraint. Formerly the president of a university was truly its Chief Executive Officer. Over time, owing no doubt to the collegial nature of university life, each faculty had devolved into an independent power centre. It was the faculty which had large powers to influence the careers of its members through promotion and, therefore, pay, tenure and sabbatical leave. Faculty interests seemed to come before university interests. Add to this a staff union which was the epitome of conservatism in the worst sense, and the difficulty of dealing with the need for change and restraint in changing circumstances is apparent. Our job was to point out to the university that they could not expect to be exempted from the demands for economy facing Manitoba society generally at that time and to recommend an appropriate response to improve university financial management. We also assumed a responsibility to underline the importance of the university to the wider public and to improve government-university management systems.

The university is a collection of some of the ablest minds in the community. There are men and women whose capacities and training set them apart from the rest, and yet how difficult some of these worthy people found it to deal with the problems of change confronting them in a business-like and realistic way, even when the general interest made it necessary. In listening to university presentations made to our commission, some of the voices of faculty self-interest and of union hardliners almost drowned out the more realistic and constructive attitudes of those who saw the wisdom of reform and realignment and who understood the essential role of priorities in a period of limited means. Even though the determination of priorities and refocusing on the essential activities of teaching, research and accountability were at the heart of our findings, the report was wildly unpopular with some, but time and sober second thoughts now validate its central thrust.

This is particularly true of our two principal recommendations. First, expeditiously to double the size of our community colleges and second to strengthen the growth and development of distance education technology to open up access to educational services to all, regardless of location, age or previous qualification.

Thus in its many aspects, education was a priority for me. Starting with a refinanced elementary school system, we moved on to refound the rural high schools, to upgrade teacher training and pay, to create three community colleges, to recognize and enhance the universities, all major steps. The shared services policy and the reintroduction of French as a teaching language in the public schools failed to please all, but made their own contribution to civility and fairness in educational policy. Even the Little Columbo Plan had its uses. So all in all, we made a difference.

In the early days of the Industrial Revolution, the great humanist Robert Owen observed that public education was the most powerful instrument for good that had ever yet been placed in the hands of man. Just so. Education is not a cost or a bill or expense but a wholesome investment in human life, growth and comprehension. It is on such a foundation that successful societies are built.

seven

A NORTHERN REPORT

◆

I WANT TO START BY SKETCHING THE BACKGROUND OF MANITOBA'S affair with the North. In 1912, the boundaries of the province were extended to more than double the former area of the postage stamp province of 1870. The frontier was stretched north to the 60th parallel and east to an extensive coastline on Hudson Bay. In between was an immense forest cut by a number of great rivers, an area obviously bearing signs of mineralization. By 1958, the impact of the 1912 extension was still muted in the rest of the province. The Hudson Bay railway had been constructed and the Port of Churchill had been opened. A mine at Flin Flon had been operating for some time, and extensive new discoveries of nickel by the International Nickel Company had taken place in the isolated Thompson area. The virgin forests were almost exactly the same as when Henry Kelsey, reputedly the first white man in the area, passed through sometime in the 17th century. But in fact, Manitoba was still focused on the southern, east-west TransCanada Highway, with our new North only peripheral to our interests.

Our promise in 1958 was to include the new North in Manitoba's plans and to make a serious effort to develop the assets of this great territory. Transportation was the place to start. This is the usual problem in western Canada. The Hudson Bay railway and the Port of Churchill were long in place, but sadly underutilized. They were operated by an absentee owner, an agency

Duff Roblin

of the federal government.[11] A study presented to us envisaged a provincial takeover of the railway and the port, on the theory that local hands-on interest would produce superior results to any the Ottawa controller could deliver. Our proposal to make this move, however, arrived in Ottawa too late. When we saw then-minister of transport George Hees, he told us he had just transferred the Hudson Bay railway to the Canadian National Railway, and he could not get it back. We had to drop that idea.

The northern highways in 1958 were completely inadequate in every way. They were badly maintained, and didn't go to all the right places. Thompson, the biggest centre in the north, was left out. An immediate start was made to rebuild and upgrade the highway system in the north, extending hard surface facilities to the major centres. This investment greatly improved the situation. It was a convenience to the local inhabitants, but more than that, it upgraded economic possibilities for the area. Spinoffs included lower transportation costs in a high-cost area and improved prospects for the tourist industry. Access in general was much improved. A major goal of the highway program was to link northern and southern Manitoba more closely together.

The second great asset we looked at in northern Manitoba was hydro-electric generation. Two of Canada's great rivers run through the north, the Saskatchewan and the Nelson. At the time, they were untapped, but well-situated to be a source of hydro-electric energy. We began with the Saskatchewan River, where the Grand Rapids plant was developed. These projects were carried out by Manitoba Hydro, an independent Crown corporation, self-managed but dependent on the government. Its bonds were guaranteed by the province of Manitoba. The government interest was to assure good management and to promote the development of an asset the whole community could use.

In 1958, the manager of the Corporation was Don Stephens, a former deputy minister in the Campbell government and, in all respects, an able man. He was encouraged to seek our support to develop the hydro-electric

11 Forty years later, the absentee CNR was still in charge of the operation which, at the risk of exaggerating, was subsidy dependent and service poor. They were short on drive. Now, at last, a private owner, OmniTRAX of Denver, Colo., has taken over the railway, and hopefully local management skills and local incentive will come into play.

resources of the north. The power potential of these great rivers was very attractive to us and we hoped to put it to good use. Of course, it had to be self-supporting and not a burden on the provincial treasury. Stephens was able to demonstrate that his plans met these criteria.

Any gigantic hydro-electric plant generates an enormous and instantaneous surge of supply the moment the turbines start to run. The local market could only absorb this capacity over time, but export markets for surpluses in the U.S.A. could provide the financial and economic rationale to justify these great capital investments. We had to be sure that the exported power could, in the long run, be recaptured for the use of our own people, and this was attended to. Stephens's great fear was the competition posed by the nuclear power industry. He was concerned by forecasts which hinted that, before long, nuclear power would be cheaper than the hydro power we could produce on the Saskatchewan and the Nelson, and he was anxious to have our plants in place in good time so they could meet this expected competition. But, of course, it never happened. We put the plants in place, but the cheap nuclear power didn't arrive then and hasn't arrived yet.

The Grand Rapids project involved the relocation of a group of Native people. Hydro had put in place an elaborate plan to meet their needs which, it was thought, carried their consent. In fact, the human problems took many years and large sums of money to assuage. It is a continuing bad habit of Canadians to play down the interests of the Aboriginal people in developments of this kind. Ultimately, we must pay for it. On the Nelson, Manitoba Hydro reported that the high banks of that stream would reasonably limit the environmental problem. Later on and under another administration, the diversion of the Churchill River through South Indian Lake to the Nelson involved environmental consequences damaging to native residents and very costly to Hydro. However, these great power plants converted the free-running rivers of Manitoba's north to human betterment, and these enormous pollution-free investments in energy have ever since undergirded the Manitoba economy.

Duff Roblin

Then there was the question of Thompson to be considered. Thompson was a city isolated in the north, created by Inco to support its giant nickel mine development. Inco invested large sums to develop a model townsite and to supply a modern community with all the amenities for its employees. Inco, naturally, did a good job. Indeed it had to, because the success of its mine depended on good living conditions for their people. Inco managers displayed a strong company affiliation. Led by a driving chairman, Harry Wingate, who operated from New York City, Inco took the view that it had paid for Thompson and had every intention of running it. In effect, the company had come to northern Manitoba as a colonizer, and others were to stand aside. I had another opinion. Their presence was welcome. They deserved every consideration and were entitled to fair treatment. But they were not a sovereign power. We suggested that within a reasonable timeframe they should relinquish the operation of the town and yield to a regular municipal government in which Thompson's own citizens would have their say. In other words, the normal Manitoba municipal system should prevail. Inco had other views. No voices were raised, no threats were made, but my position was firm and clear. Inco soon saw the point. The municipality of Thompson did take shape in due course, and our relations became cordial again.

Inspection trips in the North provided their own interesting distractions. The Department of Natural Resources had developed a program for tagging caribou in the wild. There was great concern that the caribou herds, which were so important to Aboriginal people and so much a part of our natural history, might be undergoing a serious decline. The department developed a technique of putting little prominent yellow and blue tags in caribou ears so they could then be monitored from the air. The problem was how to get the tag in the caribou's ear. Owing to my exalted position as premier, I was given the opportunity to join in the exercise. It was not easy. We went north almost to the 60th parallel, the border with the Northwest Territories, in high summer. The country was seamed with lakes and rivers, and the caribou would come down to the edge of a body of water and try to swim across to the other side. Our role was to hide behind a little clump of land, and, when the herd of caribou reached the centre of the body of water beyond the point of no return, to dash out in a motorized canoe to intercept it. I was stationed in the bow and given a long shepherd's crook. My job was to put this crook around the head of some poor inoffensive animal as it swam, drag it up to the motor-boat, and then attach the tag to its ear. It sounds a simple procedure, and it was. The only problem was some of the caribou thought they should climb into the boat with us, and that meant a considerable struggle to keep out of harm's way. Anyway, we tagged caribou most successfully.

The town of The Pas, the centre of the old North, was a stagnant community. It had a splendid history interwoven with the Hudson Bay Company and the fur trade, but its future was doubtful—except, that is, for the possibilities of the forest that lay all around it. Elsewhere in Canada, forest-based industries had proved to be very valuable. They had been the lifeblood of their communities and a principal source of jobs and renewable wealth over the years. But in northern Manitoba, little had been done, nor was much in prospect. It became the task of government to ascertain the true dimensions of the forest and examine the facts on the ground to consider what, if anything, could be done. A number of studies proceeded. The difficulties were numerous. It was an area of small trees, long distances, slow renewal and growth, in an isolated location. Those problems were modified by the volume and extent of the forest potential. Invidious comparisons with other well-favoured forests elsewhere in the country made it clear, however, why the forest industry had shown almost no interest in northern Manitoba.

But our technical and industrial studies continued, and they determined that, despite the handicaps, a forest industry in northern Manitoba could be visualized. It became a goal worth pursuing. Other investigation continued.

Duff Roblin

Technical and industrial problems might be solved, but was the whole effort worthwhile to the community? This led to the preparation of a social balance sheet for the forest industry in Manitoba. How would a new forest industry improve the life of the community around it? Every department in the government made its own analysis. Local government, education, health, welfare, jobs, law, and human betterment were all part of the examination. When we were finished, a positive picture emerged. The conclusion was that a forest industry could be developed at The Pas and the people of northern Manitoba would benefit from it. Thus it became a vital objective of mine. Despite the vicissitudes I shall now report, in the end this original plan produced hundreds of jobs for people in The Pas and much economic stimulus for the area in question.

The Manitoba Development Fund (MDF) was set up in December 1958. It was given powers independent from the government and was envisaged as a hands-off stand-alone entity. Its task was to promote the industrial and regional development of the province, and its main activity was to be the lender of last resort for those who might wish to apply. Management was straightforward. A board of directors composed of competent and respected businessmen from throughout the province assumed responsibility and management of the fund. The general manager of the fund, Rex Grose, was also deputy minister of Industry and Commerce. That seemed to be an advantage at the time. A sound operation was established. From the start, the fund lent more than $43 million, without any losses, to a number of different developments. Thirty-five hundred jobs were created, with an annual payroll of $12 million. It was generally regarded as a model of success, and Grose's leadership and management of the fund under its directors established his credit and his high reputation, both within the government and in business circles as well. The Manitoba Development Fund, therefore, was well-suited and legally empowered to perform an important task. It was given the leading role to set up a forest project in the north. Its task was to safeguard any subsequent public investment and ensure that prudent management was in place at all times. Its past record was impressive and lent confidence to the expectation it would do this job well.

MDF then began searching for a forest operator. The natural disadvantages of The Pas, and the competition from other, more desirable, forest areas had to be overcome, which meant a set of unusually favourable inducements had to be developed. In doing so, the Fund tried to achieve a balance sufficient to attract applicants, but not too generous as to be impractical. Few offers were made. Of those received, the one from Churchill Forest Industries (CFI) was deemed by the Fund to be the best. Because CFI was an unknown quantity, the Fund proceeded to investigate its credentials. Banking sources, technical sources and various consultants were extensively canvassed. Their references were taken at face value, and that was no small mistake. In retrospect, some of these enquiries concealed more than they revealed. For example, Dun & Bradstreet, a business information service, told the Fund that CFI's head, Alexander Kasser, was born in Budapest, Hungary, in 1910 and graduated from both the Sorbonne and Grenoble University in France. Much later, both universities denied having a student by that name. Kasser had claimed he was Secretary-General of the Swiss Red Cross in Hungary during the Second World War, a claim that also proved to be false. Later on, the commission of inquiry into the CFI affair said of him: "While we cannot answer the questions as to the training Kasser had and where he obtained it, we do have evidence that he was highly competent and somewhat innovative in the pulp and paper field." He had, indeed, a proven record in the development of pulp and paper resources in other places. He was in the avant-garde of technological change that had been well documented. There was reason to believe he was suited to develop the virgin forests of Manitoba.

CFI and Kasser took refuge behind the Swiss tradition of secrecy. Risks in providing financing to such a group were clearly present, but they were deemed manageable. MDF's risk-control system had been carefully worked out over time, and had successfully secured satisfactory performances. They could enter into an agreement which would give the fund maximum security. MDF took power to control the disbursement of funds on proof of value received, and took power to bar the recycling of profits of affiliates or any other devices that might be employed to weaken the operator's capital investment. Excessive fees charged by related parties were prohibited. Control of funds by MDF was critical. The distribution of funds was the chokehold MDF exercised in supervising the operation. The agreement that was entered into was designed to give MDF iron-clad control over the money, and did so. It was structured to give the fund the upper hand, if only MDF would use its powers. When the MDF directors approved the CFI agreement and so advised the government, we undertook to provide the necessary funds.

In 1967, before I left office, the official Opposition under Gildas Molgat tabled an extensive series of well-framed and cogent questions concerning the Manitoba Development Fund, CFI, and Kasser. The answers to these questions were prepared by Grose as MDF Chairman in the normal course of events. When they were presented, they did not satisfy the opposition. They should not have satisfied me. Grose's position was that although flaws had been revealed by this series of questions, they were not fatal and the project could proceed. It's difficult to explain now why I was able to accept his assurances that all was well and no serious problems had been disclosed. It had something to do with the nature of the project and with having worked with him for seven years and having previously been able to repose full trust and confidence in his integrity and judgment. I wish now that I had breached the hands off arms-length position of the MDF and gone directly to the fund directors to secure further confirmation.

As subsequent revelations disclosed, the precise, diligent, and conscientious application of the CFI agreement by the Manitoba Development Fund and exercise of its power of control goes to the heart of the matter. This was the key to what follows. Walter Newman was in charge of the money. Newman was the fund's legal adviser, entrusted with the administration of the agreement and empowered to preside over the disbursal of government funds. The task was to secure the rights of the MDF, to protect the public investment and safeguard the funds. This he did, doggedly and with determination. His book, *What Happened When Dr. Kasser Came to Northern Manitoba*, describes his efforts and documents in detail his success in performing that task. The CFI agreement gave him all the powers he needed to keep an undisciplined and unprincipled borrower in line, and he did so. The task was not easy. There were constant altercations with the CFI people, but every time Newman insisted on his point, CFI complied. But in July 1968, after my departure from office, an unpublicized and fundamental change was made in MDF procedures and its relationship with CFI. Here Walter Newman picks up the story. In his book, he tells how he was dropped and the benefits of financial control exercised by him were gradually abandoned and given away. The catalyst for this move seems to have been discussions over a new CFI proposal, unknown to me, to greatly expand the scope of the project and institute four new separate operations involving substantial new provincial financial commitments. They were: Churchill Forest Industries (Manitoba Limited); River Sawmills Co.; M.P. Industrial Mills Ltd.; and James Bertram & Son (Canada Ltd.).

Grose presented this plan to the government led by Walter Weir, who succeeded me as premier, and was told, properly, that it was a matter for the MDF to deal with. Newman reports that Grose represented this government decision to the Fund directors as a cabinet directive to proceed under his powers as chairman, thus reducing the directors to a nominal capacity. At the same time, assurances were given by Grose to the Weir government that the board of directors was, in fact, actively continuing to monitor and control CFI activities. Neither representation was correct. The Weir government did not give instruction to the MDF board, and the MDF board was not continuing to supervise the operation of the contract. As Newman related, the effect of the change was to put Grose in full control of all aspects of the CFI file. Thereafter, MDF financial control under the agreement was progressively weakened. Grose became the paymaster and relied for his payments on the certificate of the Arthur D. Little Group, consultants to MDF, who were now very much in the thick of the financial action. For a time after Newman's departure, the original system of validating claims continued. But the MDF was becoming the watchdog that refused to bite. The Weir government was defeated in July 1969 and Edward Schreyer's NDP administration took over. From this time on, there was a drastic change in the way money was paid out. The CFI people would make an application for funds, Arthur D. Little would freely certify pay-

ABOVE: SHEDDING LIGHT
ON NORTHERN HYDRO-
ELECTRIC DEVELOPMENT

ABOVE: HIGHWAY 10—BUILDING NEW ROADS TO THE NORTH

ment, without any real check or validation. On that say-so of the Arthur D. Little Company, Grose would issue the cheque. During my term of office, in 1967 little money was actually disbursed. Up to the end of Walter Weir's term in June 1969, the sum of $16.5 million had been paid out. But from August 1969 to May 1970—a period of less than a year—$59.7 million was paid out in an unrestricted and unsupervised fashion.

June 1969 marked the defeat of the Progressive Conservative Weir government and the election of the New Democratic Party. The NDP had campaigned on a vigorous pledge to deal with CFI, but such was Grose's reputation and indeed his power of persuasion that when he met with the new premier and his cabinet committee on July 31, 1969, he was able to tell them in a convincing fashion that the MDF was fully functioning and all controls were in place and working. After that meeting, in spite of the election rhetoric, Schreyer was able to say publicly that no further investigation was needed into MDF and CFI at that time. In the months that followed, up until July 1970, it was business as usual at MDF, and nearly $60 million was handed out without let or hindrance.

All was quiet until March 1970. Then Philip Mathias, a journalist with the *Financial Post*, raised the hue and cry. He had been examining some of Grose's public statements and had come to the conclusion they were inconsistent and implausible. Public concern was at a height. The NDP cabinet then demanded a further explanation from Grose, but it appears to have been unsatisfactory because his resignation followed quickly. Much later, Premier Ed Schreyer described the meeting this way:

"In appearing before the entire Cabinet, he was visibly nervous, and disturbed. At first, I thought it rather strange in the sense that he was one who'd been for many years, used to dealing with so many different people on short notice, etc., under the most—one assumes—under the greatest degree of pressure, negotiations of deals of large amounts, etc. During the course of the questioning, his nervousness, if anything, increased rather than abated."
Mr. Schreyer went on to say that:

"Mr. Grose stated in front of the entire Cabinet that in fact the figures he had given Mr. Mathias were wrong ... when asked to clarify whether they were intended to mislead, in effect, he admitted so, and gave as the reason that the *Financial Post*—had been an obstacle to the interests of economic development, in Manitoba." A sad end to a fine career.

In January 1971, a commission of inquiry was set up to find out what had gone wrong.[12] Three and a half years later, at a cost of $2 million, they produced their findings. They excoriated persons and institutions, not overlooking the injunction by memo of Alistair Stewart, a former NDP member of Parliament, to smite the Tories hip and thigh. Stewart had been instructed by the Schreyer administration to investigate the state of affairs in the MDF, and his preliminary report disclosed the chaos that existed. He blamed it entirely on the previous Conservative administrations, accepting no responsibility for what happened after Schreyer came in to office. The commission found

12 It was during testimony at that inquiry that Mr. Schreyer recalled Mr. Grose's explanation.

plenty of shortcomings. Its 3,000 pages are full of evocative descriptions of fraud and skulduggery. It accused the two previous Progressive Conservative governments of sloppy research and insufficient financial controls. It called the affair a disaster and debacle masterminded by a man of "insatiable greed." Every procedure and policy endured their scorn, but any sort of balance or wisdom in their observations is hard to find.

The fact is that the northern Manitoba forest project was not intrinsically doomed for failure. The structure of the original project was not basically unworkable. With all the mistakes, that project was viable, except for a final mistake. The decision to jettison the powers conveyed by the agreement to exercise strict financial control over the operator was indeed a fatal error. If one were to reduce it to personal terms, when Grose dumped Newman, he opened the door for Kasser. The looting of public funds was preventable. At the start, Newman used the agreement to enforce compliance. The nefarious and greedy plans of Kasser would never have worked without the witting or unwitting laxity of Grose and the Arthur D. Little Group.

During the course of the CFI inquiry, allegations were made by Grose that a committee of four cabinet ministers hammered out the initial deal with Kasser in one long hot afternoon. These were false. No such meeting was held. In fact, at no time did the cabinet as such negotiate with Kasser over the CFI arrangements. This was the function of the MDF. The allegations were accepted as true, however, even though the commissioners had the sworn testimony of three cabinet ministers contradicting the claim—the fourth was dead. Those cabinet ministers were Sterling Lyon, Gurney Evans, and myself. Maitland Steinkopf had died. The commission chose to disregard that testimony and accept the testimony of Grose, whose ability to confuse the truth had already been aptly demonstrated before them in the course of their studies.

When cabinet first came to consider the advisability of providing funds to the MDF for the northern forest development, all the public interest consider-ations that I have expressed were on the table. A very thorough study had been made of the technical and financial problems of setting up such a project, and the social balance sheet I referred to had been carefully examined. When this discussion was over, and before the final decision was made, I remember clearly saying to my colleagues, "This project is not without risks. If the risks materialize, the consequences for us politically will be grave." I was referring, of course, to the feasibility of the original project in the market. I had no idea that the risk we were facing was a different one, the misadventures of a principal actor on the stage, Rex Grose. That came as a shock and a surprise.

I had worked with Grose for seven years. I had appointed him to be the deputy minister of Industry and Commerce, and it proved at the beginning to be a good choice. His record as deputy minister was exemplary. One of his projects, for example, called COMEF, Committee on Manitoba's Economic Future, was a very intelligent and well-structured endeavour to plot the future development of the province and propose co-operation between all sectors of the economy to get things done. His reputation as a doer was first-class. He was extremely active in promoting the industrial and regional development of the province, and the MDF was partially his creation.

He was also a man possessed with a vision to develop the northern forest, which I mandated and fully endorsed. After I left office, the original CFI project I had known suffered a sea change into a more ambitious, expanded, and costly four-company proposition. For the sake of the new plan, Grose sidelined the MDF directors, disposed of an inconvenient financial controller, Walter Newman, and presided over an improvident payment of $60 million to a man who proved to be a crook. It came out at the enquiry that in 1968, Grose was negotiating a job for himself as president of a CFI company with what was at that time a handsome salary and extensive perks ($50,000 a year salary, with the promise of an indefinite consultancy if he were fired, at $25,000 a year, and an inheritance of $15,000 a year to his spouse if he should die). He did not proceed with this arrangement. Apparently, he consulted with his boss, Gurney Evans, who told him it would be a conflict of interest. Indeed it was, but it does throw some light on Grose's mental state at that particular time, and also it may throw some light on his subsequent conduct.

I feel a certain sympathy for Edward Schreyer. He came into office the vic-

Duff Roblin

tim, as most successful politicians are, of his own oratory and his own pre-
conceptions. He had pledged to investigate CFI root and branch, and do it fast.
He and his cabinet committee seemed to have relied entirely on Grose's
status report. In view of what they had said in the election, it seemed unusual
that they didn't go beyond that verbal assessment. One can forgive initial
hesitations on assuming office. That might be natural. The government did
initiate further internal studies, but they allowed a year to pass while the hemorrhage of money continued without taking further action.

My direct knowledge of CFI affairs ceased after I left office in 1967. I
worked in Montreal for the next six years. Philip Mathias's exposure of
Grose's activities in 1970 came as an unbelievable shock. When I handed over
affairs to Walter Weir at the end of 1967, the Manitoba Development Fund had
been firmly in control of CFI affairs and was exercising its powers under the
contract in an effective manner through Walter Newman. Grose's strong and
experienced leadership could be relied on. What happened? The proceedings of the subsequent committee of inquiry, who by the by heaped coals of
fire on my head, failed to satisfy me that it indeed had the answer. When
Walter Newman's book appeared, it gave a more convincing, realistic, and
hands-on analysis of the course of events. In its findings, the inquiry attacked
Newman's integrity, overlooking his evidence. I believe Newman's account is
more nearly right. Grose's success in obtaining single-handed power to rene-
gotiate the greatly expanded and much more ambitious and costly four-plant
proposal in 1968 set the stage for the payout debacle of 1969 and 1970. It is
a reasonable speculation that the fear generated in Grose and CFI by the
campaign promises and the election of the NDP government in July 1969 may
be the trigger that released a cataclysmic effect.

Nevertheless, as leader of the government until 1967, I affirm my commitment to the original The Pas forestry development policy, and I accept the
responsibility of office. There may, however, be something to be said for the
final outcome. Without minimizing the difficulties in the situation, at least for
the last 20 years, 600 to 800 northerners have had jobs, millions of dollars

worth of product has been sold, and a contribution has been made to the welfare of the people of The Pas.

On a related subject, I am acutely aware of the risks of presumption in proscribing the future of another culture, but I will take my chances because Manitoba must recognize, more successfully than it has yet to do, the unique place of First Nations within our borders. It is true that under the constitution it is the federal government that is responsible for their welfare, but their presence in the society must be the concern of all. Nowadays, First Nations comprise over 10 percent of the provincial population, and that number is growing. Demographers advise that soon one Manitoba child in four will come from an Aboriginal family.

Treaty Indians, in the language of 1958, were the constitutional responsibility of the federal government and the province was not eager to assume their role. Nevertheless, we made cautious efforts to be helpful. Our first step to improve understanding was to recruit an assistant deputy minister with Aboriginal connections in the person of Jean Lagacé. We experimented with model economic programs related to reserve activities. Co-operatives in the fishery, forest pulp harvesting and retail merchandising sectors were started. Sadly, they did not take us very far. Our efforts were premature. The ground was poorly prepared. Untrained workers were brought forward too fast. Projects were proposed from on high instead of coming from local initiative. In short, we made all the mistakes. Both Aboriginals and the government were very low on the learning curve. Now we understand much better how important it is for people to take their destiny in their own hands.

We did better on the job front. The advent of large hydro-electric projects in the north supplied the opportunity. Room for First Nations construction workers was arranged. Here, pre-job training was much better. Even so, cultural influences could not be avoided. There was some muttering among management about efficiency, but hydro contractors and Aboriginals soldiered on, each learning from the other.

In 1958 when I came into office, most Aboriginals still lived on their reserves, often in remote locations, where the traditional livelihoods of trapping, hunting and fishing supported a traditional culture. The federal Department of Indian Affairs provided some services in a highly paternalistic fashion. But revolutionary changes were on the way. The extension of the franchise, both federally and provincially, stimulated Aboriginals to emerge from the paternalistic shadow of government to assert their own place in the sun. A process of exploiting democratic rights to strengthen the First Nations agenda had begun.

At the same time, as a product of improving health and living conditions, a rapid increase in Aboriginal populations also began. This explosion in numbers led to such pressure on the natural economic base on reserves areas that there was only room for some to continue in hunting, trapping and fishing as their fathers did. The rest, refusing to decline into a welfare ghetto, began a dramatic and wrenching shift of population to urban centres, mostly to Winnipeg. Thus Manitoba's Aboriginal citizens are split—roughly half on reserves and half in Winnipeg.

On reserves, leaders speak of life with poor housing, with alcohol and drug problems, and with idleness as a wasting disease. Continuous large payments by the federal government seem to be endlessly ineffective in improving conditions. Demands are raised for more, with some chiefs threatening civil disobedience to dramatize their claims. The well-run reserves and wholesome family situations sadly receive less attention. A clear appraisal of the issue is obscured when, in some reserves, too little value is placed on a system of accountability and responsibility on the part of those band authorities in charge. This must change. Both the reserve populations who are the intended beneficiaries of government support and the taxpaying public who provide the funds can make such a demand as a basic political right with no threat to the Aboriginal culture.

Responsibility should be an accepted principle in the urgent question of Aboriginal reserve self-government. This concept of self-government may vary or be different in different First Nations communities. An unwitting sort of cultural apartheid is a danger. Cultural heritage is all very well, but good relations with non-Aboriginals does not demand the sacrifice of a heritage. In Canada, we know it is not contradictory to maintain the two things—distinctive culture and general citizenship—at the same time. On April 1, 1999, the district of Nunavut was created in the eastern Arctic. On this barren but multi-textured land, four times the size of France, 25,000 largely aboriginal people will practise local self-government.

First Nations communities can well expect to undertake management of functions like culture, language, education, health and welfare, and local economic development though they will perforce continue to rely on federal financial support to do so. Lack of an adequate reserve tax base renders this inevitable. Again, reserves will require access to provincial resources, especially for education and health services. Native peoples indeed want to end the present disheartening climate of dependency; however, sovereignty is not the right word to describe this process in Manitoba. Responsibility is a better word, both philosophically and as a description. To achieve this goal with all deliberate speed is an urgent requirement for the sake of Manitoba's society as a whole. Only to mention the grotesque proportion of Aboriginals in the prison population makes the point.

But half of the province's First Nations population does not live on reserves. They live in Winnipeg, and the population is growing. This fact needs to be reflected in the distribution of federal support and in provincial policy. Urban Aboriginals are alert to their condition. Youth gangs are prominent in the public mind, both as a threat and a reproach. Self-help groups are giving youth an alternative. There are cultural interests to be nurtured in an urban setting. The Neeginan project in the central city gives a physical home and spiritual focus to these aspirations.

Happily, there are indications that First Nations youth also understand the need, through education, to master modern life. Seventy percent of the students in Keewatin Community College in The Pas are Aboriginal. The figures at the Assiniboine College in Brandon is 30 percent and in the larger Red River College in Winnipeg is 10 percent. The University of Manitoba graduated 200 Native students in 1998 with degrees in seven professions including four doctors of medicine. The University of Winnipeg has a similar record of success. The Winnipeg economic community is beginning to recognize the First Nations presence as a potential economic asset, while a few Aboriginal self-starters are appearing on the business scene.

These are significant developments but they still leave too many Aboriginals in limbo. Under-educated and chronically under-employed, they express a basic challenge to be addressed. To co-exist happily in a modern society, education is a key. Indeed, Aboriginal cultural survival in productive terms depends on blending its essential features with a working knowledge of the wider world. Education makes this possible. Starting at the base public school level—Grades 1 to 11—Aboriginal achievement is less than half the general standards. This must change. Parents must take the lead, see what needs to be done, and induce their children to understand the opportunity. Language and culture will be part of the school system, but general community norms will also be met. Let the wider community stand ready to help, but let the Aboriginals themselves lead in decision making and lead the responsibility to carry them on out. Thus First Nations self-worth and dignity will receive their just recognition.

This would herald the beginning of a sea change among Native people and within the society as a whole. The payoff in social harmony and human development and economic rewards merits the strongest support from First Nations, governments, and the public alike. Investment in education is a foundation on which vibrant cultures and successful societies are built.

eight

HUMAN BETTERMENT

MANITOBA IN 1958 MUST HAVE PRESENTED AN INTRIGUING PICTURE to students of social change. Over the years, Manitobans had developed a strong ethic of self-sufficiency and self-responsibility. You took care of yourself, and you took care of your family. Drought and the Great Depression shook this sentiment, but even then, those forced to accept relief or the dole felt a certain stigma. But the province's deep pioneer roots were being disturbed.

Local government and local property taxes carried a large part of the social welfare role. Sentiments may have remained fixed, but the real economic world in which people lived was changing. Coping with the economy was no longer only a personal matter, where individual responsibility could be invoked. It was instead becoming a far-reaching, impersonal thing in which factors beyond the control of individuals were at play. Before 1958, our social structure had not kept pace with this changing environment. In those years, health and social welfare were basically private matters, though provincial and municipal responsibilities were emerging.

Social welfare policy issues were included in our debates in opposition and in our 1958 election campaign. I have referred to my reading during World War II of the U.K. Beveridge Report. Our own intent was to recognize need as a suitable basis for reformed social welfare policy, one tailored to the province's financial capacity. We attempted to marry commitment to individual responsibility with public concern for individual need. In fact, we called our policy the Needs Policy. This meant that the principle of universality in social policy was rejected. We did not intend to do for the competent what they were able to do for themselves. We were our brother's keeper, indeed, but only so far. We would extend our hand to people in need—the elderly, children, single mothers, the physically handicapped, those fallen upon evil times, and any in the community who could not help themselves. They were entitled to the compassion and support of society as a whole. If the provision of these services was to be universal, and everybody got the same allotment, the rich would get something they did not need, and the poor would fail to get the more they did need. The principle of need would take priority over universal entitlements so that limited public resources would recognize priorities. Our social needs policy provided humane, dignified, and efficient assistance, both in human and financial terms. It met the need, and more should not be required of it. We called it our social allowance policy.

The opposition said, "What you're talking about is a means test." But I maintained that both the psychology and the practice of our needs system were quite different. Under a means test, the question is, "What have you got?" Under the needs test, the question is, "What do you need?" When need is established, then the means available, augmented by public assistance as required, are used to meet it. This concept was accepted by the people of Manitoba, and the needy were provided for. In the process, the municipal welfare burden was relieved. Province-wide standards were set, but to give the needy citizens the assurance of fair treatment , we established a system of local social allowance appeal boards. These were set up in the various localities and staffed by local men and women. Those in need could appeal to the local board if they felt they had not been fairly treated by the system. It was the mission of these boards to see that equity prevailed. It seemed to work well and to the satisfaction of all parties.

Better access to hospitals and medicare came next. The private Blue Cross hospital insurance plan, based on voluntary premiums and run by the hospitals, was in full swing. Indeed, I had helped to start it in 1938, so I knew how it worked. Enrolment of the population was extensive, and the system was favourably regarded by the public. In 1958, we adapted the Blue Cross system to make it a public plan, but those who could, continued to pay premiums. Those who could not, had their premiums paid for them by the province. No public distinction was made between insurance cards paid for by subscribers and those paid for by the public. Hospital care was available for everyone, but the direct cost of the premiums for the needy and paid for from the provincial treasury was affordable. The premium payment system had the additional real advantage of informing the general public directly of the costs of their insurance. This public exposure had a salutary effect on hospital service providers. They were stimulated to police the efficiency of their own management and thus the level of premiums.

We followed the same practice of need in bringing medical care to all. This time we employed the existing, proven voluntary medical insurance plan run by the medical profession and widely supported by a premium paying public. The name of the plan was the Manitoba Medical Service, but the same principles of need were adopted. Those who could, paid their premiums. Those who could not, had their premiums paid for them by the government. In the operation of the plan, the doctors had an important responsibility—they policed their own profession and made sure the services of the doctors were in line with good practice and sound operation. The premiums were kept in line. When premium increases were required, it was the MMS people who had to take the message to the public and make sure their rationale was accepted by those who were called upon to pay the premium. As it was with the hospitals, need was in and universality was out, yet everybody was served in a self-respecting manner.

A feature of the MMS arrangement that greatly satisfied me was how socially effective the program was. It delivered the goods and it was socially disciplined; the doctors policed their own members and established their own premiums. The providers were in direct contact with those who paid the premiums, so the providers were in the front line justifying their costs to the general public.

Duff Roblin

This was our position in Manitoba in 1966 when Prime Minister Lester Pearson proposed a federal universal compulsory medicare system.[13] Under this arrangement, the federal government would pay half the costs of medicare for any province that would join on federal terms, but no flexibility whatever was provided for provincial variations. If you wanted any of the federal money, it was the federal plan or nothing at all. For a province to stay out, or for Manitoba to attempt to go it alone with our own plan, would indeed carry a costly penalty for our taxpayers. They would be in the position of paying a federal tax, getting no federal benefit, and at the same time helping to pay the medicare costs of other provinces. Indeed, a Catch-22 situation. I strongly urged Pearson to be more flexible and to accommodate our successful self-help, needs-based medical program in Manitoba. Stiffened by the rigid attitude of the federal bureaucrats, he refused to accept my proposition. It became apparent that if I wanted to get elbow room for Manitoba I had to get behind a bigger player and push. Manitoba didn't have the clout to do it on its own. In this case, the bigger player was the province of Ontario.

Premier John Robarts and I had come to office at roughly the same time, and I had formed not only a high regard for him, but also a good personal relationship. I explained to him Manitoba's dilemma. He listened to my plea for help and, to my great satisfaction, told me that he liked the principles we had adopted and would do what he could at the federal-provincial conference to help us. Indeed, he agreed to support us publicly, so I was hopeful. The next day at 10 a.m. the conference opened, and I met John at the door. As we made our way to our seats, he took me by the arm to say he had discussed my proposition with his cabinet colleagues and unfortunately they had not agreed to support our position. "Sorry, Duff, I can't go along," said John. "My cabinet balked." So, willy-nilly, it was the Pearson plan. In the days that followed, the federal bureaucracy took charge. Our people were considered bit players and expected to do what they were told. The wise men in Ottawa were laying down

---

13 Appearing for Manitoba before the Hall Commission on Health in January 1962, I set out our medicare need-based, voluntary insurance plan. Those able to do so paid premiums. Those unable to pay had their premiums provided by the government, thus providing a universally available medicare service. Our recommendations included a request for 50/50 federal-provincial cost sharing for the benefit of premium payers, and flexibility in administration.

the law and delivering the most detailed regulations we were expected to adopt. It's ironic to note that years after, when the federal money ran low, Ottawa then left Manitoba to face an unhappy public alone. It was an unresolved problem of the first importance to Canadian federalism to accommodate the use of federal spending power for shared programs in fields of provincial constitutional jurisdiction so that provincial rights were respected. A new protocol was urgent and essential.

Meanwhile, the provincial health infrastructure was growing rapidly. A rehabilitation hospital was commissioned for the city of Winnipeg. New regional hospitals were dotted across rural Manitoba. Extensive changes were made in the mental hospital program in the province. All of these important public services flourished under the energetic, practical, but idealistic leadership of George Johnson who was the minister in charge until 1963. The pioneer spirit lingered on, indeed, but modern social needs were also being satisfied.

The expansion of the social structure that took place during my premiership upset some local communities. That was to be expected. Old rivalries between locations were revived, and new special interests appeared. A couple of good examples can illustrate the point. Take the question of the new larger high school system. When the prospect of a new high school appeared on the horizon, every locality wanted the school within its boundaries. The communities of Crystal City and Pilot Mound are only 11 kilometres apart, and they have always been the most enthusiastic competitors. When the high school question arose, the issue of which town would receive it was of intense interest. Both towns sent delegations to see the ministers—not once, but several times—because if one had come in with one argument, the other appeared the next day to give another. Private solicitations were attempted, and pressure from MLAs was in the mix. Business self-interest was carefully disguised in this confrontation, while the values of education—inevitably—received somewhat less than due notice. The suggestion made by Solomon Roblin was that the school should be located between the two towns. Obviously, that satisfied nobody.

When the new rural hospitals were being planned, the same kind of issue arose. I particularly recall the town of Hartney, which refused to go to the town of Souris, some 40 kilometres away, for its hospital service. Hartney told us its tale of horror, of long cold winter drives to the Souris hospital for those Hartney people who needed medical attention. They rang all the changes of pathos to persuade us that Hartney should also have its own independent hospital facility. Much else was adduced by the Hartney folks in successfully advocating the interests of their town. Obviously, it had ceased to be a local health issue and had become a local business question. I am afraid this sort of pressure gave us one or two more rural hospitals than we really needed.

Soon after taking office, we faced a medical emergency. It was the threat of another of the polio epidemics which had ravaged the province from time to time. Science had developed several vaccines against polio, and at the time, the vaccine of choice was delivered in a lump of sugar. The public seemed rather leery of this innovation, even if offered without charge, and did not trust it enough to use it. To set these fears at rest, George Johnson came up with a great public relations ploy. Under the gaze of the media, and in the rotunda of the legislature, he lined up the entire cabinet and fed all of us our lump of sugar to prevent polio. Enough said. The force of example worked.[14]

After the Second World War, when I was an active member of Winnipeg No. 1 branch of the Royal Canadian Legion, I learned something about another pressing social problem. Many members of No. 1 branch were old sweats from the First World War and had arrived at that time of life when the need for old folks' housing loomed large. Comrade Jim Cowan, an old friend and later a caucus colleague from the Winnipeg Centre constituency, took the lead in mobilizing Legion action. He organized a legion housing project to meet this need for elderly veterans. He shared his trials and tribulations with me, and I knew well the problems he had to solve. The need was real, but the means were decidedly limited. This issue was not limited to legionnaires—it was widespread—so sponsors of various stripes were available. Local communities wanted to make provision for their senior citizens. They were particularly interested in provid-

14 The editor of the *Winnipeg Free Press* found a lack of principle in a free program and called it a bad omen for the government's future.

ing services in places where the client was close to friends and to family. After 1958 we set up an elderly persons' housing program. This was intended to help provide capital funding to build these institutions that kept rental costs low and made it possible for the sponsors to take responsibility for operations. Spaces were soon filled, and we found this program filled a growing need. Sponsors and people from all parts of the province responded positively.

Decisions about where to build highways also brought local interests to the surface. Most towns were happy to use bypasses, provided good access roads connected them to the highway, and this we were careful to arrange. But the village of Kenton was different. Barely a dot at four crossroads, Kenton wanted its corner on the highway preserved so that whatever traffic there was would be sure to take note of its fine facilities. Villagers wanted a modern highway, but they wanted it located just where it always was, regardless of where common sense said it should go.

A fair judgment is difficult when dealing with these important local issues. The first step is to carefully examine all the facts in each party's presentation to make sure you have a clear picture. The second thing is to sort out the general policy objectives, say for schools, hospitals, and highways, to disentangle them from the local business interests and local pride. The goal is to ascertain how much of the argument is froth and how much is solid. Even when that's done, it's sometimes difficult to be sure what the right answer should be, but on the whole, if an analysis of that kind were made, we were usually able to convince the petitioners that while they might not agree with our arguments, they at least had a fair hearing. That really is the essence of it— listen, and give a fair hearing.

One of the features of the 1958 election campaign was the little red flags. Little red flags were everywhere: Their purpose was to mark the potholes on the roads, to help drivers avoid the hazards. Hardly a highway in the province was not festooned from end to end with these little red flags. This certainly made a good opening line for me when I spoke at rural meetings. "I had no trouble getting here," I said, "I just followed the little red flags, the best highway markers I've seen for some time." This wisecrack epitomized the run-down state of provincial roads, and everybody got the message. So we had to do something about it, and we had to do something big. Soon there was activity throughout the province. Roads were extended. The quality of the highways was raised everywhere because we saw good highways as an essential public investment. This was the way to connect the various parts of the province—north to south, east to west, town to city, and town to town. An efficient highway trans-portation economy is essential in a modern society, and we intended to provide it. From time to time, we would raise the gasoline tax in order to cover the carry-ing cost of the highways investment without significant public complaint.

Good highways had one unintended consequence: they spelled the decline of some smaller rural settlements in the province. Railways had originally been laid out to service stations placed about 10 kilometres apart. This 10-kilometre factor was a reasonable distance limitation for horse-drawn transportation coming to the rail-head, but with the coming of cars and trucks on good highways, the spacing system was obsolete and so were the small towns strung along it. The larger business centres were now easily reached by automotive traffic while other smaller places withered. This was the price of change. Later on, Walter Weir, as minister of highways, took over an additional 6,400 kilometres of municipal roads which we added to the provincial highway system. He included in this plan arterial streets in metropolitan Winnipeg, which was a benefit to city taxpayers who had previously paid to maintain them.

The growing towns around the province were also eager to have regular sewer and water services in their localities, just like those that larger centres enjoyed. This had presented a substantial financial and technical hurdle for them. We provided financial and technical help, and in a few years, thousands of privies were gone from the smaller centres around the province. Supplying pipes and conduits was the first step, but the supply of water itself had to be arranged. Some communities were not conveniently situated, and we had a policy of promoting water supply at a distance so the largest number of citizens could be served. These things were attended to, and the people had modern amenities in their homes. In fact, the sewer and water program had come to some 42 smaller communities by the time I left office.

The area called Greater Winnipeg demanded our attention. There was the city of Winnipeg itself, with twelve satellite municipalities of various sizes and capabilities which had established their own personalities over time. But as urban development began to grow, this multi-municipal structure became unwieldy and ill co-ordinated. Essential common services for the whole area had to be pulled together, and it took a new plan to do it. We called our solution the "Metropolitan Corporation of Greater Winnipeg." A number of services for which central-area management seemed best were entrusted to this new body. The responsibilities included zoning, land control, tax assessment, transit, sewers and water, major streets and bridges, major parks, and garbage disposal. As well, their planning authority was extended some distance beyond their official boundaries to anticipate urban sprawl. The Metro Council was deliberately to be elected from area-wide wards to minimize parochialism and given powers of management and taxation. We did not consolidate the existing municipalities. They continued to have a significant role. Under their aegis came such matters as local streets, police, fire, parks, and snow removal. They were left on the job and for a very good reason. These functions could still be very well-managed locally in future as they had been in the past. They did not involve area-wide responsibilities.

Past experience led me to respect the management of these satellite municipalities. They were cost-conscious, economical administrations. They were close to the people, and we asked them to carry on. It was particularly important to respect the Franco-Manitoban identity of the municipality of St. Boniface. At the time, the original councils found the change hard to swallow, but only the City of Winnipeg bucked and fought a rear-guard action. Mayor Steve Juba, a consummate local politician, felt his wings had been unduly clipped, and he didn't like it. Juba was a good mayor for Winnipeg. He brought a fresh view to council which drew on his own personal background and experience. He had a way with the media that any politician would envy, along with a capacity few could match of attracting the support of the citizens. Before elections for the new Metro government were held, and to get things started, Richard Bonnycastle was appointed first chairman of the council. He came from a Manitoba family with significant pioneer roots. His adroit style of gentlemanly management, understanding of human nature, and skill in getting things done soon settled things down, but not Steve who remained unreconciled.

Municipal governments whose tax base also supports schools exist by virtue of provincial legislation and are indeed creatures of the province. The province can at any time change the arrangements under which municipal governments operate. The power of municipal governments to act is limited by their capacity to tax, and they are largely restricted to taxes on property. In recent years, it has become obvious that this tax base is limited, and inequitable in several respects. Other sources of revenue have been actively pursued. All kinds of licences are in force, and the provinces themselves, including Manitoba, have made special grants from general revenue to municipalities for municipal purposes. Municipal politicians cry that this is never enough. A new factor in play is the changing place of the major cities of Canada within their provinces. This is particularly true in the province of Manitoba, where the capital city represents 65 percent of the province's population yet still plays the traditional municipal and educational role, with the result that property taxes are so high as to be oppressive.

Governments must now consider how to deal with the so-called city state because that appears to be the development we must expect—Toronto in Ontario, Vancouver in British Columbia, and particularly Winnipeg in Manitoba. My own preference would be for the province to assume those responsibilities that cities now exercise over the welfare of persons as compared to the interests of property. Let the city look after matters which pertain to property and for which property may be fairly taxed, and let the provincial government deal with other services, like education, which should be paid for by charges against the general revenue. This is nothing more than the continuation of a trend we ourselves began in 1958.

The year 1967 was an important date on my calendar.[15] Together with 1970, we were confronted with the happy circumstance of a double centennial period, one for the nation and one for the province. Something special had to be done to mark these significant milestones, and it seemed that a birthday present to ourselves would be appropriate in a form that would be a permanent commemoration of the two events. Parks were on this agenda. Previously I had my eye on a handsome piece of provincial property on the north side of Broadway, across from the Legislative Building. In addition to being well-suited as an open space, it would serve to round out and complement the Legislative Building. It was with some chagrin that I realized in 1958 it was not provincial property at all. In fact, as a parting gesture, my predecessor Douglas Campbell had given it to the city of Winnipeg as a building site, and it soon became clear that Mayor Stephen Juba didn't want to give it back. I was only able to retrieve it by offering him a considerable soliatum to soothe his feelings and bolster Winnipeg's treasury. In due course, in 1962 we dedicated this pleasant space as a memorial park to those who had served Manitoba in days gone by.

Later on I had also taken note of the real estate manoeuvrings of the Canadian National Railway. They owned a splendid piece of property on Lake Winnipeg called Grand Beach that was gifted with a magnificent sandy shore. The CNR originally had operated Grand Beach as a resort as it was not far from Winnipeg and found it good for business on their railway line. Now, however, they were backing away from resort management and wanted to abandon the railway line that served that facility. When I found out the property might be available, they agreed to part with it for a bargain price. After we had put in a first-class road connecting it with Winnipeg and modernized its amenities, Winnipeg weekenders discovered the new Grand Beach park in droves. Andrew and Jennifer and Mary liked it, too.

Bird's Hill Park was a little different. We were looking for a park site close to Winnipeg, but the prospects were meagre. Then one sunny day, acting on a

---

15 I suggested to Prime Minister Pearson that it would be a useful symbolic gesture of national unity if the Queen, during her Centennial visits, would make the provincial premiers Canadian Privy Councillors. I was happy when she did so.

Duff Roblin

BELOW: ANTICIPATING THE SALES TAX—NOT ALWAYS
MUSIC TO EVERYONE'S EARS

ABOVE: CARTOONIST KUCH'S
EFFORT TO HELP NAVIGATE THE
ISSUES OF THE DAY

BELOW: MUNICIPAL SKIRMISHES WITH MAYOR JUBA –
SET TO DUFF

hunch, Buck Witney, minister of natural resources, and I took his car on a prospecting mission around the region. Bird's Hill came within our ambit. It was uniquely situated on high ground left behind by glaciers and Lake Agassiz. The Bird's Hill area, it turned out, was relatively undeveloped, although prospectors were nosing around. We discovered, as we toured on the trails hither and yon, old gravel pits, abandoned fields, a cemetery, lots of bush, wrecked cars and barbed wire, but it was on high ground, close to Winnipeg, and there was plenty of it. Witney agreed it had the makings of a park, so we decided to see what we could do. The land was mostly vacant, but not quite.

Mr. and Mrs. Charlie Ives had established a home for themselves in this location. When the time came to acquire property, all went reasonably well, until we came across the Ives, and in their instance, price was a serious problem. The government assessors were tough in their evaluation perhaps, but we soon found out that Molly Ives was a good deal tougher and her idea of price much higher. The Ives were long-time friends of mine. At the age of 18 or 19, Charlie had immigrated from England to teach young Manitobans how to play the game of squash. I was a little younger than Charlie, and one of his squash pupils. It is a great game, and I played it for 50 years or so. Anyway, Molly took us to court. Not just to any court, but to the Supreme Court of Canada, where she won their verdict. We paid up. We should have got off our high horse and settled in the first place, but the Ives knew their rights and they got them. This was a classic case of a plucky lady defeating the heavy-handed bureaucracy. Other parks followed: Spruce Woods, Assissippi, St. Malo, and a number of others. Years later, Lily and Rachel, my young granddaughters, were much impressed by my miraculous ability to make lakes and beaches appear at St. Malo to add to the ones at Bird's Hill where none had appeared before. This policy took care of the outdoor set. Now we had the arts to think about.

As an afterword, in recent days another provincial park, with which I had nothing to do but which, to my considerable satisfaction, has been given my name, has been situated in northeast Winnipeg. It offers a living outdoor exhibition of our indigenous flora of flowers, trees and grasses to instruct us

Duff Roblin

of our natural Manitoba heritage. Situated as it is on the abiding feature of the Manitoba landscape, the Red River Floodway, it displays in a kiosk the geological history of the Red River and the story of the flood control system.

Manitobans hold different views about the role of government as a patron of the arts. I was for it. To an unusual degree, the arts had long been an interest of Winnipeggers. Far from being a frill, the arts brought colour and life to our society, especially enlivening the winter scene. In days gone by, when rich people kept more of their money and the tax collector got less, we could count on private benefactors to do a great deal as patrons of the arts, and thank goodness there is still some of that money around, though it is not as plentiful as it was. But with the tax collector taking more private income for public use there was, I thought, a role for the public patron to come to the assistance of artistic activities. We had a modest budget for this purpose. To ensure that merit and initiative were fairly considered in the distribution of this money, we set up a new provincial arts council to handle applications. The council's presiding genius was Mary Liz Bayer, who consulted with all concerned about the allocation and distribution of our support. She, incidentally, came from a family with deep roots in the Selkirk settlers' past.

For our centennial celebration, we thought cultural facilities of lasting benefit to the citizens should be planned for the capital city. These included an art gallery, a concert hall, a theatre, a planetarium, and a museum. Brandon was to have a new auditorium. The province would take the financial lead, with an appeal to others to help out. The location of Winnipeg's complex of four structures had to be considered, and a site near the new city hall was promoted by those who hoped this investment would help to revitalize that part of downtown. But the art gallery had other ideas. Or rather, Mrs. James (Muriel) Richardson Sr., who was the grande dame of the gallery, had another site in mind, and she was not alone. To settle the matter, a well-attended meeting was convened in the cabinet room, and I appeared to receive the delegation. In the meeting, Mrs. Richardson laid down the law. I realized my limitations, and she knew what they were, so I made my retreat as gracefully as I could. The art gallery did its own thing.

For such projects, the matter of land assembly is a first step. I had entrusted this responsibility to Maitland Steinkopf, first as a private citizen and later after his election in 1962 as a minister. Joe Martin, then a young staffer, was second in command. Maitland was a hard-driving forceful personality. He was not inclined to pay much attention to political niceties, nor in this case was he interested in putting strict construction on the legal proprieties, but his vision was seminal. To hold his hand and restrain his enthusiasm, I engaged a friendly businessman to exercise a watchful eye as his partner and mentor. During the switch from citizen to minister, Maitland got himself in a tangle over the land assembly payment. This difficulty could be seen as compromising, but in fact it was an innocent breach of a technicality. In the ensuing brouhaha, the friendly businessman excused himself. In the debate that followed in the Legislature, the Liberals would have no excuses. They wanted blood. Their attack I could stand. My attention, however, was on the NDP. Morris Gray was the father of the house, and, in a sense, its conscience. He was the NDP spokesman on this issue. If Gray supported Maitland, we would stay the course. If not, things were serious. As Gray rose to speak, I slipped into a seat beside Maitland. My message was simple: if Gray turned against us, tradition and honour called for Maitland immediately to present his resignation. I had no doubt he did not appreciate the way I interpreted the parliamentary principle involved. But as Gray, who condemned him, sat down, Maitland arose without a second's hesitation to resign, thus putting his bona fides beyond question. Before driving him home that night, after the house rose, we stopped at the club for a scotch. For him, but not for me, that was his first and probably his last drink of spirituous liquor. In the by-election that followed, his electors understood his amende honorable and returned him to the house. I returned him to the cabinet to complete, with great distinction, the work he had begun.

One event of note was Maitland's success in persuading Samuel Bronfman to make a handsome contribution towards the cost of the planetarium but on condition that the planetarium be named for him. To convince Sam that this condition offended our naming policy for centennial projects

ABOVE: CAUGHT IN THE ACT, FINGERS   ABOVE: A WINNING FOREHAND SMASH
ON THE CHANTER

took some heavy persuasion, but in the end we settled for a nice memorial plaque on the planetarium wall. Thank you, Sam.

It is natural that elements in the population seek public recognition from the community. On occasion, this takes the concrete form of statues on the Legislative Building grounds. The Scots and the Icelanders were already there. The Ukrainians thought they ought to be. I thought that a good thing could be carried too far so that new monuments were not encouraged. But Canadian-Ukrainians were a special case. In effect, they had no homeland as the Soviet imperium seemed unmovable. The alienation of some Ukrainian religious bodies was particularly complete. So they were especially eager to identify themselves in their new homeland by memorializing their greatest poet, Taras Hryhorovych Shevchenko. But how? A statue on the west lawn was allowed. But the delegation wanted the biggest statue possible—bigger than I was prepared to recommend. The logical solution was simple. No other stat-ue on the grounds could be higher than that of Queen Victoria. So one fine day the delegation and I, equipped with ladder and tape measure, examined the queen seated on her throne and established the dimension. That put the top on Shevchenko. Prime Minister Diefenbaker joined me and an immense crowd on the day of dedication. When it came my turn to speak, I offered a few words in my fractured Ukrainian to rapturous applause. This was the sole occasion I was able to upstage the chief on the platform.

There was another important issue. Manitoba is a province with many small entrepreneurs on its farms. It is obviously unlikely and unreasonable to expect an industry structured in this way to perform by itself the agricultural research it requires. I thought government should take this matter in hand, first to help fund the research programs, and secondly to help the farmers make use of what was learned. Once in office, we greatly increased the research funding for operations at the University of Manitoba, and expanded the agricultural farm extension services to make sure farmers were able to put this new knowledge to work. The impact of science on better farming in Manitoba has been remarkable. I took a special interest in seeing farmers adopt new business methods. They could trace the inputs and investigate the outcomes of their activities in field crops and livestock. They could look into the capital investments that were required. They could reckon the cash flow. In short, they could know more about what was being done and how well it was being done.

In 1958, we established a new farm credit agency. The existing federal farm credit facility was useful up to a point, but we wanted more. For example, there was a need for credit for young farmers. When generations change and farmers hand over their farms, credit is needed to finance the transaction. The new provincial agency helped to make this possible. Family farms were strengthened, and credit repayment records were satisfactory.

Crop insurance presented a greater challenge to us. Farming is often, indeed, one might say always, a risky business. No matter how well they perform, farmers face two basic risks, both of them beyond their direct control. One is the price of their product, and the other is what nature does to them while they're in the process of production. Price was beyond us, but maybe we could do something about nature. We developed a plan of crop insurance against natural hazards. When in opposition, we had put forth this policy, but of course had been told it would not work. Private insurance was available against hailstorms, but that was all. We had been told that nobody else was doing anything, and when we checked with Lloyd's of London, we got a rather dusty answer. They weren't insuring crops, so we became world-wide pioneers. Ralph Hedlin and Merrill Menzies advised, and Clay Gilson, a young economist at the University of Manitoba, was our point man. I found a place for Clay in the basement of the Legislative Building, where he set up shop. He prepared estimates of the financial risk, including the terrible prairie droughts of the 1930s. Various types of insurance coverage were laid out. When the facts and the probabilities were weighed, we decided we would go, but we would not go alone. We needed to lay off some of the risk elsewhere. Constitutionally, agriculture is a shared responsibility with the federal government and the provinces, so Ottawa was naturally an obvious choice for a partner.

Alvin Hamilton, the federal agriculture minister, liked our plan. In fact, he liked it so well he arranged to have the federal government share the risk with us. But pioneers must be prudent as well as adventuresome. We did not jump in all at once. We made a careful start with three volunteer test areas, in order to find out if our plan was workable, and if farmers liked it enough to pay their share of the premiums. We did, and they did. Building on this experience, we led the way in helping farmers mitigate nature's tantrums. Our 1958 crop insurance plan was a successful worldwide first.

nine

DUFF'S DITCH

IF POSTERITY IS TO REMEMBER ANYTHING ABOUT THE SECOND
Roblin to be premier of Manitoba, it will be because of Duff's Ditch. My
policies for education, welfare, hydro and roads probably did more for
Manitobans, but the ditch has captured the public imagination. It is obvious, it is big, and its protection works for all to see.

The first thing to know about the ditch, officially known as the Red
River Floodway, is that it was designed to protect the city of Winnipeg from
high water in the Red River Valley, and the first thing to know about the Red
River Valley in Manitoba is that it is very flat. The river starts in the United
States beyond our jurisdiction, 600 kilometres south of Winnipeg. It flows
north into Canada for its last 150 kilometres. Its course is rather sluggish
and tortuous. Its banks are low; at Winnipeg it is joined by the Assiniboine
River, a smaller stream coming in from the west, traversing the flat Portage
plains. In the nineteenth century, the record of the Selkirk settlers told of
the monster floods in the valley, one in 1826 and another one in 1852. The
few farms and some small settlements of the time had to be abandoned and
their inhabitants sought safety at Bird's Hill and Stony Mountain to the
north and on high ground on the prairie to the west. In this century, people knew the Red had been cantankerous at one time during the spring
thaw, but serious flood dangers, in spite of the Selkirk records, were consigned to the history books. The truth is that very serious flooding on the
Red is to be expected on an irregular basis. When it comes, the river rises

Duff Roblin

to cover its broad flat flood plain, possibly to a width of 30 miles in places, and threatening the whole valley from Winnipeg to the U.S. border. An extra hazard occurs to Winnipeg if the tributary Assiniboine crests at the same time as the Red. In 1950, for the first time since the city and valley were heavily settled, history was revisited and the Red River and the Assiniboine rose to the highest level of the twentieth century to that date.

In the spring of that year, nature set the stage for a flood. Snow was deep. The thaw and run-off water were late. Water accumulated south of the border and slowly but inexorably pushed north. One after another, the valley towns succumbed. Farms were overwhelmed and Winnipeg itself inundated. As the Assiniboine also rose simultaneously at the forks in the centre of the city, water was everywhere. No one was prepared. Frantic defences were improvised with sandbags as the weapon of choice. Each day that spring, the rise of the river seemed to the man in the street to be inexorable. The government appeared to be paralyzed, apparently bunkered down in the Cabinet Room. Citizens began to take initiatives on their own.

On a personal level, 1950 was a watermark for me (pun intended). That spring I had just completed my first session as a member of the Manitoba Legislature, sitting as an Independent on the opposition bench. As the crisis deepened, and as the government failed to show the flag, public concern mounted. There was no sense of leadership in what the premier and cabinet were doing. We heard little about it and we saw little of them. Though but a junior MLA, I knew I had my own responsibility to act. A community meeting was called in the badly hit Riverview area; the chairman was Obie Baizley. I attended. The people were confused and frightened and noisy, but under Baizley's direction, a community spirit began to emerge. Afterwards, in a small boat, Obie and I toured the flooded homes to assess our situation. It was grim. Later on, Obie became an effective MLA and a valued cabinet colleague.

This contact with the danger stimulated me to organize a sandbagging phalanx myself. I was an officer in a veterans' association of former RCAF personnel. I set up headquarters at my business premises at 235 Main Street and called out the troops. At once we had a disciplined and hard-driving crew for 24-hour sandbag duty. One of our targets was the St. Boniface Hospital, right on the river bank. We laboured night and day to protect it. The sandbags held. The hospital was spared. Similar ad hoc self-help efforts sprang up all over, but the river was not to be denied. At the eleventh hour, when the army was called in and General R.E.A. Morton took command, there was a feeling that at last someone was in charge and confidence rose. Nevertheless, 10,000 homes were flooded, tens of thousands of people were evacuated, and the transportation systems linking the city with the outside world were almost lost to the waters. That would have truly been a dangerous threat to food and water supplies. Urgent plans were made to evacuate the rest of the city. By dint of extraordinary efforts by citizens led by the army and bolstered by an equally extraordinary wave of support and assistance from all over Canada, we survived the crest.

But survival was not enough. Indeed, I knew a 1950 flood could come again. People and businesses and homes were still exposed. Our reputation as a safe place to live and work was at risk. We had been warned. In the aftermath, we should not and could not settle back. My own exposure to the crisis drove that lesson home to me. Meanwhile back at the Legislature, a slow reaction began. The Prairie Farm Rehabilitation Administration (PFRA), the water expert of the federal government, was asked to advise on flood protection. Historical records were validated and measured. The probability and size of potential future floods were estimated. At least one big one, probably as big as 1826 and 1852—certainly bigger than 1950—could be expected sometime in each century. Then possible defensive measures were studied. In Canada, the flat valley made control dams useless. Basins to contain overflows were non-existent. Widening and deepening the river itself was considered—every option was on the table. With other possibilities eliminated, the final proposal was to construct a diversion or floodway around Winnipeg itself, to give the river a second channel through which floodwaters could be released. From a technical and engineering standpoint, this was the effective solution of

ABOVE: Sandbag crew on Kingston Row – 1950 flood

ABOVE: Moving the first dirt on the Floodway, assisted by Andrew, Walter Dinsdale (right) and friend

choice. Of course, the threat from the Assiniboine was part of the problem. The upper reaches of that river could be dammed and Lake Manitoba near Portage la Prairie offered a holding area. So in 1953, the PFRA Report recommended a 48-kilometre-long floodway around Winnipeg to handle flooding on the Red, plus a holding dam on the Assiniboine upstream at Shellmouth and a channel at Portage la Prairie to divert Assiniboine water into Lake Manitoba.[16] This plan lay before the Campbell government.

Naturally I demanded action. Every year that passed brought us closer to another crisis. What we were offered was yet another commission, this time to establish the benefit-cost ratio of the PFRA recommendation. This, of course, was a vital consideration, but with the life of the community at stake, as I believed, and as subsequent events confirmed, a second study should not prevent the declaration of a flood protection policy. The government did not oblige. Thus in the 1958 general election I made flood protection a major plank. Not long after we achieved a majority government in 1959, the benefit-cost report came in. A majority of the commissioners endorsed the PFRA plan and established a highly favourable benefit-cost ratio. But it came with a significant price tag of $63 million. Thus, while accepting the report and committing ourselves to proceed, I concluded that it would be a good idea to find a partner to share the burden and that federal-provincial cost sharing was in order.

Under the federal PFRA system, federal-provincial cost sharing on water projects was provided with the federal share being about one third, and the province responsible for the balance. I thought Ottawa should do better than that. My reasoning was simple. The Red was an international river. Most of its course lies in the United States. In fact, most of the water arises in that country beyond our control. There is an important international aspect to our problem. In a fit of hyperbole, I speculated that if to protect Manitoba we dammed the Red River at the 49th parallel and flooded back well into the U.S., its international implications would be clear. So began over-lengthy discus-

16 Ironically the benefit-cost study awarded the Portage diversion sector the highest benefit/cost ratio. But when we came to build it later on, our own political friends in Portage felt their area had been sacrificed. As a result, two legislative seats were placed in hazard.

sions with the federal government which at first refused to budge from the PFRA formula.

Meanwhile I had the legislature to deal with. Starting in my own caucus, not all our members were enthusiastic about paying to protect Winnipeg, but they were susceptible to persuasion and soon became convinced supporters. But political opposition in the Legislature was vocal. They were sceptical of the plan. They rejected the cost. The whole proposal was unnecessary. A flood like 1950—to say nothing of a greater one—was quite unlikely. Even if that was not so, they questioned the effectiveness of the recommendation. They finally fell back on the assertion that the interest carrying charges on the money would sink the project. That prompted some one of them to coin the epithet "Roblin's Folly" to underline their disapproval. Our firm public undertaking to proceed with flood protection had, they said, let Ottawa off the hook. Expect little from them. But we stuck to our guns. We would go ahead and Ottawa would help. Meanwhile, negotiations with the federal government moved slowly.

Alvin Hamilton, the minister in charge of PFRA, was intransigent on the one-third federal share. Gordon Churchill and Walter Dinsdale, our representatives in the federal cabinet, weighed in on our side to improve the federal offer. But it was soon clear that John Diefenbaker and I would be called upon to settle the matter. So on one of his visits to the province, the two of us met in a small pokey hotel bedroom in Winnipeg. Negotiating with John was an experience. He manoeuvred me up one side of the question and down the other. Relations with other provinces, federal financial capacity, national water control policy, the PFRA rules, provincial constitutional responsibilities after the 1930 transfer of federal natural resources to the province, our personal and political relations and more were explored in detail. Precedents were invoked. Legalities abounded. Personalities were weighed in the balance. Diefenbaker had been well-briefed, and he held to his brief. I was equally persistent. All the arguments that had been in play were reviewed, and Manitoba's position was reiterated. Even the 49th parallel dam got into the argument, as international relations were trotted out. Diefenbaker brushed that off, but at 55 percent federal share, 45 percent provincial share, he stuck. It was a question of take it or leave it. I graciously decided to take it. It met my minimum target of 50/50. Even so, the provincial share was a cool $26 million, but I felt we could manage it.

Of course, $26 million scandalized the opposition.[17] They renewed their attacks with even more vigour, and they had help. A small committee of leading Winnipeg businessmen called on me one day, urging me to think again. They warned, as others had before them, that we didn't need it, and even if we did, we didn't want to pay for it, indeed we couldn't pay for it. They meant well, but they were wrong. So was the opposition. Our policy was long-term, and the protection was worth it. But there was one point to watch. If the money was borrowed, the interest cost of borrowing would be significant. I wanted to avoid that. It was decided we would pay for our share of cost of the floodway and the ancillary works out of current revenue, cash on the barrelhead. We did this by spreading the work of construction over several years. Indeed, the very magnitude of the floodway itself recommended such a course.

George Hutton was our minister in charge. He organized Manitoba's private sector's earth-moving capacity: 100 million cubic yards—almost a second Panama Canal had to be shifted. The 48-kilometre-long floodway was brought around the east side of Winnipeg. The average depth was 30 feet, the overall width 450 feet. The design capacity was 80,000 cubic feet per second, more than doubling the capacity of the old Red River. The tributary Seine River was siphoned under the channel so that it could proceed on its way to the Red. A score of road and rail bridges were installed. Local land owners were naturally apprehensive about access to their property and level of water table. George and I held public meetings to ventilate their fears and answer their concerns.

Work began October 6, 1962. My son Andrew and I were on hand to put the first earth-moving machine in motion for its first bite of dirt. Walter Dinsdale from Ottawa was there to share the glory. As a three-year-old, Andrew was unimpressed, but I was satisfied. In time, Roblin's Folly became

17 At that time, the total provincial budget was $653 million dollars.

Duff Roblin

Duff's Ditch. I am content with this new description. Since its completion, the Red River Floodway has been used 18 times, but the flood of the century came in 1997. While the river rose, on the April night when the diversion was put into operation, I was there. Premier Gary Filmon invited me to press the button activating the flood control gates. A satisfactory moment. Winnipeg now could withstand the worst the Red was likely to do.

But the valley towns south of Winnipeg were still at risk. After the diversion was completed, a series of ring dikes was proposed and installed to gird those settlements from the river. A plan, unfortunately only partially fulfilled, was envisaged to raise isolated farmsteads and homes above flood level and zone new construction in unprotected flood-prone areas. There is work still to be done to protect the whole of Red River Flood Plain.

The 1950 flood was a traumatic and defining experience for Winnipeg and Manitoba. My part in that test made me determine to do what might be necessary to deal with a similar future threat to life in the valley. That was the basis of our policy. Duff's Ditch is there, and Duff's Ditch works.

ten

FEDERAL FORAYS

---◆---

MY FORAYS INTO FEDERAL POLITICS OFFER A WRY TALE OF FAIR intentions compounded by mishap and miscalculation. In 1967, chaos reigned in the upper reaches of the Progressive Conservative Party of Canada. Diefenbaker, the old chief, had been invited to retire, and a swarm of potential successors buzzed around. It was decided to submit the issue to a national leadership convention. At an earlier time, Diefenbaker had mused approvingly about me as his successor. Everybody knew this was not a serious gesture. Only death or force majeure could create a vacancy, and Dief was not expecting either. Still, it was a kindly pat on the head.

Gordon Churchill, MP for Winnipeg South Centre, was Manitoba's cabinet minister. We were firm friends, for we had worked together in the common struggle when both of us were in opposition. Gordon was a teacher turned soldier turned politician. His word was his bond, and he was a Dief loyalist to the bitter end. In office, we worked together very well on projects such as the floodway and the nuclear establishment at Pinawa. Two years before the 1967 leadership campaign, Gordon had organized some of the federal MPs to sign a telegram urging me to enter federal politics. It was a very respectable list of some 50-plus members of the federal caucus. I was not able to do anything more than thank them for their interest at that time. That telegram, however, was the genesis of a meeting Gordon later set up between Diefenbaker and myself in which Gordon planned that Diefenbaker was to validate that invitation by asking me, personally, to join the federal field.

Duff Roblin

I didn't encourage Gordon in these efforts. Nevertheless, on one of Dief's visits to Winnipeg, the indefatigable Gordon got the two of us into a meeting room at the Winnipeg airport.[18] John was bubbling over with glee. That very day, George Hees had made his submission. George had previously left Diefenbaker's cabinet in a huff, with some rather cogent criticisms of the Chief. Now he was back, penitent and seeking absolution. John's triumph was the sole subject of his conversation on that day. Nothing was said to me about becoming a federal politician. When John issued his own memoir years later, this incident was turned upside down. According to him, I was invited, and refused. At the time, poor Gordon Churchill, waiting outside the meeting room, was upset when I reported to him what really happened—nothing. I was relieved.

When the 1967 federal Conservative Party convention date was announced, I was in the 10th year of my premiership. Many of the things my colleagues and I set out to do in 1958 had been done. The prospect of a new challenge offered itself. There were signs of substantial support. I had to take the matter seriously. Diefenbaker, of course, would run again. Other strong western names were being put forward. In fact, a fairly large and impressive field of candidates was emerging. Bob Stanfield had just successfully won re-election as Premier of Nova Scotia. In that contest, he was called upon to declare his federal intentions. He undertook, if elected, to complete his term of office in Nova Scotia. I regard-ed that undertaking as genuine, as no doubt at the time it was. This miscalcula-tion on my part was serious. Believing Bob to be a non-starter, I thought I had plenty of time for tactical delay in making my own announcement. Meanwhile, Dalton Camp came calling. Sterling Lyon, Ralph Hedlin, and I met with him at Sterling's house. In a tête-à-tête with Dalton, I made it clear I was not ready to announce my intentions. Afterwards, Ralph drove Dalton to the Winnipeg Airport. Dalton told Ralph that I was not going to run. Ralph, who knew me bet-ter, told Dalton that I was. Ralph was right. Shortly after my meeting with Dalton,

18 This abortive meeting between Dief and me influenced the measure of support I eventually received from MPs during the 1967 leadership campaign. Those MPs who urged me to run in 1965 never heard from me that no invitation was ever later issued by their leader. In fact, I think Dief probably led them to believe he had asked me. Indeed, he says so in his autobi-ography which was quite inaccurate. So naturally, some of them were a little nettled when I came around in 1967 asking for their help. One wouldn't be surprised if they were a little sulky, which helps explain why the federal caucus was decid-edly lukewarm to my candidature.

and to my surprise, Stanfield entered the race. What Dalton told Stanfield, I do not know, but the campaign began and I was in, willy-nilly.

My abiding impression of the 1967 leadership campaign is the way in which my campaign committee organized itself out of thin air. Late in the field, dropping their usual activities, indeed foreclosing their usual lives, a number of unknown faces from the West—young men between 30 and 40, a crew of gifted amateurs—together produced a remarkable effort. Finance, strategy, a campaign schedule, all came together quite without me. Contacts were established in every province, somebody got a hold of a small jet plane from Calgary, and my transnational tour was under way. By air, from St. John's to Victoria and back, we were unfailingly on time and on target.

The campaign for Mary and me passed as a sort of a high-speed blur. Movement was everything—reflection was to come later. At every stop in the West, a reception committee materialized. Joe Martin briefed me on who and what. Harry Mardon handled the local press. Mary looked after me and delighted our well-wishers by her appearance. In spite of strong, local, western rival candidates, the western reactions were first-class. Atlantic Canada was courteous, but its heart was elsewhere. In Quebec we moved by motorcade, often at hair-raising speeds. In *les cantons de l'est*, it was a succession of *vins d'honneur* with Maurice Arpin as my devoted presenter. The new western Canadian face who could bring a message in French aroused some surprise. Quebec City was a more structured event. *Deux nations* got a good working over, particularly with my friend Martial Asselin. Bearing in mind that in the West there are more "nations" than "deux," I framed a careful statement of good will that did its job. My French improved daily. I even went so far as to submit to a *viva voce* question and answer on French television and survived. After all, Maurice was a good coach. But Chicoutimi and Lac St-Jean were the most fun. The unilingual French-speaking crowds were not only interested, but enthusiastic. They wanted to see and hear for themselves this stranger from the far away West who was interested in them and had brought a sense of their unknown country to them. At all times, the quiet but steady support of Daniel Johnson and his friends smoothed the way and encouraged the cause. His emissaries, Jean Bruneau and Jean Bazin knew the temper of their people.

Duff Roblin

LEFT: THE LEADERSHIP CAMPAIGN
PLANE IS LEAVING

ABOVE: PRESS CONFERENCE TO THROW HAT IN THE RING

LEFT: BIG SHOES TO FILL

Daniel Johnson, Senior, and I had met a decade earlier. In 1957, Nova Scotia had been celebrating an anniversary of the establishment of responsible government in that province—a Canadian first. A grand banquet in Halifax was on the program. Bob Stanfield had invited a prominent New Englander to speak, but at the last moment the guest declined. Bob phoned me to fill in. On the way down, as fate would have it, Dan Johnson and I—then perfect strangers—were seated side by side on the Montreal-Halifax flight. Naturally we struck up a conversation to discover that he and I were going to the same affair. Dan, a junior cabinet minister in the Quebec government, was going as his province's representative at the celebration. Thus began a warm friendship that lasted until his sad and untimely death. He was a skilful, adroit, effective politician who understood his province of Quebec very well. His shoes have never been satisfactorily filled. Later on, Dan brought his two teenaged sons on a visit to Manitoba, showing them their country in a cross-Canada tour, and I had the opportunity to meet them. Daniel Jr. and Pierre-Marc—later both would be premiers of Quebec themselves, though oddly with different parties. When Sterling Lyon and Campbell Maclean paid him a quick visit in Montreal in 1967, his support was instantly given. During the campaign, Dan's help was enormously effective in securing support for me in the Quebec delegation. His work was unofficial and done in a quiet way, but everybody knew where he stood.

In Ontario, a similar plan was in place: to visit as many important locations and see as many delegates as possible. But alas, John Robarts was no Dan Johnson. When Sterling and Campbell called on John who was fortuitously visiting Kenora, he was amiable but non-committal. His reaction was tempered by a certain careful neutrality which in the event became support for Stanfield. Early on, I dropped in on former premier Leslie Frost to receive an avuncular pat on the head, but no more. Indeed, no more was expected. The Toronto Tory press was effectively hostile, and that did hurt. Ontario's big blue machine, which helped elect a long procession of Tory governments, was strongly in support of Stanfield. Dalton Camp and his brother-in-law, Norman Atkins, were in charge of that expert operation. In contrast, the people in my campaign were all amateurs. But the writ of the blue machine only ran so far. Ernie Jackson, Dick Dillon, Nancy and Bill Poole, and John Cronyn were among many Ontarians who stepped into the breach on my behalf. The Manitoba Mafia's enterprise and enthusiasm performed prodigies. The Maritimes excepted, support came from all over.

Matters such as public relations, finances, campaign literature, transportation to numerous venues, delegates' meetings, and delegate chat-ups, convention floor management, the candidate's appearances, and statements were all miraculously in place as the campaign unfolded. The momentum was maintained and morale was heightened. It was a heart-and-soul effort. No man was supported by better friends. The actual convention proceedings in the suffocatingly hot Maple Leaf Gardens were in turn exhilarating and sad. In the interests of civility, I made a special effort to visit John Diefenbaker, and received the inevitable rebuff. A sad parting. Sidney Spivak, Arthur Mauro, James Burns, Duncan Jessiman, John MacKay, Donovan McCarthy, Ralph Hedlin, Joe Martin, Laurie Mainster, Harry Mardon, Campbell MacLean, Gordon Pollock, Wally Fox-Decent, Garnet Kyle,

Duff Roblin

Bill Neville, Hugh McDonald and my cabinet colleagues, particularly Sterling Lyon, Walter Weir, Thelma Forbes, and George Johnson, and so many others marshalled our forces. My wife Mary, Nancy Poole, Diane McDonald and Lenore Dinsdale enlivened the proceedings with their presence.

Hospitality rooms were staffed and monitored. Every collection of delegates was targeted and none slighted. We decided to parade from the Royal York Hotel to Maple Leaf Gardens with a brass band. The only problem was to get a permit to walk through the streets in this fashion. Poor Don McCarthy had to place his life on the line in order to get clearance and had to promise to lead the parade himself. It was not a productive enterprise, as it turned out, but it certainly made my friends feel good. My team took me everywhere, usually with that brass band. Sometimes we misfired, with hilarious or serious results. My appearance to register as a delegate was to be a media event, only somehow my credentials had been mislaid, which botched the event. On one formal call on an important delegation, I was ushered off the elevator at the wrong floor, and found myself gate-crashing the Stanfield headquarters, which raised a few Maritime eyebrows. My handlers also decided that a display of umbrellas, coloured a brilliant yellow and marked "Roblin for Leader" would make an interesting display on the floor, particularly as the vote was conducted. Unfortunately we were told by the management that umbrellas were out of bounds, so the idea never materialized.

A serious breakdown occurred at the Young Progressive Conservative all-candidate session. Somehow my team reported to me that this was to be a simple question-and-answer meeting with no formal speeches. This seemed to be a reasonable assumption, but on the platform I found out differently. It was actually a full-dress speech occasion, and an important one at that. Bob Stanfield delivered Dalton Camp's speech to great effect. I stumbled through some warmed-over comments. It was the low point of my performance in the convention. The other candidates seemed to have got the program right. The actual nomination by my proposer, Darcy McKeough, a rising young Ontario cabinet minister, and my seconder, Madame Paul Sauvé, widow of the former Quebec premier, did me proud. I owe them my gratitude and respect for their support and encouragement. My own nomination speech benefited from the tender ministrations of Arthur

Mauro and Maurice Arpin, and it seemed to satisfy my friends. Such are the timeless issues of Canadian federal politics that it could be well understood by listeners today. National unity and provincial relations topped the list, followed by development and jobs. I spoke in both English and French.

Voting in the humid environment went on through an excruciating afternoon and evening. It seemed endless. Mechanical snags in the American voting machine that delayed the count into the sweltering night added to our discontent. Mary had to bear it all beside me. On the first ballot we ranked second, and so it was destined to stay until the end. Meanwhile, Sidney, James, Ralph, and the rest kept watch over the also-rans, Fulton, Hamilton, and even Diefenbaker. Sidney shadowed John Robarts to keep him away from Stanfield. During the voting, parleys with other candidates, particularly the three westerners, were attempted. If Alvin Hamilton and Davie Fulton had come in to join me soon enough, they might have tipped the scales. But no one budged. I remained No. 2 until the final count. Through all this searing test, Mary was with me to encourage and to console. I had the stimulus of action. She had to stand by in reserve. As events unfolded, I remember telling her we must brace ourselves for defeat. She responded with dignity and calm. I tried to do the same in acknowledging Stanfield's victory from the platform, after the final vote was called.

It was a great adventure that came to nothing, but I'm glad I tried. After the convention, and on the flight back to Winnipeg and home, Mary and I tried to comfort our despondent friends. Though we ourselves were tired and downcast, we were not disconsolate because we knew that Andrew, now aged eight, and Jennifer, now aged six, were waiting to meet our plane, and that made all the difference to us. I think defeat hit my supporters harder than it did me. Naturally, I understood the calculus of defeat. They never allowed themselves to consider it, so it was doubly hard for them when it came. I grieved for their distress. I knew they deserved better. I left Toronto deeply attached to these friends and supporters, but not heart-broken. Mary was with me, my children greeted me when I landed in Winnipeg. My best had not been good enough, but I regretted nothing. It was time to turn to other things.

Duff Roblin

In the course of the leadership campaign of 1967, I hinted, and maybe I did say, that come what may at that convention, afterwards I was going to leave both the legislature and the government. After 10 years as premier, the programs that I began had been accomplished; I'd done what I set out to do, and the time had come for a new voice to be heard. There is a cycle and a life to a political administration. In my experience, 10 years is the cycle. The stress of office, the psychological and physical wear and tear, make themselves apparent, and the need for new blood arises. For I must frankly say that the provincial legislature at that stage in my life had lost much of its savour and appeal. I certainly was ready for new things, and I had no doubt the province was, too. I resigned in November 1967 and was succeeded by Walter Weir after a contest in which Sterling Lyon, Stewart McLean and George Johnson participated. Naturally, I was neutral in that particular struggle.

Walter Weir was an excellent minister. Two of his portfolios—highways and municipal affairs—dealt mostly with rural people and rural problems. He handled them with skill and finesse, and no doubt he attracted their interest when the question of his own leadership came to the fore. Like the rest of us, he was a creature of his own background. He had little feel for urban affairs, particularly for urban politics, and he surrounded himself with men of his own stamp. In 1969, the caucus honoured me with a reception, and when that was over, Walter invited me to join him for a chat in his office. It turned out that he was contemplating an early election, which he announced shortly after my visit with him, but which never entered into our conversation. He didn't mention his intention, nor did he give me an opportunity to say what I thought about it. Perhaps he knew very well I would recommend caution and delay. Perhaps he ignored one of the advantages of my retirement from the premiership so soon after the successful 1966 election. One of the thoughts that ran through my mind was that my early retirement, besides suiting me, would give my successor time to settle in and establish his own following. So it was quite unlikely I would be in favour of an early vote. I thought it was unwise tactically and unnecessary politically. Anyway, I was not consulted. Fortune has proved my case.

When I left the Manitoba legislature in the spring of 1968, a federal election soon followed. Gordon Churchill was not contesting his Winnipeg South Centre seat, and thought I should try to take his place. Today it seems rather self-serving, but I had a private quixotic notion that I had a duty to run. Stanfield had beaten me in 1967. This was not the time to sulk like Ajax in the tent, but to rally to the cause. No doubt I hoped my provincial record would help, but the opposite occurred. The provincial sales tax was my nemesis. Years before, in a careless moment, I had told a reporter a sales tax in Manitoba was as dead as a dodo. Times had changed, but public memory had not, and I was squarely in the voters' sights. During my door-to-door canvass, their mood was clear and election night confirmed it. E.B. Osler, my Liberal opponent, who ran a gentlemanly campaign under the impetus of Trudeaumania, went to Ottawa.

I ran my final election campaign in 1974. To call the sally in Peterborough foolhardy is right on the mark; disastrous would be a better word. My motives for trying to make another federal run were mixed, and I shall not try to disentangle them at the present. Suffice to say that when two Peterborough nabobs, Sam Murphy and Sandy Fleming floated the notion that I run in their constituency, I decided to accept their proposition. I came to an amicable parting with my employers, Canadian Pacific Investments Ltd. in Montreal, and entered the fray. Truth to tell, up until my stint with CPI, I had always been my own boss and I liked it that way. Moving out of the corporate embrace was not disagreeable. It was time to move on.

Peterborough is an attractive small city, well-situated and agreeably laid out. It had a sound economic base of services and professions resting on manufacturing and industry. The surrounding countryside outside the Toronto ambit was picturesque and attractive. The citizens were of solid Ontario stock.

Things began well. The local party people were welcoming and encouraging. Bill Neville, a Manitoba friend then teaching at Trent University in the riding, came down to Peterborough to help. He put an organization of local people together. But no one more than I should have been alert to the peril facing a parachute candidate like me. Naturally, the Liberal candidate, Hugh Faulkner, and his friends made sure that everybody knew I was an outsider. That was strike

No. 1. Strike No. 2 was Bob Stanfield's election platform. Without consultation, he surprised us with a call for "wage and price control." Wage control presented a problem. There were a lot of wage-earning voters in the Peterborough constituency, and they were clearly worried about what Bob's wage control plank meant for them. Then Pierre Trudeau came up with his inspired riposte. Wages? Zap, you're frozen! The voting chill was in, even though Trudeau amply displayed the folly of that policy when he cynically brought it in himself soon after. Those problems were bad enough, but strike No. 3 was the killer. The CFI case in Winnipeg was coming into the public domain. The newspaper coverage was juicy and devastating. It did not matter who did what or who said what, it all stuck to me in Peterborough. At any rate, that was the line in the *Peterborough Examiner*. I was represented as a fugitive from Manitoba justice attempting to foist himself off on the good people of Peterborough. It was no contest—I was down and out. The surprise was how many of my Peterborough friends stuck with me. They saved my deposit. My deepest regret was in bringing Mary and our two children, Andrew and Jennifer, into the campaign. They had to live through that tribulation. They never spoke of it, but I knew that they suffered for it.

eleven

SENATORIAL DAYS

———◆———

ALTHOUGH I SPENT 18 YEARS AS A PARLIAMENTARIAN IN THE
unicameral legislature of Manitoba, I thought little of the second chamber
in our bicameral Canadian Parliament until I was summoned to join it. And
that summons was entirely fortuitous. In a decision that became him, in 1978
Prime Minister Pierre Trudeau concluded that as a result of the long Liberal
reign in Ottawa, Progressive Conservative numbers in the Senate were so
depleted as to reduce the opposition in that chamber to a submerged rump.
Their numbers were too small to function effectively. Opposition Leader Joe
Clark was invited to propose suitable Progressive Conservative candidates to
replace Tories who resigned or died. My name came up. A telephone call
from the prime minister followed to ask if I would accept the Governor
General's commission as a senator. I had never sought this distinction, but I
took the oath of office as senator for Red River with pleasant anticipation.
Experience on the job made me a firm believer in Senate reform of which
more later.

Parliamentary business in our legislatures and in the House of Commons
is conducted under well-developed rules. Every procedural contingency has
been provided for. The role of the opposition is recognized, but the
parliamentary process leads to the orderly conduct of government business
and timely decision-making. Debate is encouraged. Opposition obstruction is
tolerated, but within prescribed limits. So important are the rules of procedure

Duff Roblin

in Parliament that after my first election in 1949, John Diefenbaker sent me an autographed copy of the parliamentarian's bible, *Parliamentary Rules and Forms*, edited by Arthur Beauchesne, with instructions to learn it well. In fact, Dief inscribed it with these words: "The sound knowledge of the rules is the most important working tool of parliamentarians." And so I found it in the Legislature of Manitoba.

Alas, in the Senate I found I could very well leave Beauchesne at home for, at the risk of some exaggeration, the Senate had no rules at all. At least, those it had were too rudimentary to be useful. The Senate operated, or seemed to operate, quite well on good-will and compromise, the old boy system. When a procedural skirmish arose, the leadership of both sides would find a compromise in open discussion across the floor of the House. Beauchesne counted for little. That system was good enough for calm weather but dangerous if the weather should change, and change it did.

The Senate remained unreformed during my term there, but a storm was brewing. In accordance with tradition, the government leader in the Senate is a cabinet minister, usually the only one from the second chamber. Jacques Flynn was my chief in the Senate. He was a wonderful combination of the best in francophone charm and Irish sparkle, though liable to explode if vexed. He was good to work with. He drove the team with an easy rein. As Joe Clark's minister of justice, he held a senior portfolio in the government. When Brian Mulroney won in 1984, I took Jacques' place as leader of the government in the Senate.

As leader of the Senate, I found myself at the head of a government minority party. The leader of the Liberal opposition, Allan J. MacEachen, led the majority party. He was fresh from the House of Commons, his reputation as a skilful operator preceding him. Question Period provided some daily excitement. As the sole cabinet minister in the Senate, I was responsible for taking all questions on every department of government and on every subject the senators might wish to raise. I found myself fielding most of them with a combination of general knowledge and instinct. It was a stimulating process. MacEachen immediately made his mark by reversing a constructive Liberal-inspired process in the Senate called "pre-study." Its effect had been to deepen and facilitate the study of legislation on the bills expected from House of Commons. I rather liked it—it was efficient. Allan J. did not, so his Liberal majority insisted on banishing a good Liberal idea to nobody's benefit.

When Brian selected me to lead the Senate and thus become a member of the cabinet, I was naturally gratified. I knew my job was to manage Senate business and speak for the government in that chamber. I also expected, as the only Senate cabinet minister, to have some say in the formation of government action and policy generally. In the event, I found myself having no part to play in this second expectation. Policy was settled by the prime minister and a select group of his cabinet colleagues. The rest of the cabinet were, of course, informed but expected to conform. This was especially true of the Senate. If no use could be made of my views on policy and programming, the role of Senate leader in the cabinet was more honorary than challenging. I concluded that two years in that capacity was enough. In February 1986, when reporting on my Southern African Development Co-ordination Conference visit to Joe Clark, then Minister of External Affairs, I told him of my intention to leave the cabinet, though I did not say why or when. Things came to a head in July. Brian had too many cabinet ministers in Manitoba—four. He wanted to make changes, and I was ready to have him do so. He courteously invited me to become lieutenant-governor of Manitoba. But I left the Senate leadership and declined the honour of the new position. This marked my withdrawal from frontline politics.

During my time as Senate leader, however, with occasional hiccups, the opposition majority allowed the government minority to get the job done. Later on, when I was no longer Senate leader, the weather changed and the brewing storm broke. The cause was the Goods and Services Tax. The public hated the GST. To explain that it largely turned what had been a hidden tax on manufacturers' sales into a less regressive and fairer public tax on sales with credits for the poor availed nothing. The Liberal Senate majority saw this conflict as an opportunity to put themselves forward as true defenders of the people—and why not? The new government leader in the Senate was Lowell

Murray, and he faced two problems. The first was that he lacked a majority. There was a solution to that. When they wrote the Constitution in 1867, the Fathers of Confederation inserted what I call the Senate joker. The prime minister of the day could, under certain conditions, appoint eight extra senators so his party could gain a majority. This clause had not been used, but it was available. Mulroney used it in 1990 and the government minority became the government majority. Liberal senators were transported with fury. Their political ace had been trumped. The eight brave new Progressive Conservative faces suffered an unequalled degree of scorn and contumely from Liberal benches.

But there was more to come. Murray's second great problem was how to get the government business done. The Senate rules, such as they were, and as I have previously described, provided no sure means to ensure that government legislation could even be introduced, let alone debated and voted on in a timely manner. The power of obstruction of even the minority opposition was complete. Closure, or anything like it, was not in the Senate books. What followed plumbed the depths of uncivilized parliamentary behaviour.

When Murray attempted to introduce the government's GST bill, the opposition howled him down, refusing to allow him to speak. Protest escalated into pandemonium. Liberal senators threatened violence to intimidate the Speaker. The Speaker was assailed, vilified, and defied, though he held his ground courageously. They danced in the aisles. They crowded onto the floor. Random noise filled the air. Shouts, ranting, song. Party noisemakers appeared. The sergeant-at-arms was jostled. In short, bedlam, a 1960s students' riot. No voice could be heard. Those on the government side who tried to speak were shouted down. When Murray, the leader of the government, rose to speak, he was confronted by noise and howls that rendered his words inaudible across the floor of the house. Jean Chretien, then the Liberal leader of the Opposition, appeared in the gallery to wave to his colleagues below.

Each day the Senate met, and each day no business was done. The noisy Liberal mob ruled. MacEachen, the Liberal leader, missing from the chamber at the start of the brouhaha, turned up in the midst of this malign misconduct.

The minute I saw him, though no longer government leader, I went to him and drew him outside the chamber to insist something be done to end anarchy and to restore order. His reaction told me he was perturbed, so negotiations to return to order began. Then followed several days of quiet, almost clandestine, meetings between the two of us, slipping in and out of each other's office. As a plan for regulating procedure began to be roughed out, other senators were brought in on both sides, including the leader of the government. Bargaining was intense. Murray was suspicious. In the meanwhile, a truce, or a suspension of the operations in the Senate, was arranged.

In the end, both sides agreed on what to do, and the full Senate confirmed it. The main thrust of the agreement was to provide a lengthy series of opportunities for the opposition to have its say and to make amendments. We set out in exacting detail what could be done, when it could be done, and how long it would take to do it. During a lull at the end of that agreed procedure, the Progressive Conservative caucus met to consult. I urged that when the Senate sitting resumed, our undertakings having been fulfilled, we move at once to put the question and take the vote and so it was. Thus when the Senate sat again, the terms of the agreement having been fully played out, Senator W.L. Kelly arose immediately to move that the Speaker put the question. This the Speaker did. The opposition cried foul, but their heart was not in it. The motion carried, and the crisis was over. This episode exposed the folly of a Senate without rules. All haste was made to fill in the blanks. The Senate adopted new rules, in my opinion, overreactive, as one might expect after that experience. Nevertheless, these new rules would prevent the future recourse of a divided Senate to similar anarchy and obfuscation. It is, however, a considerable irony that after this senatorial Armageddon, Liberal senators quietly swallowed both the GST and themselves when their days of parliamentary power returned.

As a postscript to these proceedings, that perennial Canadian political chestnut of Senate reform occupied my attention, raising the inevitable question, what price a Senate. When the Senate of Canada came into existence in 1867, the Fathers of Confederation had a clear purpose in mind.

Duff Roblin

ABOVE: LEADER OF SENATE AND LEADER OF GOVERNMENT ON THEIR WAY TO THE OPENING OF PARLIAMENT

ABOVE: GENTILITY PREVAILS IN SENATE STYLE PRESS SCRUM

All democratic federations such as Canada have parliaments consisting of two chambers. The Lower House, the Commons, is based on the principle of population—one man, one vote—where numbers only count and where popular majorities give the executive and the government their legitimacy. The Upper House, the Senate, in sharp contrast, is based on the principle of territory, giving regions, regardless of population or area, equal numbers of senators. In our case, the three original senatorial regions or divisions of Ontario, Quebec and the Maritimes were allotted 24 senators apiece. Regions outnumbered in the Commons were expected to defend their interests in the Senate. Thus, while sheer numbers rule in the Commons, empowering populous regions and marginalizing the others, in the Senate, each region, regardless of population, speaks with an equal voice. By this arrangement, a federal state attempts to strike a working balance between the interests of the people as a nation (the Commons) and the interests of the people in their territorial divisions (the Senate). To this end, the Senate was given powers in most respects co-equal with the Commons. But not the power of the purse nor votes of confidence.

From the beginning, however, this best laid plan went awry. The Senate failed to make itself a House of regional interests, and for a practical reason. The Crown, meaning the prime minister, was given the sole power to select senators by appointment. Once appointed, even with all their powers, senators constitutionally represented no one and were responsible to no one, surely an unacceptable anomaly in a 21st century democracy. But there is more. In practice, a prime minister expects the senator he appoints to support the prime minister and his party, and the senator appointed indeed expects to do so. Now Pierre Trudeau never expected that of me so there are exceptions. But for most appointed senators, the old song said it all: "Gonna dance with the guy what brung me." Thus the power of prime ministerial appointment accounts for a tame Senate, where regional interests are muted, and thus its main reason for existence obscured. Though the Senate has other public values that are considerably more than marginal, in the public mind it has become a byword and a political anachronism. Thus, as a private member, and particularly as a westerner, I attempted to make reform a priority on the Senate agenda.

Duff Roblin

This agitation on my part received a rather lukewarm reception, as if I was tilting at windmills. Nevertheless, visits were authorized to the House of Lords in Great Britain and the Senate of Australia in Canberra to examine other second chambers in the parliamentary tradition. Of course, the Lords was a non-starter. But I did observe their practice of making literally hundreds of amendments to Commons' bills that were regularly accepted by the Commons, making our Senate's usual semi-acquiescence look tamer than ever. The Lords were careful, however, to respect the principles of Commons' bills. Sober second thought in the Lords and the primacy of the Commons thus rubbed along tolerably well, even if in some tension.

But there was paydirt in Australia. Their parliamentary system is almost identical to ours, with the great exception that the Australian Senate is elected, by the people, and much more than with us, serves its purpose of regional representation. Furthermore, the manner of electing senators is unusual. The single transferable vote system is used to elect their house of representatives in single-member seats, but Australian senators are elected by the people directly through a system of proportional representation in which each state is a single constituency electing six senators at one time. All nominees, perhaps 20 or so, are listed on a single ballot paper. Voters mark their choices, starting with their first choice and going down the list. A quorum is set that the successful candidates must reach. Voters' preferences are tabulated and transferred as necessary until six candidates reach the quota. This voting method struck a chord with me for it was under just such a system I won my first election in 1949, with proportional representation in a four-member seat in Winnipeg South.

This election formula could well be adapted for an elected Senate in Canada. Following the original pattern of confederation, five senatorial regions could be established, namely, the Maritimes, Quebec, Ontario, and two new ones, the Prairies, and British Columbia with the North. Each would elect 24 senators by proportional representation. If thought convenient, a senatorial region could be subdivided, say, in two.

As in Australia, proportional representation would make it likely that no one party will dominate the Senate, and Independents and minority parties may appear. Easy acquiescence with the majority in the Commons may not be routine, awkward for the management no doubt, but perhaps a desirable check on overweening prime ministerial power. In Australia, disputes between their two Chambers can be fierce, but Australians make it work and show little disposition to change. However, it is possible that we could improve on their model by putting into place, up front, a reasonable dispute-settling mechanism so that parliamentary deadlock would not threaten good government.

I valued my experience in the Senate, but I soon learned to be dissatisfied with important parts of the way it worked. It needs to discharge its duty of sober second thoughts outside the shadow of the House of Commons and outside the heavy hand of the executive. It could recapture its original mandate of regional representation. It is my submission that the direct election of senators by the people is the sovereign remedy. Indeed, 21st century notions of democracy demand nothing less.

Sadly, pressure for change is weak. Political parties and political interests like the Senate just as it is. Inertia holds sway. Constitutional amendment is out of fashion. The public when it takes notice probably wants the present Senate to be abolished and is unconvinced of the useful potential of a reformed institution. It may be tilting at windmills now, but Senate reform is an issue that will not go away.

twelve

PERAMBULATIONS

—◆—

WHILE SENATE LEADER, I HAD A WALK-ON PART TO PLAY IN THE government's campaign against apartheid in South Africa. An end to apartheid in the republic of South Africa, formerly a member of the Commonwealth of Nations, has been a strong policy objective of Canadian governments. I remember John Diefenbaker's initiative to expel South Africa from the Commonwealth when it refused to modify its apartheid policies in the 1960s. More recently, Mulroney led the charge against that detestable regime. South Africa's neighbouring states of Botswana, Swaziland, Zimbabwe, Zambia, Malawi and the Portuguese-speaking nations of Angola and Mozambique regarded themselves as front-line states in the struggle against South African apartheid. South Africa was, however, the economic powerhouse of the region with whom close economic links were unavoidable. Nevertheless, this group of seven states joined under the banner of SADCC (the Southern African Development Co-ordination Conference) to assert their feelings and their interests.

Under SADCC, each member was assigned a leadership role in one segment of their joint economies. The aim was to strengthen the whole against South African economic domination. In fact, the main virtue of SADCC was not economic. To be blunt, not much progress was made along that line. But it helped develop a spirit of mutual solidarity, self-help and confidence. Canada expressed its support for the group's aims by sending a message of interest in its conclaves, and I was the bearer of the message in 1985 and 1988. My presence at their deliberations was intended to personify Canadian sympathy and support for their cause and to reinforce the efforts our diplomats on the spot were making. I had previously visited southern Africa under other auspices. I had met President Kenneth Kuanda of Zambia, waving his white handkerchief around and talking in grandiose platitudes. I had visited the astonishing wildlife preserve on the Luangwa River and travelled by local train to the spectacular Victoria Falls. I recommend train travel in southern Africa. It gives a good bird's-eye view of how local people make out.

The first SADCC meeting was held in Harare in Zimbabwe and was a serious business. In spite of the efforts of our High Commissioner, President Robert Mugabe of Zimbabwe was not available to casual visitors so I was presented to Canaan Banana, the president of the republic, who is now before the courts. He seemed a small insignificant man occupying a sinecure. I called on Joshua Nkomo, leader of an opposition group, who provided quite a contrast. He was large, almost a giant of a man, with an impressive political persona. He was at outs with the president and the parliament, and he gave me his grumblings. Going to church in Harare is an experience in Christian zeal and enthusiasm. In the course of the service I was invited to speak to the congregation, and as a reward for my contribution was asked to accept a chief's walking stick, a heartwarming privilege.

During a SADCC visit, I took a side trip to Malawi, the smallest SADCC member. It was feeling rather neglected because it had had few official Commonwealth Canadian visitors, and I was nominated to fill the gap. The president for life (almost), Hastings Banda, invited me to attend a community ceremony with him. Waving his fly whisk on high, the ancient president descended to the arena and danced, or rather shuffled, with an enthusiastic mob of supporters, mainly women. Afterwards, I sat beside him on the podium. His cabinet members seemed to kneel as they approached to consult him. Together with Banda, I inaugurated a Canadian agricultural aid program. With our High Commissioner, I made contact with and spoke to groups with a Canadian connection, showing the flag. I opened a Canadian-supported nursing station up-country, filled with pathetic patients. I was taken to inspect the magnificent new boys' school, modelled on Eton and teaching the Eton curriculum. The scholars, of course, were strictly limited to the elite.

Swaziland was another world. An old-style African tribal monarchy persists there, with a type of democracy more honoured in the breach than in the observance. Leopard skins were proudly worn by the dignitaries. Dinner in the shape of a young ox was paraded before us for inspection. The strips cut off the roasted ox later in the day could have done with some tenderizing. Swaziland is called the Switzerland of Africa and in many ways it is, but snow is rather hard to find.

South Africa itself is a beautiful country. The last time I was there was just after Nelson Mandela came to power. This time I came with a Canadian Institute of International Affairs party which concentrated on Capetown, Johannesburg, the new politics, and business prospects. Cabinet ministers, academics, opposition politicians, and businessmen, black and white alike, gave us their take of the future prospects of South Africa under the new regime. Their universal determination to make the new South Africa work was inspirational. Even F.W. de Klerk, the former apartheid president, spoke in positive terms. It was like watching a miracle unfold. SADCC could now relax, but their optimism, if not euphoria, will be needed, because even a little acquaintance with the depths of black deprivation and despair exposes the size of the challenge.

When Tanzania's President Julius Nyerere visited Ottawa, I was at the Governor General's guest house to offer the official welcome. It seemed I had acquired a reputation in some government circles as being the resident "africanophile."

A little noted work of the Senate is in the reports that its committees issue on matters of public interest usually not otherwise studied in parliament. The recommendations in these reports are reached by consensus and party political interests usually find little resonance. My Senate committee interests settled around foreign affairs, defence, energy and finance. When on-the-ground investigation seemed useful, a Senate committee would travel to the scene of action. One such study focused on the Near East and what is euphemistically called the Arab-Israeli peace process.

I first visited Israel in 1949. My Israeli hosts knowingly matched me up with a compatible guide, a university student and the son of a Winnipeg alderman, Marcus Hyman. The two of us visited the biblical Israel from Dan to Beersheba. We stood where Deborah, the judge in ancient Israel, stood on the Tel by the waters of Megiddo and the river Kishon where "the stars in their courses fought against Sisera." We walked in the quiet meadows around the Sea of Galilee and Capernaum. Near Eilat, I sweltered at the site of the putative mines of King Solomon. I watched Bedouins and their camels cross the Dead Sea Desert. About the only thing I missed was the stone David used when he smote Goliath, though a facsimile could have been provided.

But I did talk with real live Blue Helmets of the United Nations Peace Keepers on the borders of the Gaza Strip. I visited the former RAF pilot, Ezer Waisman, a hero of the 1946-7 Arab war and later Israeli president, to exchange World War II gossip. I lunched with Golda Meir in her dominating prime where the problems of nation building were laid out with clarity and force. I got the message she wanted Canadians to hear. My last call was to No Man's Land between the Arab and Israeli armies, near the Mandelbaum Gate in Jerusalem where other Blue Helmets led by a Canadian, Colonel Steele, were posted to keep the peace. Shortly after, a sniper's bullet felled the gallant Colonel, a martyr to his duty. But over all, the pioneering spirit of the kibbutz and the valour of the men and women of the citizen army marked the people and the land.

The visit of the Senate committee in 1983—some 30-odd years later—opened on a different scene. There were still elements of Pan-Arab-Israeli confrontation, but it was more narrowly focused on the Israeli-Palestinian clash. Israel was transformed from a defensive entity focused on survival to one that had surmounted the struggle to exist to become the dominant regional military and economic super power. But first we surveyed the Arab states starting with Egypt. Our hotel in Cairo, built in the last century to accommodate visitors to the première of Verdi's Aida, looked out on the Great Pyramids across the Nile. We could ignore the Roy Rogers fast food bar in the lobby. President Hosni Mubarak expanded on his experiences of the Sadat Peace with Israel and impressed as a constructive if cautious player. Other ministers and business-men were less reassuring, but all in all a reasonable entree to the region.

At the Saudi capital, Riyadh, our interlocutor was the Minister of Foreign Affairs Prince Saud Al-Faisal. Though not able to follow Egypt's lead on Israel, he took a large view of Near East problems with a wary eye on Iran. We next met a senior officer of the National Guard, however, who took the traditional strong Islamic line about the holy places in Jerusalem. When calling on the Minster of Agriculture, I found another delegation had preceded us. It was also a party of Canadians, one of whom—from Edmonton but unknown to me—was also named Roblin. They had come to sell agricultural equipment to wheat farmers in the desert. An aquifer was tapped to bring water to the sands of Arabia which, supplemented by outrageous subsidies, produced totally uneconomical crops of wheat. What price nationalism, or is it oil! We were housed in a vast and splendid newly built hotel. In one of the lobbies, a whole roasted sheep was laid out for our refreshment. We were invited to carve our own portions. Thankfully, the sheep's eyes were closed. We seemed to rattle around as the only guests. At a ceremony at the opening of a magnificent new mosque, the king received us.

Syria presented a dark aspect. Damascus was overrun with military security. Armed riflemen manned each floor of our hotel. An armed convoy with sirens shrieking escorted us on a cross-town visit to the semi-secret location of spokesmen for the Palestine National Council, and the Democratic Front for the Liberation of Palestine. They mainly reprobated Yasser Arafat, then in difficulties with dissidents in Tripoli as being too moderate. We inspected a local PLO refugee camp—a sort of clean squalor in a concrete war-ren filled with children and numbers of idle youth—a hopeless dead-end with escape from Syria the only prospect. They were hostages, carefully preserved but not redeemed by Syrian authority. When not otherwise engaged, I prospected the ancient Damascus souk situated among equally ancient

Roman columns. Though the merchants were mostly Moslem, a few Christians and one Jew showed their wares, observing among themselves three different holy days. Arabic handicrafts in silver and gold, bracelets, pins and bangles, with oriental hangings, fabric and carpets were staple. I picked out an antique silver and turquoise bracelet that I knew would suit my daughter Jennifer. I found the street called Straight, but no trace of St. Paul, and I looked for the head of John the Baptist, said to be enshrined in the Great Mosque. President Assad being in the hospital, we met the prime minister and foreign minister who fully represented the malign influence of their nation on both Palestinians and the peace process. This one-party state, based on force, enjoyed the role of spoiler, yet must be reckoned with. It was a relief to move on.

Lebanon was thought to be a bit too dangerous for us so we next visited Jordan. Bright, civil and relaxed, Amman was a pleasant relief from Damascus. The royal palace was modest as palaces go, without an obvious military presence. King Hussein was cordial, direct and candid. He hoped for peace with Israel and sought a firm relationship. He espoused the "land for peace" policy, but the Israeli attitude disappointed him. Nevertheless, his determination to pursue all options was plain. He struck us as Israel's best interlocutor in the Arab world. We were to cross the Jordan River into Israel via the Allenby Bridge. On the way we stopped at Jarash, one of the towns of the Decapolis mentioned in St. Mark's Gospel, long since covered by desert sands. Excavation shows a well preserved Roman provincial town to excite the imagination.

It took a while to digest the changes since my last Israeli visit. Once over the West Bank, development on every side was pervasive and substantial. Israeli dynamism had quite changed its national profile, but sadly attitudes toward West Bank Palestinians seemed stuck in a time warp. Our Jerusalem contacts were extensive, including a wide variety of Israeli opinion. The Holocaust Memorial told its blood-drenched tragedy. Peaceniks confided their fears. Right-wing spokesmen weighed in with their ambitions. A Mennonite observer showed us past Israeli building sites on the bulldozed former homes of Arabs. But it was our interview with prime minister Yitzhak Shamir that crystallized the terrible dilemma. I took the opportunity to ask him directly what he intended to do about land for peace. It's not a question of peace, he said. It's a question of security. The idea that peace was the best road to security was not on his agenda. But when I remembered that the terrible plight of the Jews of Europe was not on Canada's agenda during their Gethsemene in World War II, I held my tongue.

The Senate committee on defence opened opportunities to join in a number of meetings of the Canada-NATO Parliamentary Association. In parliament, defence and foreign affairs got pretty short shrift in the House of Commons. The Senate had an opportunity to do better. NATO parliamentary meetings around Europe and in the United States were too much like a tourist's delight to some but, nevertheless, gave a sober and practical basis for defence committee work. The task was to underscore parliamentary and national support for an informed and effective Canadian defence and foreign policy by highlighting these issues in debate and in our reports. Just as useful was the chance to raise Canada's profile with our allies, particularly with fellow NATO parliamentarians, set out our Canadian-made views, and to demonstrate our distinct contribution as the other North American state in NATO. This latter role required steady attention and a good brief. On a lower level, NATO ideas on economic issues sometimes evoked my strong Canadian response. NATO and U.S. agricultural subsidies and the fish war were two such. I put in a strong case for a level playing field for Canadian farmers. During a visit to Spain, Canadian, Portuguese and Spanish views on overfishing threatened to hijack other proceedings, sort of a pre-taste of Tobinism. But the ending of the Cold War and the astonishing appearance of Russian field marshals attending in uniform at the NATO table opened up a new era and new hope in NATO and world politics.

About that time, I had invitations to visit Eastern Europe. One was to Poland. In the dying days of his dictatorial regime, General Wojciech Jaruzelski, moved no doubt by domestic reasons, extended a quixotic invitation for the Speakers or representatives of NATO legislatures to convene in

Warsaw. I was sent to speak for Canada. We assembled in the Polish Sjem, and when it came to my turn on the podium, I challenged my Polish hosts to adopt a true democracy. Of course, my speech had nothing to do with it, but that happy outcome occurred soon afterward. Warsaw was a testimony to the martyrdom of Poles and Jews at the hands of Stalin and Hitler. I visited the scenes of some of these crimes. The second state with second thoughts was East Germany which also sought a visit from a small NATO delegation, in which I was included. I landed in West Berlin. The Wall had just been breached in one or two places. My West Berlin cabby got through the Wall all right, but when searching for the government guest-house where I was to stay, found himself in uncharted East German territory. He finally dropped me in what I hoped was the right neighbourhood, and so it proved—I didn't have to walk far. Our party viewed the ragged departure of the demoralized Russian garrison from Potsdam. We inspected a unit of the disintegrating East German army on the nearby Polish frontier, but the East German officials who had invited us and with whom we expected to consult were so ineffective that their invitation was fruitless. No business was done. There was really no one to do it with. Collapse seemed complete. During the same period, a relatively minor blow-up occurred between Canada and the Soviet Union. As a gesture of conciliation, a small parliamentary delegation, of whom I was one, was set to assuage Soviet feelings. Our most satisfactory visit was with Aleksandre Yakovlov, the former Soviet ambassador to Canada and confidante of Chairman Mikhail Gorbachev. Hopefully the right message was delivered.

The Canada-United States Parliamentary Committee is another valuable international but North American connection. Here, Canadian commoners and senators met with their counterparts in the United States Senate and House of Representatives. An agenda covering the never-ending points at issues between our two countries was debated vigorously. An important Canadian goal was to explain and defend Canadian positions and politics to American legislators, some of whom only listened with half an ear. Americans from border states were usually attentive, but it was from representatives of the deep south that we found a gratifying comprehension, particularly on

Duff Roblin

ABOVE: SPEAKING AT A NATO PARLIAMENTARY MEETING IN EUROPE

ABOVE: MEETING EGYPTIAN PRESIDENT MUBARAK IN CAIRO

trade. Nevertheless, both sides learned something. In particular, I learned the workings of the congressional system and how best to approach it. Leave the president to the diplomats. Concentrate on the individual congressman. Harder work, but it pays. To my surprise, members of the lower American House often displayed a wider appreciation of the outside world than some of the senators on issues like free trade and Canadian national interests. Senators may be keyed too closely to their states. Certainly they could easily overlook us, enjoying a certain arrogant ignorance. On occasion, it took the help of some of the southern U.S. representatives to take our part and bring senators around to more reasonable attitudes.

In retrospect, I marvel at how easy both foreign and defence policy issues were in those days. We had the Russians on one hand and the Americans on the other. We knew which side we were on and had no doubt that our proper course was to co-operate with the western world and take our place in NATO as a firm supporter of the United States and Europe. I am sure that while the situation has vastly changed since the end of the Cold War, we should not entirely abandon the alliances we made in those days. After all, our national security is highly dependent on alliance partners to act in concert when threatened. As a nation who lives on trade, particularly with the United States, we have to take the closest interest in what goes on there. We have to take an interest in the future of NATO. We have to do our best to act as candid friends to the Americans when they involve themselves in other people's business. Carryovers from the Cold War have value. They must be reassessed no doubt, but they must not be ignored. However, the old certainties are no longer there. We are now in a world where there is just one superpower which only fitfully takes an interest in the outside world, and when it does so, seems most of the time to be as ham-handed as any imperial power ever was. Still, whether they like it or not, the U.S. is entitled to our careful and considered good offices. We have a modest influence to exert.

Looking at the wide world, what is our foreign policy now? There is much merit in excusing ourselves from the status we acquired in World War II as a major military power, which indeed we were. We now have to consider how that role is changing in the new world. We've muddled up our military policy between being soldiers in the World War II offensive sense and being soldiers in the peacekeeping or perhaps peacemaking sense. I conclude that with our limited resources we should choose which of these two is the most important. Peacekeeping and peacemaking under the auspices of the United Nations, or NATO for that matter, should have priority in our new defence and international relations. My public and private travel in foreign parts prompts me to speculate about Canada's place in the shifting comity of nations. In its early days, carried along by the currents of the 19th century, the United Nations consecrated the concept of the sovereignty of the nation state. The nation state, according to the United Nations, was thought to be free, independent, and inviolable, standing among its peers fully sovereign. Now there are so many sovereignties. Canada is one of them, or so we may think, until we recall our history first *vis à vis* the French and British connection and secondly *vis à vis* the United States. We have learned that with a little trouble we can accommodate ourselves to the limitations of our situation as good neighbours are constrained to do.

So from the beginning, our vision of sovereignty has had a Canadian flavour. Indeed there are now clear signs that show the advanced world seems to be leaving the traditional notion of the sovereign state behind and moving toward a different model. Important and leading states are willing to pool a significant aspect of their sovereignty in order to underwrite the peace and in the interests of economic co-operation and integration. The proud and ancient nation states of the European Union lead the way in accepting a common economic rule that limits their national sovereignty. NAFTA and the World Trade Organization strike a similar note. The United States, the sole super-power of the day, agrees, at least in a minimum sense, to accept common economic rules and to be regulated by a dispute-settling mechanism in those two great international organizations. Thus supranational organizations are developing aspects of sovereignty of their own. While we observe these developments, it is ironic to note that the United States, the erstwhile creator of the United Nations and leader of the free world, sometimes seems to forget its role and hanker for things as they were in the past. Senator Jesse Helms comes to mind. All these aspects of sovereignty are in the process of yielding to a greater concern, the concern for human rights. In the name of human rights, world opinion has begun to override the sovereignty of nations, and no one yet knows how far that challenge will take us. Suffice it to say a new principle of human rights is now at work in the world, and those who will the ends, will be called upon to will the means.

None of this means that we give up being Canadians, any more than the Germans in Europe give up being German. There is a natural apprehension of an American cultural imperialism which nowadays stretches across the world. We have been exposed to it longer than most, perhaps since the last century. While its influence has been pervasive, if not indeed oppressive, somehow our own "distinct society" not only survives but flourishes. State support for culture in this process helps when it is not merely feel-good politics effective only at the margins. Our Canadianism will make its way with or without artificial aids. We need fear no loss. We can be Canadians and we can also be citizens of a wider world at one and the same time. Our foreign policy can be comfortable in this interdependent world, and our input in that world can still count. I take note of the fact that there will still be rogue nations outside this beneficial circle, and they will continue to play old nation-state hardball in their own league, and when we play with them, their rules will apply.

Within our own league, and in our interconnected world, our place is well established. We are a middle power, with malice toward none, looking for an even playing field, and willing and able to help keep the peace, or rather to see how peace-keeping and peace-making can work together. Peace-making is not a task that we eagerly seek, but it is likely to become a practical and necessary option. Peace-keeping is largely between two or more nations. Peace-making is largely within a single nation. So there is a profound difference between peace-keeping and peace-making. Peace-keeping eschews force. Peace-making ultimately relies on an appeal to force, and with it comes profound risks to soldiers' lives and limbs. Persuasion may thus translate into force.

Defence policy must, therefore, take both these types of operations peace-keeping and peace-making—into its account. An Armageddon is remote and we are not preparing, nor need we, for a World War III, but we will undoubtedly be confronted on the international scene with internecine struggles and domestic slaughter, rogue states and terrorists. So while we may dispense with the arsenal of aggressive war, we do need the means to be fully armed and capable to deal with the tasks we can see. This calls for an elite rapid action force trained to persuade, yet ready to fight. Let us also continue Canada's leadership and support in the Commonwealth of Nations where good can be done quietly and by example. It is a society of friends and worthy to be cherished. Let us also respond actively to the rising significance of the Pacific Rim. Economically and politically, we are fixated on the United States. That's today's concern, but tomorrow it will be Asia—let us be ready. When China fully masters democratic capitalism, she will be a world power par excellence.

So Senate committees had work to do, and some led to results that I found satisfying when helping to write a number of reports on foreign affairs, defence policy, energy development, and public finance. Most Senate reports do not make much of a splash when they are published, but their recommendations often turn up as government policies later on. In normal times in Senate committees, political interests are usually muted, and good practical work gets done. Committees also provide an excellent forum to hear from the public about current issues and to receive public briefs and presentations. Good but not good enough.

thirteen

MET ALONG *the* WAY

◆

MY YEARS IN POLITICAL LIFE BROUGHT ME INTO CONTACT WITH some remarkable people, the great, the good, the powerful or the intriguingly eccentric. It is easy for a bystander to assess the qualities of other men, their good points and bad points. It is much more difficult to put oneself in their place, to struggle with the problems they confronted, and then judge fairly their success. In my case, free opinions invite free rejoinders. Here are a few of them.

The first federal/provincial conference I attended was at John Diefenbaker's invitation, in 1958. Ontario was there, ready to set a good example to other provinces, really needing nothing for itself. Premier Leslie Frost spoke from a position of confident authority. He displayed it in an avuncular manner which perhaps might even be called bland, but full of good will. Frost was the user, if not the inventor, of a wonderful phrase called 'social betterment,' which in my mind describes a position of conscience without the dogma that sometimes accompanies it. He was a formidable personality, obviously a leader.

Quebec's premier, Maurice Duplessis, was fiercely protective of provincial rights, and quick to resent any federal encroachment, no matter how well-intentioned.[19] Later on, he even rejected federal aid to universities

---

19 Duplessis was always cordial to me. When I went to the province of Quebec on an official visit later on, he gave me what is now referred to as the "big hello" and dinner with the cabinet: A very friendly gesture toward the province of Manitoba in those days.

on the grounds that this was a trespass on the provincial responsibilities under the Constitution. So he put his mouth where his money was, so to speak. But on this occasion, he was good-humoured and perky. In fact, in a very short speech to Diefenbaker, he said, "I can tell you, Mr. Prime Minister, what brings me here. I can express my sentiments in one short four-letter Anglo-Saxon word." He had our attention and he spelled it out, "C-A-S-H. Cash. If there's no cash, and cash without strings, I think I might as well go home." That interesting riposte could not camouflage his autocratic hold over his province.

W.A.C. Bennett was the B.C. premier at the table in 1958. I think you could call Wacky Bennett the ultimate British Columbian. He was not anxious to talk about his origins in New Brunswick. He seemed to have very successfully lived those down. For him, the mountains were not only a physical presence, but a psychological barrier. B.C. was B.C., and he was only half-interested in what was going on elsewhere in the nation. He was not obstructive, but on the other hand, he wasn't particularly helpful in national affairs. Wacky was a hard-headed man of business, backed by a rich combination of natural resources in his own province—forest, mine, oil, power—all of which he seemed to take personal credit for. Anyway, it enabled him to operate in a rather expansive way. His fixation, which he seemed to mention as I recall on more occasions than one, was the cost of building roads. British Columbia is full of mountains, the prairies are full of prairies. It's cheaper to build roads on the prairies than it is to build roads in the mountains of British Columbia, and he felt that fact ought to be, if not written into the articles of Confederation, at least decisive when financial matters were on the table.

Ernest Manning, of Alberta, was riding on a very comfortable wave of extraordinary oil revenues. Due to the discovery of these unexpected and gushing resources, he had been transformed from a prairie populist pushing the Social Credit economics of William Aberhart's day to a fiscally conservative and orthodox manager. Ironically, the oil money gave him the wherewithal to run what I thought to be a rather free-spending administration, and yet he was accorded the reputation of running an economical government with the lowest provincial taxes. The latter was certainly true. His expenditure on education and welfare measured on a per-capita basis, made Manitoba look pretty sick. My Social Credit opponents in Manitoba were always urging me to run an Alberta spending program on a Manitoba revenue base. No dice. Later on, when Manning and I were both friends in the Senate, he would talk of virtues of uniting right-wing parties. Though he had long since given up Major Douglass Social Credit funny money schemes, he was still too much right-wing Alberta to appeal to me. Preston Manning goes even beyond his father.

Tommy Douglas of Saskatchewan was a most attractive figure who lubricated his socialist propositions with a pungent and telling show of wit. He was gifted in that way, and yet his strong sense of fiscal responsibility mostly kept his extreme followers within bounds. His record, particularly in the field of Medicare, challenged me when I came into office because Manitoba was then far behind Saskatchewan in the social welfare and health fields. Saskatchewan, though not a role model, certainly challenged us to show that we could do for our people in our own unique Manitoba way what Douglas was able to do in the province of Saskatchewan, and so we did as I shall show.

Robert Stanfield, as I observed him at federal-provincial conferences, seemed the quintessential Nova Scotian who happened to be a Tory. His demeanour and deliberate manner reflected Nova Scotia as a pre-Confederation entity of its own with the first legislature in Canada to have won responsible government. A certain gravitas was in order. But as he intended to use the bounty of the federal transfer system to the fullest, he displayed a cautious prudence about irritating his federal patron. The qualities of quiet, unaggressive persistence that made for success in Nova Scotia politics did not resonate so well when he entered the federal arena and became leader of the Progressive Conservative Party. Early on, a defeat of the Pearson government on a budgetary vote was allowed to pass. Later, his 1974 election promise to bring in wage and price control fell by its own weight. He won respect but not devotion. His was regarded as a safe pair of hands but failed to ignite enthusiasm. A personal comparison with his predecessor John Diefenbaker and his competitor, P.E. Trudeau, was inevitable. He won esteem but, alas, not the prime ministership. My relations with Bob, if not warm, were always respectful and good natured. I envied his wry sense of humour.

Joey Smallwood of Newfoundland was the only living Father of Confederation, and he never tired of telling us so. An engaging gnome of a man, Smallwood was master of all he surveyed on the Rock. He could talk, though. Once granted the floor, say, at dinner at Sussex Drive or elsewhere, he seldom let it go until he had covered every current topic at hand. So let others stand aside. But he tried with reasonable success to make a place for his province on the national agenda. We knew he was there.

Hugh John Flemming of New Brunswick and Alexander Matheson of Prince Edward Island make up the balance of the premiers at the 1958 meeting but my contact with them was brief.

Brian Mulroney is a very complex character. There are two sides to him. One is what I call the private Mulroney, the other is the public Mulroney. From my contact with him, they could hardly be more different. My first knowledge of Brian Mulroney came during the seven years or so that I was living in Montreal. At that time, the Progressive Conservatives were absolutely nowhere in the province of Quebec, though Mulroney was playing a leading role in the organization within the province. I was surprised in 1983 when he again offered himself for the leadership, but interested, because during the campaign he brought a very potent message. He urged that Quebec could vote Progressive Conservative with him as leader. I have to say that in spite of being interested and impressed by this claim, I was a little sceptical. I decided to continue my support of Joe Clark, a worthy if not entirely successful politician, but one whose candidacy I thought deserved continued support. When the chips were down, I voted for Joe. Mulroney won, and I loyally accepted that decision, as did Joe. In Canada, it is essential that a national party be well-represented in Quebec. It needn't have a majority, but it needs substantial support. Mulroney not only gave us those voters, he gave us a majority, and that was a significant achievement. I was much impressed with many of the members from Quebec in Brian's administration. A few of them were rascals, no doubt, but there were also a number of very worthy folk indeed, whom I was honoured to work with. This was particularly true in the Senate.

In the caucus, Brian Mulroney was everything one could expect a caucus leader to be: modest and sympathetic and adept. He listened to the observations of his caucus; even the most far-out rants did not escape his attention. His respect for ministers in difficulty with the caucus, or for minority opinions within the caucus, inspired confidence. He made himself available to members who wanted to talk to him. He elucidated government policies in the caucus in a way that made them convincing, and he command-ed his members' support. He in no way used his position to impose his personality on the caucus. He let them have free rein, he listened, and he responded in the most constructive and helpful manner one could hope for. Though I myself ceased attending caucus after 1988, I was one of very few who did so, as I explained earlier. The caucus was exceptionally loyal. This might sound strange to people who only know him from his public persona. That is the riddle of his character.

In public, he gave the appearance of a backslapping politician of the Lyndon Johnson persuasion, with an arrogant and partisan approach to issues. At the risk of exaggerating myself, no simple statement would do when an exaggeration was available. He was identified with a low brand of reward politics which alienated even friends. This clever gifted personality came adrift in the public mind. He gave bold leadership on free trade. Even his ded-icated and dogged efforts to reintegrate Quebec into the structure of Confederation at Meech Lake and later were frustrated by a public who could not quite trust him. Courage in the great issues he did not lack, but sadly he is perceived by too many to fail in the test of character.[20] He presented to the public mind a personality that was just the reverse of the one I knew in the

---

20 I remember vividly his visit to Winnipeg in 1983 when he was leader of the Opposition, and the question of the bilingual character of the country was being hotly debated. The Progressive Conservatives in the province of Manitoba were hostile to the then provincial NDP government's plan to make Manitoba a bilingual province. He asked me to introduce him at a party meeting on the issue, which I did with vigour to a sceptical audience. He then delivered a speech which was a courageous defence of francophone rights. It showed he was not afraid to confront opposing opinions, even if they were within his own party.

Duff Roblin

caucus. I only regret that the caucus personality did not prevail. As to his policies, imitation by his successors is the sincerest tribute as history will record.

Pierre Trudeau shot like a brilliant comet across the Canadian political
spectrum, with his own unique aura. His sharp intellect and style of politics
commanded respect. His rapport with the hopes of his fellow Canadians was
astonishingly evocative, as Trudeaumania showed us. Yet his perception of
Canada was curiously incomplete. His gradual emergence as a perceived voice
of arrogant eastern indifference won few hearts and less votes in the west.
He appeared to be satisfied with the certainties of what I call the Cartesian
method, that if something was theoretically attractive and intellectually
satisfying and logically complete, it was therefore right. He omitted to apply
what I would describe as a more typical Canadian test: Will it work?

The human factor escaped him. Bilingualism may be a good thing
in itself—I decidedly thought so and still do—but as a partial answer to Quebec
separatism, as I believe he intended it to be, it failed. Separatists don't care
about French outside Quebec, and they limit bilingualism inside Quebec.
The National Energy Program had a theoretical rationale that looked good
to central planners in Ottawa, but it contributed to western alienation
and a distrust with the centre that still lingers, and time has demonstrated its profound futility. Repatriation of the Constitution satisfied a certain self-respect
in Canadians, but the way it was done left a sore in Quebec which still festers.

Meech Lake was a valiant attempt to reconcile Quebec to the Constitution
and to put matters right for the sake of Quebec federalists. Trudeau's attack on
Meech Lake before the Senate on March 30, 1986, was a brilliantly argued case
that clearly satisfied him. My distress at what he was saying drove me from the
chamber. He trashed a great hope for national reconciliation while Liberal
senators hung on every word of his excoriating eloquence. It constituted a
destructive triumph in personal justification.

The Charter of Rights and Freedoms exposes us to a growing
Americanization of the Canadian psyche, where the rights of individuals are
enshrined and collective rights are muted, where the courts are positioned to

supplement Parliament in the making of the law by judicial decision. Let the record show that with reservations I voted for the charter in the first place, but the fruit of unintended consequences leaves a bitter taste. Trudeau made me a senator. I owe him my respect, but he never asked me for my judgment, nor did I give it.

Joe Clark came to notice as a promising young Alberta member of Parliament who so impressed a Progressive Conservative leadership convention in 1976 that to the surprise of some, they chose him to succeed Bob Stanfield. Just as surprisingly, he went on to defeat Pierre Trudeau in 1979 to lead the nation. As prime minister, fate foiled many good intentions. The press made him the target of their superiority, magnifying his mishaps and belittling his good points. He did commit some egregious political errors. As leader of a minority government, he took for granted those opposition politicians he should have stroked. Back in opposition, he deemed the support of two-thirds or so of a convention to be unsatisfactory, and in the next convention he really did lose. However, the strength of his character was convincingly displayed later on when he became a member of Brian Mulroney's cabinet. His conduct of foreign affairs and his interest in human rights, especially in South Africa, was distinguished. His willingness to take on the unity file was courageous. His efforts to engage Canadians in the process were unappreciated, but the title of 'Good Citizen' belongs to him. Nothing more justified this claim than his second appearance as leader of the national Progressive Conservative party. The cause is just, the labour will be long, and the outcome is veiled in probabilities. But I thank him.

One day in 1964, Peter Lougheed, then contemplating his role in Alberta politics, visited me in the premier's office to discuss his political problems. He had observed the way in which we had successfully replaced a well-entrenched government in Manitoba, and he wondered how he might be able to confront the might of the Social Credit Party in his province. Alberta appeared to me to be ripe for a change. It required courage and determination to enter the legislature in that province with a few friends, perhaps, no more, and start building to prepare for the change that was coming. We talked about

Duff Roblin

ABOVE: GREETING POPE JOHN PAUL II WITH PRIME MINISTER BRIAN MULRONEY AND FORMER PRIME MINISTER JOE CLARK AT RIDEAU HALL IN 1984

what we had successfully done here in a somewhat similar circumstance, with our emphasis on finding good candidates. Ernest Manning, who had been impregnable but was about to retire, left office after a successful term of many years to be succeeded by a weaker administration. That gave Peter the opportunity he was looking for. Alberta was ready for Peter because he had the ideas and the instinct of the new generation—what the province badly needed. His subsequent success, therefore, was no fluke of fate. He had the advantage of being the leader of a province with enormous natural resources of which I was, of course, rather envious. But he certainly was well worthy of the responsibilities entrusted to him. He is a uniquely respected Alberta statesman.

I first met Gary Filmon when he was running for city council in Winnipeg in 1975 and he asked if I would accompany him in canvassing his ward. Immediately, I found him to be a very agreeable and attractive personality, quite easy to elect as councillor, so it was easy to be helpful. I took no part in the provincial leadership campaigns in which he was a participant because I felt it was not part of my duty as a former leader. It was up to the party faithful to choose their leader and discover the merits of the candidates on their own. However, I did appear on the scene in one of his elections. At that time, the caucus was a little unruly. A couple of members were a little outspoken about whether Filmon had the necessary nous to carry the day. I was asked to become the nominal head of the election committee, and I emphasize the word nominal. My real function, however, was to knock heads together: to put aside differences in the interest of party unity during the campaign.

Filmon's task as leader of the government has not been easy. He came in at a time when provincial finances were not in good order—some might even say wildly out of control. The real question was how to pay the bills without disturbing the supply of public services more than absolutely necessary. It required hard decisions and good judgment to determine how far you could go in reorganizing the structure. Once people are used to a government service, it becomes almost sanctified, and any change in it is met with suspicion and resentment. That's natural, that happens, and you just have to cope with it as best you can. I think that, all things considered, Manitobans probably suffered less dislocation of their public services under Filmon's economic measures than people in most other provinces, although not all Manitobans are so philosophic. He has stanched the hemorrhage of the provincial deficit and brought the treasury into good order. I think he has been farsighted and courageous in bringing the province out of the dismal swamp of deficit and debt. As a result, we are poised for new economic growth here so that public services can be attended to.

One of the most outspoken objectors to my 1953 speech on the sad state of the national party was Alvin Hamilton. At that time, Alvin had been trying to get elected in the province of Saskatchewan. He had run on a number of occasions, both federally and provincially, and very bravely carried the banner in a province where Conservatives were exceedingly scarce. When Diefenbaker came to power in 1957, Alvin Hamilton came with him. He had a remarkable gift for promoting new ways, particularly in agriculture and northern development. He was a fount of ideas. They were not all ideas that would work, but he was a prairie original and open to new concepts for the development of the nation and of government policy. He ran against me in 1967 for the leadership of the Progressive Conservative Party of Canada and was a factor in splitting the western vote to my loss.

Other quasi political characters I've met around the province are easy to recollect. R. Maxwell Moore was thought to be a remittance man from a distinguished English family, but I never saw any remittances. He called himself President of the Imperial Immigration League of Manitoba, whose project was centred in the thick bush in southeastern Manitoba on a whistle stop of the Winnipeg Water District Railway. The natural assets consisted of acres of Christmas trees. I cannot say if any immigrants were in evidence, but Bobby Moore certainly was. He appeared before many legislative committees with a message. His brief was not always germane to the issue nor brief. An appeal for order from the chairman only encouraged him. He would gradually work himself up to the end of his presentation with a positively frenzied conclusion. Some wanted to remove him, but citizenship carries certain rights, and I said, let him be heard. Afterwards, though my staff officiously tried to keep him out, he would appear in my office and after a brief chat, which appeared to satisfy him, he would take his leave. He lent a little colourful flare to the business of politics.

Bob Russell was a trade union leader of the old school. He arrived from the old country in good time to take part in the 1919 Winnipeg General Strike, and his leadership in that labour dispute is a matter of record. I was aware of Bob, but our paths really crossed in a big way when he became the spokesman as secretary for the Winnipeg Labour Council. It was the custom of the council to seek an annual meeting with me and my colleagues in order to tell us what they thought about the government of the day, and in particular what they thought about our attitude toward labour. At one such meeting, Bob was reading their brief, which I had previously seen, and he came to a passage that was very critical of the government. It excoriated us in extreme terms for our lack of interest and attention to the needs of the labour movement. When he got to that part of the brief, I stopped him and said, "Bob, do you really believe that?" and without missing a beat, and in the midst of his confrères, his reply was, "No, Mr. Premier, I do not." And he kept right on reading! No wonder I arranged that in due course a school should be named after him to commemorate an honest and forthright labour leader.

Joe Borowski made his views public on a lot of issues. One year, in the 1960s, he protested an increase in the salaries of provincial cabinet ministers. He was against it, or he was against them—it is not entirely clear which. He began to camp out, installed in a heavy sleeping bag, in the vestibule of the Legislative Building, even though the weather was rather cold. Coming and going, morning and night, I stepped around him and usually stopped to exchange a word as well. One morning, he seemed rather unwell, so, seizing the occasion, I asked Dr. Johnson to pick up his doctor's bag and pay him a house call. George reported Joe had a heavy cold, but we conspired together to raise his diagnosis to incipient pneumonia, obviously a hospital case, so we bundled him off to the hospital, from which he did not return to the vestibule. Later, by fate's comic intervention, Borowski became a cabinet minister himself. His views of cabinet ministers' salaries had remarkably softened.

Public office brings pleasant occasions to greet the head of state, Her Majesty the Queen. The first royal occasion was a visit to Winnipeg in 1939 of King George VI and Queen Elizabeth. It was splendid. On a mild May day, graced with a mist of rain, the RCMP mounted squadron, carrying their lances and pennants, formed part of the royal procession that moved down Main Street with colour and pageantry galore. My mother was a member of the library board in those days, and as such she was entitled to a seat on the City Hall platform on the parade route. I was allowed to escort her. My father, with his comrades of World War I, were relegated to lining the streets while the royal procession went by. It was over in a minute, but I turned up later at a ceremony at the old Fort Garry Gate where the governor of the Hudson's Bay Company tendered two black beaver skins to the sovereign due as rent for Rupertsland on the occasion of such a visit. This was provided, of course, in the May 9, 1670, charter of the Hudson's Bay Company. In 1959, Mary and I, as premier, welcomed Queen Elizabeth II and Prince Philip to Manitoba in their first state visit to the province. I was on hand later, in 1967, when Philip opened the Pan-American Games, during which we were treated to a drenching prairie downpour which threatened to wash us all away from our open seats on the stands. I must have appeared rather nonplussed by this event, but Philip said to me, "Never mind, we'll stay. We're wet now, so we might as well stay and get good and wet." So he and I did. Afterward, he took the wheel of our jeep as we drove to Bird's Hill Park to visit the Boy Scout Jamboree. Later on, as Senate leader, I was the minister in attendance on one of Her Majesty's visits to Manitoba. At Dauphin, the people gave her a great show with a picnic lunch. I blotted my copy book by spilling the white wine from the lunch on my trousers, but it didn't disturb the Queen at all. She simply said, "Bad luck, but it'll soon dry." Sometimes the royal entourage can seem rather fussy, but never the Queen. She was well-briefed, observant, and interested in all that was being done for her. Her professionalism made it very pleasant for the Canadians around her to make her a welcome guest.

I am old-fashioned enough to remember the days when the British Empire was real. I had a map showing vast red patches on every continent as part of the Empire. The monarchy in those days was natural for a country in Canada's position. The heroic defence of Great Britain, Commonwealth and Empire refreshed our connection in World War I, but World War II was a turning point. Afterwards, the Empire was slipping away, and the United Kingdom was being retired to the second rank of world powers. The Queen remains our sovereign due to the ties of interest, affection, and memory. This is a comfort to Canadians of more than one ethnic provenance. While these ties endure, they give our nation and our constitution a unique coloration in the North American continent. The idea of monarchy fits well with our Canadian tradition. I do not recommend a change. Should time and tide, alas, install another head of state for our country, we may still acknowledge the monarch as head of the Commonwealth. This would be a comforting bond with other sorts and conditions of men and women around the world.

fourteen

LIFE BEYOND POLITICS

❖

NECESSARILY, POLITICS OCCUPIED A GOOD PART OF MY ACTIVITIES, but I do not overlook family life and my business adventures. While politics may attract most attention, there was great satisfaction along other lines. It is true that chance and opportunity and propitious times are part of any story, but preparation and intent lie beneath the flux of events. In my case, fortune's smile eclipsed her tribulations.

When the war was over and I was discharged, the RCAF got me off to a good start with a handsome gratuity. Almost six years of service, with four overseas, yielded enough separation money to buy me a yellow Studebaker convertible and a trip to Jamaica. This yellow convertible was deliberate, but Jamaica arose out of impulse. One winter's day, I picked up a holiday magazine that was featuring a view from the Shaw Park Gardens in Ocho Rios to the blue Caribbean. I was entranced. In 1947, Jamaica was both remote and exotic, a sleepy British Crown colony untouched by tourism and inhabited by a most agreeable black population with a sprinkling of British and North American ex-patriots. Of course, it was an adventure to get there—a day and a half and three different airlines, landing at Kingston at two o'clock in the morning. But I never looked back. The tropics, seen for the first time, were a glory of colour and scent and warmth. When you add the Blue Mountains, running to 2,100 metres, and the sand and the coral reef and the blue sea, it was intoxicating perfection for a prairie native. Clearly it was sometimes hard for locals to make a living, and social conditions were primitive, but nature was kind and wants could be satisfied. The people easily made the visitor feel welcome and at home. One day I caught sight of Alexander Bustamente as he began his rise, leading in due time to Jamaican self-government.

I explored Jamaica from Morant Point in the east to Lucea in the west, as far as the primitive road system would allow. Thereafter, during my annual trips, I discovered the artists' colony and many good friends, Jamaican-American-British, only some of whom are still alive. But North America was moving in and an impressive land boom took shape. I did not have the money or the courage to go big-time, but a successful small real estate speculation hit a similarly small jackpot. In those days, foreign exchange transfers were controlled so I built a modest seaside villa near Dunn's River Falls, Ocho Rios. The night breeze swept down over the property so it was called "Too Cool." In the end, the struggle to support it in the style it demanded proved too much for an absentee owner, so we had to part. It was fun while it lasted.

Meanwhile, back in Winnipeg, there was business to be done. Working as a manager in the family car dealership with my father and my brother, Rod, paid the rent. Douglas Chisholm was an insurance friend of mine who persuaded me to start a minuscule motor vehicle insurance company with him. It seemed like a bright idea to be a sleeping partner. But the risk and the loss soon woke me up. Taking a hand in Western Tools and Industries Ltd., which I have previously mentioned, was more to my taste. Organizing personnel and management, building a small plant, promoting business, scrounging finances was a sufficient challenge. The business operated at first from the garage premises, but when the automobile industry began to expand again, we had to move out. A handy location was located in the bend of the Red River in north St. Boniface where, acting as our own architect and contractor, we put up a modest but suitable plant building. When I became Leader of the Opposition, my brother assumed my interests in family business affairs.

When I left the legislature in 1968 needing a job, I was convinced something would turn up. Three somethings did: two from United States-based companies and one from a very Canadian Canadian, Buck Crump. N.R. Crump was chairman of CPR. He had met me previously when I spoke at a CPR function in Winnipeg, because CPR was always a favourite target for western premiers. I must have made an impression because he proposed my joining Canadian Pacific Investments Ltd. Joining a large corporation had not been in my program, but the prospect of working in a Canadian interest rather than an American one was enticing. The CPR had split itself in two. One part was the railway itself with other transportation interests, ships and airlines, and one part comprised an extraordinary range of non-transportation assets including natural resources such as oil, natural gas, coal, forest products, mining interests, plus real estate and hotels. Under the name of Canadian Pacific Investments Ltd. (CPI), with headquarters in Montreal, CPI extended right across the country. This range of interests in a Canadian company provided an unequalled overview of Canada's economy, and the opportunities it offered for growth and development across the country, surely unique. Marathon Real Estate, CP Hotels, Pan-Canadian Petroleum, Cominco Mines, Fording Coal, Pacific Logging, etc.—all operated under its aegis. Here was an offer I couldn't refuse, even though it meant relocation and learning to live a new life. Thus began a six-year unique business experience leading to the company presidency, based in Montreal but always on the move, to Toronto, Calgary, Vancouver, and Victoria as well.

Buck Crump was in the old school of great CPR presidents. He loved his railway, he loved his country. He had a clear firm mind, but an easy personality. He and I at the time were both cigar smokers[21], and a box of cigars appeared at directors' meetings. Unfortunately, his brand was called "House of Lords," which I have never learned to enjoy. On one occasion, Buck invited me to travel from Montreal to Toronto with him in the chairman's private Pullman car. It was attached to the tail-end of a freight train that swivelled and jerked and stopped here and there on the way all during the night. Sleeping was at a

---

21 I have to report that in the days of my premiership I could be identified as a regular cigar smoker. Not many, mind you—perhaps one a day or, at best, three a day. I found it a very handy device because when meeting delegations it was useful to have something in my hand to look at and to contemplate while I listened to the wisdom that was being offered. It somehow was a comforting thing to do. Not so much because I liked cigars—only the first half of any cigar should be smoked, the second half should be thrown away immediately—but I found it to be a handy little gadget. I still smoke them if anybody gives me one!

premium. Next time I declined the honour—once was enough. It takes a real railroader to face it.

Ian Sinclair succeeded Crump as chairman of CPI. He came from the town of Teulon, north of Winnipeg. We first took notice of each other at a hearing of one of the seemingly continuous royal commissions on transportation that took place when I was first in office. I was a witness for the province of Manitoba and spent four hours on the stand, doing what Manitoba's premiers always do—telling the CPR to get its freight rates down. Sinclair was cross-examining me and doing what CPR men always did, saying things were just about all right. When Sinclair succeeded Buck as chairman of CPI, he amply displayed an unrivalled mastery of his brief. At board meetings of CPI companies—and there were a number—Ian knew more and knew it better than some of his managers, and he let them know it. His grasp of financial matters and taste for the risks of growth and expansion made him a great business leader, but his drive overshot the mark, leaving his successors to execute a significant strategic and awkward downsizing. Later on, by one of those odd conjunctions, during my time in Ottawa he too became a senator. I was leader of the government and he was in the opposition. We renewed our adversarial attitudes of the old Manitoba days. Later as chairman of the Senate finance committee, he ruled with an iron hand like a prosecuting attorney. I have been known to intervene to moderate his enthusiasm when dealing with hapless witnesses.

CPI regarded me as an unknown quantity. By and large, CP executives come with a lifetime of experience in CP culture. The new boy had to learn to fit in. I did not find it easy to immerse myself in this new ambience. I am grateful to colleagues who did their best to fit me in. The CPI I joined was hardly your typical Canadian corporation, but in its transportation links it has been part of the epic of Canadian nation-building. In the West, it was seen as an unloved force of nature, controlled elsewhere, but dominating the land. Its Montreal headquarters, housed in the old Windsor railway station, was redolent of the 19th century. Yet it was anything but passé. Along the way, it had accumulated interest in real estate, mines, forests, coal, oil wells, hotels and much else beyond transportation. With these interests grouped under CPI, it played a master role in our 20th century economy. But it was saturated in its own culture. Some executives spent their lives with Canadian Pacific. They respected authority and tradition. They knew their place, and wanted to be part of the greater glory of CP. Their dedication to the job was a priceless advantage, but it often narrowed their view of life outside the job. Corporations don't operate in a vacuum. They operate in the context of the society, and society offers an implied contract: the right to operate, make profits and pay taxes, provided it is done with due regard to society's para-mount interest. There are strings attached to the bottom line. Among the things I attempted during my tenure at CPI was a dilution of the Montreal clique. I sought local regional representation on the boards of some CPI com-panies. Local management was given the authority and the budget to take part in local causes. Regular communication and co-operation with regional authorities and community interests were encouraged. In a word, a change of mindset from the imperial corporation to one with links to the common interest of the community. Like a great ship, CP is hard to turn, but turn it has. When later its national headquarters moved to Calgary, I sensed the turn was complete. Nowadays CPR has practically reinvented itself, re-swallowing CPI.

It was during the Montreal years and the time of the FLQ agitation in Quebec that the press took notice of my appointment as a companion of the Order of Canada. The very next day, whether by chance or through the media notoriety, at 3:30 a.m. a phone call rang and an unidentified voice announced that I had a bomb in my house. Of course, a frantic and foolhardy search revealed nothing. But for the next little while I was favoured with a police escort. So much for terrorism. As a member of the Anglo elite in Quebec at that time, I certainly paid attention. The frustration expressed in the violence, indeed, murder by a splinter group, was highly subversive, but if left unat-tended could lead to a wider malaise. Caught up with the general paranoia, I did not see it in this light at the time. The focus was on catching the perpetra-tors and on restoring public confidence. It took time for the deeper issues to be identified.

The Montreal years were challenging and satisfying. CPI gave me contacts with an exceptional variety of talented businessmen representing provincial and regional aspirations that expanded my vision and appreciation of Canada. The Montreal years were memorable. But the time came to move on. When we left Winnipeg for Montreal in 1968, Mary wept. But so appealing were our years there that when we left Montreal for Winnipeg in 1975, she wept again. After all, she had been born there.

Our return to Winnipeg was fortuitous. After I left CPI for the Peterborough adventure, my income ceased. When the Peterborough votes were counted, I returned to Montreal where nothing stirred. I began to wonder what to do next. Then my Winnipeg friend, Maurice Arpin, phoned. One of his clients had a problem and was looking for help. Maurice thought I might be interested. Metropolitan Security Limited was the client. Metropol had nothing to do with securities like stocks and bond, and everything with men and women in uniform and providing private security services. This flourishing small family business had been started from nothing by George Whitbread, a former RCMP officer. It started as a mom and pop business. Hard work and opportunity had brought success and growth. But growth was the problem. Success had put the management system under strain and Maurice thought I might help them modernize. So for several months I commuted between Montreal and Winnipeg to advise on what could be done. Shortly after that assignment was completed and I was back in Montreal, I got another call from Maurice in Winnipeg. This time he reported that George Whitbread had decided to sell his company and was I interested. Of course, by that time I had a good feel for the potential of the industry. In fact, my due diligence study had in practice already been done. I had a grasp of the opportunity and was ready to give it a try. It was particularly encouraging that the Winnipeg friends of mine, Alan Moore and John Greene, were willing to join me in financing the purchase price and later on to counsel on management as two not-so-silent partners. This combination proved a winner. My interest in a rent-a-cop venture surely raised some eyebrows, but we never looked back. The company had a good base in Winnipeg and northern Manitoba and some interests elsewhere. This gave a good start for expansion.

Duff Roblin

We began to grow—soon we were in Newfoundland, Quebec, Ontario, Manitoba, Saskatchewan, Alberta, and British Columbia. Directing widespread operations and personnel had its problems, but as usual, careful recruiting of good managers and emphasis on staff training soon raised our profile. Strategic acquisitions in Calgary, Vancouver, and Toronto hastened our growth and enhanced profitability. I was a regular visitor in seven provinces to encourage our people, consult with clients, and scout for opportunities. Over time, a substantial operation developed. In due course, the time arrived when it seemed prudent to shed active responsibilities and prepare for new owners. Another security concern offered to purchase the bulk of the operation so we bowed out. CPI taught me that successful business involves a manageable concept, timing, and people—especially people. I had them all. I can report that this late-in-life foray into private business made it possible later on to endow a professorship in government at the University of Manitoba. Generous friends led by James Burns and Kathleen Richardson added to my contribution to establish, also in my name, two valuable fellowships for promising scholars.

But since the sale of Metropolitan, I am not entirely unemployed. I enjoy a continuing business interest. I do not admit I am retired. I attend my office daily where my advice and consent is sometimes sought and sometimes heeded. I am glad that business employment and experiences both before and after politics gave balance and perspective to my life view.

My curiosity about the world and the people who live in it make travel a keen pleasure so the Canadian Institute of International Affairs has been a continuing interest of mine. Their many sponsored tours in foreign lands under qualified group leaders open doors to political, business, and social circles not usually available to travellers, and all in the company of changing but interesting groups of Canadian businessmen. The CIIA gives a valuable snapshot of peoples, attitudes, economies, and expectations unique to its activities. In this way, over time I was able to take a look at Latin-America, Central Europe, and the Orient, with samplings of opinions in the United Kingdom and the United States.

My first such experience was three weeks in the 1970s in China, starting in Beijing. Our lodging was in a newly Russian-built dormitory already a victim of gentle disintegration and neglect. We next faced a conference with a dozen or so second-rank officials and elderly generals, each of whom gave a perfunctory (or so it seemed) but lengthy recital of Chinese accomplishments in his particular areas of expertise. Much tea was drunk. Dialogue was attempted, but we were firmly informed that all was for the best in this Chinese world.

One night at the Canadian Embassy I met Canadian teachers of English who had a far less complacent take on the attitude of their classes of young adults. The next day they arranged a surreptitious visit for me to their school. Promising young linguists from all over China were perfecting their English at the capital. I gave a short speech on parliamentary democracy in Canada to be met with a barrage of keen questions and flattering interest, a far cry from the dull, bland interlocutors of officialdom. Later we were guests at a session of the mighty in the Great Hall of the People in Tiananmen Square where orderly acquiescence prevailed. The Great Wall of China, also intended to limit political activities in ancient times, improves on visual inspection. It is colossal. The Imperial City and the Dowager Empress's Summer Palace were a letdown. Incidentally, in Beijing bicycles ran wild in uncountable numbers. Pedestrians beware!

Chengdu in Szechuan province was our next stop. Security there was, fortunately, much less oppressive, and I was allowed to wander about the streets. I came across a store-front shoe factory of mom-and-pop dimensions. No words were exchanged because of the language barrier, but my distribution of Canada pins won me smiles on all sides and a tour of the premises. They had a rather simple but ingenious system of making running shoes, using heat, moulds, and synthetics. Sadly, the shoes looked as if they would melt in the rain. The official lectures continued, however, and we found hosts saying nothing interesting at great length. I became devoted to chopsticks and Chinese beer, but not to the continuous offerings of green tea which distinguished every meeting with officials. The agricultural and industrial potential of Szechuan province to which we were introduced was impressive.

Duff Roblin

FAR LEFT: JENNIFER IN A
DRAMATIC ROLE

LEFT: ANDREW WITH A SET
OF HIS FAVOURITE STRINGS

ABOVE: THRESHING GRAIN NEAR KUNMING IN THE STYLE OF "RUTH"

Kunming is a centre of China's ethnic population. It is near the old Indo-Chinese border, not far from Burma. We were allowed to visit with representatives of ethnic groups who took turns telling us how good relations were with the Han Chinese. There was no word from Tibet. A railway line once ran between Kunming and Hanoi in Indo-China. Oddly enough, it had left a curiously French flavour about the city—perhaps it was the boulevards and trees, reminiscent of the French way of urban development. We came to a collective farm where threshing of grain was taking place in the same old manner that one reads about in the story of *Ruth* in the Bible. The harvest was hand reaped and flailed. The grain was winnowed out by tossing it up in the air and letting the breeze blow the straw away. In the course of our visit, we saw only primitive techniques employed. The manager said this was a good way to keep the peasants quiet on the land.

We had a look at a Red Army barracks, austere and spartan but clean and orderly. The soldiers seemed to fit the role. When our bus made a rest stop, to our great surprise we were overtaken by a bicycle group consisting of some English-speaking Chinese tourists from Hong Kong. How they got there and made their way through the Chinese bureaucratic and red-tape labyrinth is a mystery to me. When we stopped at a small town, the locals would mob us, especially when we offered Canadian pins as souvenirs. It appears that Caucasians were seldom seen in their area and they all wanted to make sure they had a good look. In fact, they were so enthusiastic and so many, it was a bit frightening.

In Kunming, I wandered out one night and found myself in a park beside a very pretty little lake. In a small pavilion in the centre of this park, I heard some music, oddly enough in western style. When the young people who were gathered around the cassettes playing this music saw me, they stopped and the crowd parted. Obviously, they were a little uncertain as to whether I could be trusted with the knowledge of their somewhat clandestine musical interests. Yes, it was western music, and it came from cassettes made in Hong Kong. It seemed to be quite out of place in Kunming and evidently not approved by the authorities. When I proved to be harmless, the entertainment continued. Youth will be served, even in China.

At Canton, the vice-governor gave us a classic Chinese feast. The number of courses were hard to count, and the toasts were equally innumerable. The only trouble was they were mostly offered in Mao Tai, which is one of the most unattractive liqueurs I have ever tasted. However, in the name of fraternity, I downed my share manfully. An efficient train took us into Hong Kong in a few hours. There we found a frenetic bustle, with everyone trying to sell and everyone trying to buy, all engaged in profitable commerce with nothing else much on the mind. Will all China be doing this one day? If so, watch out, western business! We may all be working for them.

Duff Roblin

One occasion took me to New Delhi, India, when Roland Mitchener was our High Commissioner. Roly fed me and arranged a drive to Agra to look at the Taj Mahal. I arrived as twilight was closing in to be handed over to the local police for safe keeping. As a boy I was fascinated by Rudyard Kipling's story of Kim, a young Anglo-Indian orphan living in the twilight of the British Empire in India. As I looked around the narrow streets and markets of Agra, it seemed exactly like the Indian city Kipling had described, with its splendid jumble of noise, smells, and colours, with people of all tribes, religions and languages, and combinations, a scene of high romance. Standing on the balcony of the police station, I saw the crowd moving below. First a torchlight procession with a bullock cart appeared, with the local idol on board, accompanied by curious oriental bagpipes and a train of male dancers, eunuchs from the temple on their way to a Hindu festival. Following shortly after was a second procession. This time the centrepiece was a decorated elephant. The howdah carried a boy of about 12 being conducted to a Moslem rite of circumcision. When this excitement had gone by, an open-bodied police truck drove in, bearing the dead bodies of several local bandits or dacoits that had been ambushed nearby and being brought in for identification. They were bringing the trophies home. Next day the Taj Mahal seemed beautiful, if a bit too perfect. Travelling on the Great North Road, with its donkeys, camels, horses, carts and some trucks, again showed the diversity and variety of the people of north India. Jaipur was on my route. There, below the walls of the pastel pink city, you can sleep in the Maharajah's palace in the lake and buy magnificent coloured gems cheaply. Farther on you can climb by elephant up to the abandoned Muslim medieval city of Fateh Pur Sikri to watch daring young divers splash far down into the water tank. To these prairie eyes, exotica unfolded everywhere.

Nicosia, Madrid, Lisbon, Paris, Rome, Brussels, Amsterdam, Prague, Budapest, Vienna, Rio de Janeiro, Sao Paulo, Brasilia, Mexico City, Monterey, Santiago, Valparaiso and Buenos Aires were also on my overseas visiting list. So you can see my travelogue was extensive.

fifteen

GIVE POLITICS BACK
its GOOD NAME

———◆———

THESE ARE HARD TIMES FOR THE INSTITUTIONS OF SOCIETY AND for those in authority. In earlier days, respect for office, if not always for the office-holder, was readily accorded. Politics was a worthy calling, and I described myself as a politician with some pride. Nowadays it seems that politics is a pejorative word, although the people in politics are, by and large, just as good as they ever were. They represent the full variety of Canadian citizenship, but in the public mind, the reputation of politicians has declined. And not just politicians: Governments, business, police, professions, the courts—all face the critical assessment of a skeptical public. Information on everything, from anywhere, by anybody, floods in from every side. Some of it is good, some of it is bad, and the voice of special interests is often heard the loudest.

Among the information-providers, television takes first place. It is the main source of what we think and of what we know. It dotes on personalities, and though it may often offer only a 60-second sound bite, it can also communicate with us in unequalled depth and richness. So what else is new? In its day, I suppose, every new quantum leap in communication technology attracted a similar comment, and yet throughout it all we learned to survive and to manage the changes. But TV or no TV, if the public idea of politics is bad, politicians themselves can surely do something about it. Let me refer particularly to Parliament.

Duff Roblin

Question Period on TV does no good for the public perception of politicians. Of course, Question Period is a splendid democratic parliamentary invention. It seeks to hold governments to account. Questions ostensibly seek answers, and answers give government a chance to explain itself. So far, so good. But the present structure of Question Period, or rather the non-structure of Question Period, allows a circus-like free-for-all with members jostling one another for the TV spot amid shouts and noise. Questions thus are booby-traps, and answers are designed to excuse. Now, Parliament is not a bloodless debating society, and its members are full-blooded competitors. Yet the people may expect to see their business conducted with a more serious purpose. TV treats Question Period as infotainment. When it is over, the press gallery empties. The sober business of debate and of law-making cannot compete. It is possible to change this atmosphere. Questions should be written and submitted in advance. Then considered replies can be given orally in Parliament. On hearing the answer, the questioner may ask a supplementary question or two in order to clarify the information he has received. The circus of journalistic excitement might subside, but the real business of questions and answers would go on to the public advantage. The British so-called "private notice question," submitted in writing by noon on the day of asking, works well at Westminster. There, ministers, even the prime minister, take questions only at the time and day specifically allotted.

Over the years, the Canadian system has marginalized the ordinary member of Parliament to no good purpose. Enormous power has been concentrated in the hands of the central executive headed by the prime minister. The eclipse of ordinary MPs devalues them in the eyes of the public. The prime minister's sway is complete. This need not be so. When every government bill becomes a matter of confidence, woe betide a government dissenter. Government members are muzzled. It is a convenience for the government, no doubt, but destructive of the representative character of Parliament, and the public takes notice. Party discipline is far too strict in the Canadian parliament. We can look at the British House of Commons to see how some elbow room can be given to members without the system falling apart. Let votes of confidence be restricted. They should be declared in advance and attached to such items as the Throne Speech, the budget, and those other measures of high government policy. In other instances, where the question of confidence is not involved, all members would then be freer to vote on the basis of their own judgments. Awkward for the management, no doubt, but the public would approve.

The actual writing of government bills could be opened up to members. As things stand at present, a bill in Parliament receives three readings. The first merely records the bill's name and number. At second reading, the actual wording is revealed and members vote on whether or not the bill is acceptable in principle. But from then on, though the bill was prepared in secret by the civil service, and though no member, except in the Cabinet, has had much of a say in its content, amendment, unless government sponsored, has little chance of success. It is basically a done deal. It would not be hard to provide room for greater input by members. Simply adopt the former Senate procedure previously noted, called pre-study, and the first reading stage could be used for that purpose.[22] In this way, first reading could be accompanied by a draft of the proposed legislation. The draft could be examined in committee by members and the public. As a draft, it is capable of amendment and alteration without a challenge to confidence or government prestige. Public input could be solicited. Backbenchers would have some opportunity to take part in framing the structure of the bill before the government's seal of approval was applied. Bills on matters of confidence would be excepted from this procedure.

So if we could reduce party discipline and expand the role of MPs in actually framing legislation, if we would restrict matters of confidence to questions like the budget and vital government policy, we would go a long way toward removing the parliamentary strait-jacket which is characteristic of our present system and move toward a more open one in which members and the public are more clearly involved. This would enable us to pick up one of the

---

22 During my time as premier, after bills were drafted (except budget bills) but before being printed for first reading, our caucus undertook a clause-by-clause review giving the caucus, at least, a share in the preparation of laws.

good points of the American congressional system without abandoning parliamentary principles important to us.

One fundamental feature of parliamentary government is often misunderstood in the West—the fact that the parliamentary system is a system of representative and responsible government. It is not a system of delegate government. That means that when members of Parliament are chosen, they are expected to act as representatives of their community, but not as delegates. In other words, they must use their own judgment in the conduct of affairs, and while they must undoubtedly listen to the views of their constituents, they are not solely bound to reflect them absolutely in the conduct of parliamentary business. And pre-eminently they take counsel together in the interest not only of their constituents, but of the nation as a whole.

Edmund Burke made the case eloquently in the late eighteenth century when his Bristol constituents resented his perceived failure to act as their local delegate in the British parliament. In his words, "your representative owes you not his industry only but his judgment, and he betrays instead of serving you if he sacrifices it to your opinion." Bravo. The idea that members of Parliament are delegates of their constituents and bound to reflect the views of their constituents, and them only, is an interpretation of the representative and responsible parliamentary system which I think wrong. Merely consider the problem of finding out what your constituency wanted you to do. A voter may say, "I like my member because he does what I think he should." Another voter will say, "I don't like him because he doesn't do what I think he should." How is that member to reconcile those conflicting views when he becomes the delegate rather than the representative? Does he fall back on the latest ephemeral political poll? Who takes a view of the long-term good? If voters don't like what their members do, they get a crack at them every election day, and that is sufficient discipline to make democracy work.

When Parliament began its rise in England centuries ago, the great struggle with the monarchy crystallized in the quarrel over taxation and the control of the public purse. The supremacy of Parliament was assured when it gained the power to manage public money and control public spending. This became a supreme and basic prerogative of Parliament within our own system of representative and responsible government. But times move on. Today, an over-mighty federal parliamentary executive, namely the prime minister and his cabinet, backed by an all-knowing bureaucracy and the party whips, seem to have replaced the monarch and obscured the role of the representatives of the people in discharging their fiscal capacity and responsibility. In the House of Commons today, this responsibility is more honoured in the breach than the observance. Spending estimates, today, seldom get the examination they deserve. No doubt the sheer volume of detail tends to swamp the system and relieves the executive from the task of explanation and justification of their demands on tax resources. The record in recent times is an object lesson of unexamined programs and payments, leading to questionable if not reckless failures to prioritize, failures to match expenditures to revenues, with consequent monstrous government debts and interest payments stifling public services. Parliament must bestir itself to become the master of public expenditure.

One place to start would be the parliamentary committee system.[23] Sufficient committees, strengthened and empowered, should be assigned to inquire into departmental spending. Each committee should be assisted by full-time independent staff empowered to follow committee instructions and to which the administration is obliged to respond. The work could proceed whether or not Parliament is in session. Perhaps the chairman should sometimes be a member of the opposition. Over time, committees and their staffs could be expected to master their briefs and to hold spenders to account. Such an examination might help to relieve another important aspect of public concern, a perceived lack of accountability in the operations of government. Some more precise and timely examination of and accountability for government spending would surely serve the

23 When I was in the legislature of Manitoba, the annual spending estimates were examined in committee line by line and item by item, as were the annual public accounts of money previously spent. This was a wholesome discipline and gave members direct input into the proceess.

public interest. In particular, the all-knowing bureaucracy could be held to a public reckoning. Backbenchers would have an opportunity to prove their worth.

Parliamentary estimate committees, armed with authority, could satisfy themselves about the outcomes of past expenditures before approving more of the same. Those who benefit could be clearly identified. This accountability would apply not only to policy makers but also to the bureaucracy who some-times inspire and certainly direct the operations of government. The concept and practice of accountability would be strengthened in co-operation with the auditor-general. The whole estimate presentation can be modernized to make it more readily open to the general reader. Narrative could make plain the sig-nificance of requests. Logical connections, consequences, outcomes, and future projects could help elucidate the meaning of the figures. In addition to passing laws, parliament could then reclaim its former role of guardian of the public purse. The reputation of parliament and the relevance of its members would be enhanced. Furthermore, Gladstone would approve. As for the Senate, I give my views on that institution elsewhere.

Success in parliamentary leadership awaits the right conjunction of events. One of the essential qualities is to recognize an opportunity when it presents itself. It's a mistake to think opportunities can always be manufactured out of hand. Sometimes that may be true, but mostly they are revealed by the course of events. The vision, the wisdom, the capacity to recognize those opportunities when they appear and to make use of them is an important aspect of political leadership. Leaders thus need to have a clear idea of what needs to be done. They need a vision. They need not only to know what to do, but to have a con-ception of how to do it—how to bring it to pass, and how to persuade other peo-ple to lend their voices and their efforts to the enterprise. A political leader must seek to show the way and articulate the goal of political action.

My relations with the media have usually been good. In fact, with signifi-cant reservations I feel that, by and large, I have been treated fairly. When I came into office, I had a particular advantage because I was somebody new with new ideas, and the press is interested in new faces and new ideas. Consequently, when I spoke in the legislature or when I talked privately with members of the press, we always had something constructive to talk about. So a good relationship developed. The press taught me certain things. First of all, it taught me there are no secrets, and it's useless to think that any decision made by a government is going to be a secret for very long. It's good to be frank and up-front in dealing with the press. Sometimes, you can't answer their questions in full, or tell them everything they want to know. I find that if you frankly say what your limitations are, they respect them. I also found it was useful to give the press background information. That is, even when a policy is not fully developed or ready for public exhibition, the press would know that consideration was being given to this or that. That presented a problem, but I always found that if I said to the press, "This is the background of the situation, this is where we're heading, this is what I can tell you, and this is what you may say," those requests were invariably honoured.

When I was in the legislature, the Manitoba press gallery were leading exponents of their trade. Merely to record some of the names I can remember tells a tale. Ken MacIvor, Don McGillivray, Peter Desbarats, Peter Liba, Len Earl, John Dafoe, John Sifton, Ted Byfield, Jim Shilliday, Maurice Western, Shaun Herron, Mike Best, Ralph Hedlin, Frank Walker, and Shane MacKay constitute an impressive cross-section of the profession. Of course, you had to be a little careful with a few of them who had special interests. They weren't so much interested in the news in the prosaic sense, they were interested in startling or scandalous news. Some of them really were inclined to make that their main goal, to find nuggets of news which could be developed into stories different from the normal day-to-day bread-and-butter items. Ted Byfield, in particular, had a nose for the bizarre. When I was in office in Winnipeg, any members of the press who wanted to see me knew they had access to my office. I found that to be helpful to them and, to be frank about it, was helpful to me because I was able to give them my point of view on things.

I took note about what I read about myself in the paper, or heard about or saw about myself on radio and television. Sometimes I was distressed that my position was not fairly presented. I have to say that didn't happen often. Most of the time, my position was fairly presented, and if I didn't like what I heard or read, it was usually because I didn't tell it properly. I took the first opportunity in a non-confrontational way to make the point with the person concerned that what I had really intended to say but failed to say was such-and-such and so-and-so. Sometimes, that resulted in a further story and sometimes it didn't, but it gave me an opportunity to clear my mind of any problem on a sensitive issue. I read editorials and editorial comment very carefully indeed. Editorial writers, take heart! One politician, at least, paid attention to what was written. I didn't always agree with what I saw, but the thing in this business is to pick out the valid criticism, the points that were properly made, and not slough the whole thing off on the grounds that, "Well, he doesn't like me so I'm not going to pay attention to what he said." That's counter-productive. The thing to do is to make use of legitimate criticism and do something about it.

When I began, a politician was very largely on his own. He was not surrounded by hordes of advisers or people who thought they knew more than he did, and lobbying was not an important concern. The politician and the government were left to get on with their business as best they could, and the outside influences which are now so pressing were not seen in that degree. Maybe that's because life was a lot simpler then, and the government didn't get into areas that it gets into today. There were plenty of reasons, but it seems to me that we do have a problem in the number of special interests which now want to persuade public officials to see things their way. It starts, of course, with lobbyists. Lobbying seems out of control in these recent times. Now, people have a right to talk to their government and tell their government what they want it to do, and it's hard to dispute that in principle. It all depends on how this information is conveyed. If they seek to use special connections or special influence, or claim to have these kinds of powers, then it's a question of some concern. Lobbying should as far as possible be reported. When it is done in private, the public is naturally concerned that undue influence is being brought to bear. The remedy for lobbying, in my opinion, is openness and publicity.

sixteen

NATION BUILDING

———◆———

THE NOTION OF THE CENTRALIZED ALL-POWERFUL SOVEREIGN state is changing these days. Some of its powers are being made over to super-regional or super-national bodies, and some of its powers are devolving to local authorities within its territories. It deals with an expanding economic community around the world, and with growing local pressures within. But the state is still the indispensable focus of the national interest. The challenge is to achieve the right balance.

Canada was invented in 1867 to secure such a balance, first between the English-speakers and French-speakers, and secondly between the central government and its provinces. The Fathers of Confederation planned a central government to handle the major activities of the time. They proposed a supervisory role for the central government over the provinces, which were given jurisdiction over functions of a then basically local character. Some responsibilities were shared by the two levels of government. Incredibly, this 1867 concept of the role of the provinces persisted even in the mind of a premier of Manitoba, as late as the 1950s. I remember Douglas Campbell comparing the activities of a provincial government to those of an enlarged municipality, a view to which I objected. Nevertheless, although as premier my immediate responsibility was to serve my province, I never forgot I was a Canadian first.

Duff Roblin

This original arrangement soon began to change under the pressures of practical experience and judicial rulings. Ottawa's supervisory powers began to atrophy, and the provinces became masters of their own house. Nowadays, federalism in Canada is a sovereignty divided between federal and provincial spheres of administration. For the most part, up until the 1960s, each jurisdiction respected its own constitutional limits as they had developed. If Ottawa wished to take important policy initiatives in provincial affairs, it was possible to amend the Constitution to accommodate it. This was the case with unemployment insurance. But in the aftermath of the Great Depression of the 1930s, a provincial problem with national repercussions arose.

Some provinces, which we now call the "have-nots," found themselves fiscally unable to provide services of a standard reasonably comparable to other provinces, the "haves." The have-not tax base simply could not yield sufficient revenues from comparable taxes to support comparable services. The peril of this development to Canadian unity, to say nothing of human values, was plain. The Rowell-Sirois Report in 1940 provided a clearly Canadian answer called fiscal equalization. The federal government, with the agreement of all, would help the have-not provinces financially. The principle of equalization led to a formula devised and administered by Ottawa by which the have-not provinces would receive unconditional equalization payments from federal tax resources. The aim was to enable all Canadians to receive roughly equal standards of provincial services on a roughly equal provincial tax effort. I call unconditional equalization an unqualified act of Canadian statesmanship, and the fiscal bedrock of Canadian federalism. It carried the patriotic consent of all. In 1958, with the help of equalization, Manitoba, for one, was able to fully fund its own educational, health and welfare costs.

In the 1960s, a second significant federal initiative was introduced into provincial affairs: federal spending power. Since World War II, the federal government had made use of its spending power to promote shared cost programs in areas of exclusive provincial constitutional jurisdiction with Ottawa laying down the rules and regulations. Post-secondary education, medicare and welfare figure prominently. While this constituted an arbitrary and uni-

lateral interference with provincial policy making and, in effect, appropriated part of the provincial budget, improvements in these services were
welcomed. Tempted by the offer of federal cost sharing, usually on a 50/50
basis, provinces were persuaded to agree. I have set out elsewhere the Catch-
22 situation facing a dissenting province. Nevertheless, Quebec's reservations
have always been emphatic. Over time, the two levels of government have
rubbed along in a fairly passable fashion. But events have made it clear that an
unresolved problem of Canadian federalism is the use of the federal spending
power in fields of provincial constitutional jurisdiction so that provincial
rights are respected. An outline of a federal-provincial protocol on the use of
the spending power in shared-cost programs suggests itself.

- The spending power is constitutional.
- It may be invoked for new shared-cost programs that have the support of
  seven provinces comprising 50 percent of the population.
- Subject to appropriate safeguards, provinces wishing to follow an
  independent policy on new programs may do so and receive reasonable
  compensation to be spent on programs with similar objectives.
- A tribunal will settle differences among governments, with special
  responsibility to give consideration to national standards in services.
- The federal government will be free to deal directly with Canadian
  citizens and institutions without infringing on provincial areas
  of jurisdiction.
- Above all, clear-cut rules of co-ordination will apply.

In the 1990s, the financial balance shifted again, this time in the direction
of the provinces. Ottawa had budgetary problems, federal funds had run low,
and federal transfers to the provinces suffered a sharp and drastic decline. It
is obvious that this development would strain federal-provincial relations. A
more basic change has also gradually taken place in the economic balance
between the provinces and Ottawa, and among the provinces themselves. At
the beginning of the 20th century and probably up to the end of World War I,
Ontario was the economic and political powerhouse in the new Confederation.

Quebec had a unique and powerful supporting role. The other seven provinces weighed lightly on the scale. By the time I attended my first federal/provincial conference in 1958, it was clear a very different configuration was in the making, particularly in western Canada. By 1990, Alberta and British Columbia had become economic powers of their own. All provinces have become more competent and more confident. Nowadays, education, health and welfare are the real substance of public attention, and they all lie within provincial jurisdiction.

Throughout the world, power is devolving from central to local governments. The argument is made that government closer to the people provides a more sensitive and efficient delivery of services. But in Canada, it is not a question of a further devolution of federal powers. The transfer of federal powers to the provinces is not the issue. The issue is the federal government's intrusion into provincial affairs. The old slogan co-operative federalism is more relevant than ever, but to make it work as it should, clear and agreed rules governing federal financial initiatives in areas of provincial jurisdiction are a *sine qua non*. Unilateral federal money power in shared-cost programs will no longer serve. Federal responsibility for the economic union among the provinces should be enforced by a formal dispute settling mechanism similar to that which applies in our North American Free Trade Agreement and other international trading arrangements.

The Canadian Constitution is wonderfully made. It is sufficiently flexible to accommodate 21st century needs if we have the will to make it so. Amendment at present may be difficult, but it is not needed if we summon the will to adjust the Constitution we already have. But can this same statement apply to Quebec?

The place of the francophones of Quebec within the constitutional framework of confederation is no new thing. The BNA Act of 1867 itself gives clear recognition that while provinces may be equal legal entities, by no means are they treated in identical ways. Quebec's position, however described, is firmly established as different, yet the articulation of that difference has never ceased to concern us. We should not be afraid of difference. Provinces may be equal, but they are certainly not identical. The Constitution in its workings has always been able to make room for special arrangements to meet special needs, and not for one province only. As a child, my mother took me to a certain Madame Daigneault to discover that "La plume de ma tante est dans le jardin." Though I never became truly bilingual, I have described my adventures in the French language elsewhere. When I was premier, and during the 1967 leadership campaign, Quebecers made this not quite bilingual westerner feel unfailingly welcome. Their feeling for their language or culture is no different than mine for my own: the desire to be recognized and to be welcomed for what they are within the Canadian circle. Now in 1999, what is it that Quebec wants? Just what it always wanted. Quebecers want to feel at home as Canadians with their own language and culture, especially in their own province, and they want their provincial government to be able to protect, preserve, and promote their language and their culture. Whatever the state of Quebec's interests within our federal structure and with other provinces, Quebecers rely on the Quebec government—their own government—and society as their shield.

Confederation has been made to respond to that need. In 1867, the Civil Code, the Senate, the Supreme Court, a degree of bilingualism in federal institutions, control over education and welfare responded to Quebec's interests as perceived at that time. Since then, the Privy Council spoke for provincial rights, including Quebec. By Quebec's own efforts, the protection and development of the French language and culture, immigration and pensions now lie within its ambit. The Caisse de Depôt is a financial powerhouse presiding over the Quebec economy, though truth to tell, the gap with Ontario continues to widen. Quebec receives a full share of federal expenditures as well as a generous payment of unconditional equalization. Francophones generally have successfully equipped themselves to occupy the commanding heights of the Quebec economy and not of Quebec alone. The Constitution, with or without amendment, has proven Confederation flexible enough to encompass developments within Quebec and within Canada not dreamt of by Georges Etienne Cartier in 1867.

Duff Roblin

ABOVE: DUFF ADDRESSES THE ISSUE OF NATIONAL UNITY AT HIS EIGHTIETH BIRTHDAY GALA

A solid case may, therefore, be made that, within Confederation as it has developed, Quebec's language and culture are not only safe but capable of full expression and development. What added assurances are needed? Francophones federalists in Quebec must give that answer. Being a major player in a united Canada, punching considerably above its weight in the federal arena, Quebec can feel an assurance of power and stability that an adventure in independence is unlikely to match. Quebec is strong in Canada today.

But that is not so for separatists. Quebec francophone separatists—the "purs et durs" hardliners—reject that argument entirely. They will be satisfied with nothing short of a completely separate and sovereign state of their own, however tactically mealy-mouthed the referendum questions have been. Constitutions cannot reach them, and they live in a political world of their own construction. To date, Quebec referendums have been held in that make-believe world with the hard choices carefully camouflaged. Independence is presented by its enthusiasts as an easy natural option without significant adverse consequences, at least for Quebec and with all Canada constrained to agree to Quebec's terms. Reality discloses a different scenario. However reluctantly, federalists must require that the next referendum vote ensure a clear question with the highest quality of balanced consideration of the issues. To propose that separation will follow smoothly on a simple majority vote is preposterous. Separation is not an act that can be repealed after the next general election. All Canada has a right to insist on a reasonable majority because all Canada will bear the consequences. To say that the question must be clear and unambiguous is to state the obvious, and the adverse political and economic effects of separation must be reckoned with and openly debated.

Internally, it is idle to suppose that the territorial integrity of an independent Quebec along present boundaries would be unquestioned. Strangely, separatists maintain that it is normal for a minority within Canada, namely themselves, to unilaterally rupture Canada's integrity, but that the same reasoning does not apply to unwilling federalist minorities within Quebec. They cannot do to Quebec what Quebec can do to Canada. Externally, it is idle to finesse à la Parizeau the question of world opinion and recognition. Let France do as it will, the recognition that counts is recognition by the United States, especially for NAFTA. The United States senate, with its predominant power, would ensure that any independent state of Quebec, recognized by them, would conform to American defence and economic interests. In Canada, Quebec francophones speak from strength. As a minor state, which an independent Quebec would be, the French fact in North America risks being marginalized, and that is just the beginning of the reckoning. Cutting established political, economic, fiscal, social and customary ties is like separating Siamese twins. They may survive. Certainly they will never be the same, and both will be sadly diminished. Incidentally, we should take note that by adopting the Euro, the members of the European Union undoubtedly foretell a diminished state independence in a growing federal system.

Separatists will consider the raising of such questions as spiteful and malign, but all Canada has a vital stake in the issue. Separation is irrevocable in its political, social and economic consequences which we have scarcely begun to understand. A nation like ours dismembered and split in two will experience in every part a political and economic crisis of the first magnitude. Every part will feel the pain. One hears, especially in the West, that all provinces are equal, and this mantra is used to allege that they are to be treated identically and to deny Quebec the recognition that history and the facts assert. Provinces may be equal, but they are decidedly not the same. They are different, and proud of it. Just ask any Nova Scotian or Newfoundlander. We must let francophone federalists in Quebec know we understand their right to be different, and our Confederation can accommodate that difference in a manner they can accept. Political unity does not require cultural uniformity. Let us remember that Quebecers themselves will decide the issue and that Quebec federalists are Canada's advocates in the front line. All Canada will not vote in any Quebec referendum, but all Canada can help arm Quebec federalists to carry the day.

But these continuous nagging bouts of challenge and response are soul destroying and economically wasting. We need not set out to establish milestones on our road to folly. We need not reject reason. We do need to understand the better angels of our nature: that politicians in some parts of English-speaking Canada must lay aside an unbecoming provincialism in favour of the nation; that all Canadians recognize the need for Quebecers to fulfil themselves within Confederation; that Quebec is an essential part of our national essence; that Quebecers recognize that they can find a North American guarantee of their self-identification within Confederation. Let the motto be fraternal recognition. Indeed I delivered that very message to a record gathering of friends and Manitoba faithful who met to celebrate my eightieth birthday.

Canada is a nation in a class by itself. On our half of this continent, we have created our own independent North American personality. We hold a good working balance between rugged individualism and community values. We understand the constructive role of the state and the virtue of personal responsibility. We are willing to join with others to support peace and human rights at home and abroad. We are beginning to reconcile ourselves with Aboriginal Canadians. The world looks on us as fortune's favourite, as we are. We will set aside unworthy feelings and secondary concerns to show the world and prove to ourselves we are equal to the opportunities which providence has bestowed. Vive la Confédération canadienne.

seventeen

WHAT NEXT?

———◆———

ABOUT THE FUTURE, IT IS TRUE THAT I CAN KNOW NOTHING, BUT that will not prevent me from having a decided opinion. That opinion is heavily weighted by the expectation that the present favourable trends I can see are a guide to the future, and what I cannot see, I can hope for. So the first thing to say about the future is that I am greatly hopeful, and that present trends underline that hope. I will speak of my province only. In 1949 when I began in politics, Manitoba was a province of survivors. First the Great Depression, reinforced by a bitter drought, brought our economy to its knees. Then we faced austerity as we dedicate ourselves to victory in World War II. We were stretched thin, but the worst never happened and we came through strengthened and revitalized. For some, it has been a long and trying 50 years since then, but our material, social, and cultural growth have indeed been spectacular. We have learned as we have built, and what we have built has not been by our efforts in Manitoba alone, but in the company of other Canadians across the land. The key to Manitoba's future is simple: it is to make the most of what we have.

Let us take a look at the economy which supports our culture and quality of life. Manitoba started out as a farming province. Building on that base in recent times, our agriculture has almost reinvented itself. Crop diversification has added to our wheat culture. Local value-added activities working from a broadened base that includes a significant livestock sector gives us export strength. This will develop into new opportunities. Manufacturing for export has shown excellent growth with a strong diversification of product. This small and not-so-small entrepreneurial community in Winnipeg and in the countryside shows vigorous growth. "Green" compatible hydro-electric power is a hidden asset. Sound provincial government finances is confidence-building. The power of information technology to transform the economics of location favourably is good for Manitoba. People no longer face the same pressures to go to work. The work can come to them.

We cannot match the natural resources of some other provinces, nor the advantages of a more convenient location, but in the now dominant services sector of the world economy in which We share, these factors count for less. Winnipeg began as a national east-west railway centre. The Panama Canal and the growth of larger centres further west rendered that service obsolete. The new prospects of Winnipeg as an air and road nexus for intercontinental traffic are promising. Indeed, our old role as a transportation nexus may be revived. For many years, our population growth has been steady but very slow. The loss of young people to other areas has been painful. That is doubly so in the current climate of skilled worker shortage. I have strongly urged the centrality of education to give our people a grasp of traditional and space-age skills that power the modern economy. Of course, this endeavour should not lead to a neglect of the liberal arts that undergird our society. So education is the key. Without being complacent, we have made respectable progress in bringing those concerns to the favourable notice of many Manitobans, but much more work needs to be done. Let us look at education not as an unavoidable bill of expenses but as a wholesome investment in the possibility of human life and growth. Clever, innovative human beings are the ultimate competitive advantage.

It would help if the demands of the state weighed less heavily on the productive enterprise of citizens. High taxes on employment and incomes hold back the animal spirits of the economy. This means that ultimately there are less resources available to raise the quality of life for all, including those in need. Again in human terms, reconciling Aboriginal lifestyles to the wider community and vice versa is a major challenge. We travel more hopefully, but we have not yet arrived. People are doing things, but they are not doing things anything like as much or as well as they can. The future belongs to those who have the ability and the education to make the modern world work for them and their community.

My forbears tested just about every variety of mainline Protestant Christianity, and some others. In this post-Christian world I find myself an Anglican. Anglicans live in their own space. The liturgy and the language are superb. Without the dogma of infallibility, an accommodation of views permits a broad church to comfort questioning souls. Anglicans are Catholic by tradition, but Reform by events. As the prayer book says, "There was never anything by the wit of man so well-devised or so sure established which in the continuance of time hath not been corrupted." The Anglican problem, of course, is the problem of humanity. There are just some things we can never know for sure. Faith is what goes beyond knowledge. I call the human mind the great miracle of the cosmos, and it is hard to think or to admit that this mind is in itself limited, and that when the finite grapples with the infinite, the finite comes off second-best. I can only trust that an energizing spirit gives a purpose to existence. But lay these speculations aside. When Goethe said, "I am here to wonder," he said it for me.

ABOVE: DUFF UNVEILS PLAQUE COMMEMORATING HIS GRANDFATHER SIR RODMOND'S BIRTHPLACE IN EASTERN ONTARIO, ACCOMPANIED BY MARY AND ONTARIO PREMIER JOHN ROBARTS

INDEX